KATE WATSON
BABY LLAMA DRAMA

Copyright © 2023 by Kate Watson

All rights reserved.

Cover by Lucy of Cover Ever After

No portion of this book may be reproduced in any form without written permission from the publisher or author, except as permitted by U.S. copyright law.

For all of those women who long for motherhood but whose bodies or circumstances have made it impossible in this season of life.
It sucks.

AUTHOR'S NOTE AND CONTENT WARNING

This book deals with themes of loss, abandonment, anxiety, pregnancy complications, divorce, codependency, infertility, and chronic illness.

A lot of women live with infertility. Some get to become mothers through adoptive miracles or medical miracles, some don't. I am inexpressibly grateful that my medical infertility eventually ended in both kinds of miracles. But for many, many years, it felt like an eternal, absolutely never-ending trial.

If you're going through that now, I'm so sorry. It sucks. I hate it for you.

CHAPTER ONE

MILLIE

*I*s it weird that I'm thinking of a little girl I met a few months ago?

Yes, yes it is.

I stare at a picture of the two of us on my phone, eyes crossed, tongues sticking out at the camera. You can hardly tell she'd been crying moments earlier. We both look too goofy.

And happy.

I look so happy.

I took the picture six months ago while I was visiting Sugar Maple for work with two of my best friends. Our marketing firm had been hired to rebrand a famous farm, and our CEO, Jane, had flown out, alone, to start on the job before the rest of us could make it. She fell for the new owner ... eventually. That new owner was throwing a dinner party on the night in question—and babysitting his goddaughter.

I spotted Lottie holding a cheese board under a table and

crying because she missed her dad, who was away for work. So I joined her.

I've always been good with kids—I'm a child therapist, after all—but this was on another level. Lottie stayed glued to my side that whole weekend. It made me feel whole in a way I haven't in years.

And then, I went back to Chicago.

I had just about recovered from the impact that weekend had on me, when I saw her only a few days ago. She was with her aunt at Jane's wedding to the farm owner. When Lottie saw me, she squealed my name and laughed and cried and held me until she fell asleep.

Now I'm missing the feel of those little arms wrapped around my neck.

At first, I wondered if I connected with Lottie because she reminded me of my niece, who I miss to my very core. But no, Lottie is special in her own right.

Since my friends and I relocated to Sugar Maple, South Carolina a few weeks ago, I've been watching for Lottie's chestnut pigtails to go bouncing down the street. This is her hometown, after all.

And because I'm all about punishing myself and don't have anything else to do, I roll my chair to the second-story office window to peer at the people below, just in case she comes by.

Autumn is in full swing, and the trees are mid-change, with every shade of green, yellow, orange, and even red. A few workers I recognize from the Sugar Maple Farms factory walk into the hardware store across the street while an SUV with out of state plates drives past and stops in front of the vintage thrift store. Four women pour out of the vehicle, laughing so loudly, I can hear them through the glass. When they walk into the shop, I snort. The surly owner does not enjoy loud, giggly women.

Learned that one the hard way.

A gold Lincoln Continental, older than I am, pulls into a

spot outside Sugar Maple Diner. The passenger door opens, and Mr. Beaty shuffles around to the driver's side to open the door for his wife. She's dyed her hair, and I'm not sure if it's a trick of the light, but it looks distinctly pink.

Rock on, Mrs. Beaty.

After another minute of watching, no cute little girl bounces into view. I sigh and force myself to look at my too-sparse calendar on my phone. My next client is in twenty minutes, but it's a telehealth client I brought with me from Chicago.

I blow my lips out like a horse.

I need more work.

Or at least a Diet Coke.

I'm just turning away from the window when something new catches my eye.

Or, rather, someone.

He's walking toward my building from somewhere up the street wearing a fitted v-neck sweater and light jeans that seem both broken in and tailor made for his muscled thighs.

The closer he gets, the better view I get of him, and let me tell you: *better* is right. This Greek God with a creased brow and hands in his pockets is like a younger, blonder, hotter version of Gisele Bündchen's ex-husband. You know, the football player guy? What's his name?

My friends would mock me mercilessly, but I have no head for sports. I know Gisele because she's a fashion icon and because she has an umlaut in her last name. I'm a sucker for cool style and cool spellings.

This specimen of a man who looks like that famous model's famous husband ... whew. How is he just walking around the streets of this small town looking like that without getting mauled? Or having panties thrown at him?

For the record, I do not approve of mauling or panty-throwing.

But wow. Dude is sexiness on sneakers.

Stop objectifying him, I tell myself. But I struggle to listen to my own advice.

That is until I get a deeper glimpse at his face right before he comes into the building. He looks ... wrecked.

And now the objectification doesn't just feel immature, it feels callous.

The Jane & Co. marketing firm is on the first floor of this building. He's probably received some bad news about his company and needs help, and if that's the case, I'll get the opportunity to meet him soon enough. I still work part time with them doing consumer behavior—

The door chime rings.

I pop out of my seat, straighten my cream smocked dress, and peek into the lobby through the blinds in my door.

It's him.

I try to push away my disappointment. It's wildly unethical for a therapist to date a client.

Not that we were destined to date, but I'm still bummed. As much as I can appreciate a hot guy, it's not often I *feel* it. I'm pickier than a vegan at a steakhouse.

But I'm the queen of compartmentalizing, so I put away my attraction and my disappointment and instead focus on curiosity.

His back is to me. With his hands jammed in his pockets and his shoulders up around his ears, he looks uncomfortable. Defensive, even. That devastated look I noticed only a minute ago rounds out the image of someone in deep pain.

"Hi Ms. Angie. I, uh, didn't realize you worked here." His voice is muffled through the door, but I hear him well enough. His accent is mild but as warm as sunlight through a window.

My receptionist, Angela, smiles. "Hiya, hon. Are you hoping to speak to a clinician?"

"I-I don't know what that is."

I'm about to come out and introduce myself, but the warm

brown skin around Angela's eyes crinkles softly. "Just a fancy word for the therapist. We have two."

He's so hesitant that the spot in my heart that was hollowed out years ago aches like a phantom limb. His reluctance is common, especially among men. They think therapy somehow makes them weak instead of realizing that it gives them the tools to be even stronger. "Do they ... have any experience with kids?"

Angela nods and gives him my coworker's impressive bio, including her ten years doing family therapy. Then she gives him mine. Graduated with an MSW from University of Chicago, interned for a year doing animal-assisted therapy and another year at the top children's hospital in Illinois. Three years corporate consumer behavior and private practice experience.

He nods and I catch a glimpse of his profile. He looks like a rabbit staring at headlights. He's in over his head. Even something as simple as deciding which clinician to talk to has him stressed to the max.

He puts his hands on Angela's desk and shakes his head. "You know, I think I made a mistake coming in. Sorry for the misunderstanding."

Angela tsks but says goodbye. I come out as soon as he leaves the lobby.

"Not ready, huh?"

"Not yet, sugar, but give him time. I know his daughter, and she's been through the ringer. He's a good father. He'll come around."

A few minutes later, I take my telehealth appointment in my office. The face of therapy has changed over the last few years, and more and more people have found that they can get the same quality of help without having to travel to an office. If I wanted to do strictly telehealth, I could fill my calendar in a snap, especially now that I'm licensed in both Illinois and South

Carolina. But I have the opportunity to do animal-assisted therapy in Sugar Maple, and no work makes me happier.

When my friends and I officially moved from Chicago, I planned to continue doing consumer behavior analysis and help with rebranding for our company, Jane & Co. I had every intention of seeing a handful of clients virtually at nights and on weekends, as I have for the last two years. But the farm owner, Tripp, talked to me about the possibility of animal-assisted therapy at the farm. My heart melted into a puddle of warm goo. He asked if I'd consider working with them, and I couldn't say no.

I love working with my friends, but my heart is in helping kids. With our recent successes following the Sugar Maple Farms account, we have enough paid interns and consultants that I'm only needed part time at the firm.

Now I just need enough clients to make up that other "part."

After my virtual session, I take a lunch break. I walk past my friends' offices downstairs, but they're all in meetings or in the middle of work, so I head for the diner alone.

The weather is mild enough that I leave my cardigan in the office. Another welcome change from the Midwest—it's October, and I'm not even wearing a jacket.

What is this sorcery?

Maple Street filled up in the hour I was in a session. The pumpkin patch over at Sugar Maple Farms has dramatically increased the town's traffic, more so because it's Friday.

I smile and wave at everyone I see, both on the street and in the shops. I'm too new to know who's local and who's not, but I've delivered baskets of Sugar Maple Farms goodies to each of the shopkeepers and owners along Maple Street and was welcomed warmly enough.

Except by Nico, the man who owns the vintage shop.

The vintage shop, of all places! Vintage is my jam!

Nico is probably sixty, yet he looks like he hasn't missed a gym day since before I was born. He's grizzled and tough and everyone tells me has a heart of gold.

For me, he's all scowls.

My friends and I came in months ago when we visited Sugar Maple, after signing the lease on the Jane & Co offices. I was browsing while he was watching sports on a small, ancient TV behind the counter. When I asked him if he ever got in vintage Burberry pea coats, he held up his finger to me in the universal "wait a second" gesture.

"Oh. Sure," I said. I have a service industry background, so I may have sounded a bit surprised that he was pausing a customer to watch a game. Anyway, I think he assumed that I was being rude, because he eyed me something fierce. Unfortunately, in that exact moment of glaring, someone in the game kicked a ball into a net, and his team appeared to score the winning point, and he missed it.

I tried to apologize for my timing, but he mumbled something in Greek.

Now he *only* speaks Greek to me. I'm pretty sure they're all curse words.

When I wave through the glass, the smile on his face drops and he looks away. I sigh and continue my last dozen steps into Sugar Maple Diner.

The place is appropriately packed. It's everything a small town diner should be: friendly, charming, and delicious. I've come frequently enough since I moved into my office that I'm already a regular. I smile at Mr. and Mrs. Beaty, who eat here every meal, as far as I can tell. They look like they're finishing up, but I know from experience they'll stay another hour.

Mrs. Beaty shakes her unmistakably pink head at me. "Child, didn't your mother ever tell you not to wear white after Labor Day?"

"It's cream, Mrs. Beaty. Besides, I know you have 'winter white' in the South," I say in a teasing voice.

Mrs. Beaty has a lot of opinions about my clothes. She doesn't think I wear enough color. I told her last week that redheads don't get to wear the same colors that everyone else wears, and she studied me for a beat before agreeing.

"That may be true, but that just means you should wear the colors you *can* get away with. Just no red or pink."

I wonder how much trouble I'd get in if she found out I'm wearing a hot pink bra at this very moment.

After I compliment Mrs. Beaty on her hair, I catch Tia's attention. Tia is my favorite server here. She's more than a server; she basically runs the place. The owner moved to Charleston a couple of years ago, and since then, half the town thinks Tia should buy the place from him.

The fact that she brings me a Diet Coke on her way to help someone else tells you everything you need to know: I'm Team Tia.

"Bless you!" I gush.

"You know I got your back." Tia has on dark red lipstick that looks amazing against her olive skin. With her black hair in a high bun on her head, she looks like a 1950s Filipina pin-up girl. "Listen, I'm just clearin' a table so give me two seconds. I'll wave you over. Oh, and I need some advice, so I'll pop by on my break."

I make a point of not sighing. In the few short weeks I've been here, I've had a lot of people ask me for "advice." I have boundless energy for my job, but "advice" is draining. "Advice" doesn't happen on the clock. It can happen anytime, anywhere, and without boundaries.

I sip my soda until my mood perks back up. It's amazing what a good Diet Coke can do.

A couple of minutes later, Tia waves from the back of the room. "I got your table, Millie!"

Over the low drone of conversation, a little voice cries, "I want Miwwie!"

Recognition spreads from my heart all the way to my fingertips as I weave through the cramped space. I know that little voice! I look from table to table for those dark, thick pigtails.

At the same time that I'm trying to find Lottie, I notice movement nearby. Only a few feet away, the Greek God of a man from my office stands. He walks backwards, making a placating gesture with his hands.

And then he whirls around and bumps right into my drink.

Which dumps all over me.

I gasp in a wave of ice cold shock. He gapes down at me.

"I'm so sorry!" he says. He grabs napkins from the table next to us and dabs at my face when I grab them from him.

"I got it." I wipe my face, squeeze the excess from the bottom half of my hair, and then look down.

My dress—my fabulous, smocked cream dress that hits right above the knee and flatters my curves like it was tailor-made—is soaked in Diet Coke.

And I'm wearing a hot pink bra.

To be extremely clear, it does not normally show through the fabric—*at all*. But evidently, when this dress gets wet, my bra shows.

Information that would have been more useful to me this morning when I put the stupid thing on.

This spectacular Gisele-Bündchen's-Ex-Husband looking man only lets his eyes drop to my bra for a moment before they snap back up. "Sorry, I swear I wasn't trying to check you out. The ... the color surprised me."

"You and a hundred of your closest friends," I say, gesturing to the enraptured room. People are even taking their phones out! Are they *recording*?

He reaches into his back pocket and pulls out a thin yellow blanket like some weird magician. Then he drapes it over my shoulders.

I pull it forward until it covers my bra. "Thanks."

"Can I help?" he asks.

"I'm just gonna run to the restroom," I say, then dart for the back. Tia stops me just outside of it and hands me a backpack. "I always keep a spare outfit on hand for just these occasions."

"Bless you again," I tell her. "Nothing like having a room full of people ogling your favorite bra."

"That's why you only wear nude bras with white, hon," she says as she zips off to clean up the mess.

"I'm a redhead. I don't get the chance to wear pink if it's not on my bra or on my shoes."

"Then keep it on your feet," she says with a wink.

"She has a point," a voice drawls from behind me.

I look over my shoulder and see the hot stranger, a half smile on his face. He followed me? And is smirking about my bra?

"Uh, yeah, I'll take it under consideration for the next time someone accidentally dumps Diet Coke down my dress." I close my eyes. "Sorry, I'm probably not at my best right now. Hot pink humiliation, and all that."

His lips twitch further upward, revealing dimples. *Because the man isn't content with perfection.* He has a dimple in his chin *and* in his cheeks, and my knees tremble just looking at them. Also because of the ice cold soda.

"If it helps, I think they were looking at me more than you."

I can't keep my head from cocking to the side. "Because of your height? I don't follow, sorry."

It's his turn to look confused. "No, because of who I am."

"I'm new to town, sorry. Are you the mayor, or something?"

He looks left and right, as if trying to find the hidden camera. "Are you joking me?"

Just then, I hear the same little voice I heard earlier yelling my name. "Miwwie!"

He groans and squeezes his temple. "If I have to hear that name ever again ... " I look past him for the little girl calling my name but can't see her. She sounds like she's across the restaurant.

"What do you mean? It's a fabulous name."

"Then you haven't heard it ten thousand times over the last couple of months."

What on earth is going on here? I feel like *I'm* the one being punked right now. I hear my name again just in time to see the cutest little girl running for me. The handsome stranger wheels around, and the girl pushes past him and launches into my arms.

"Lottie!" I squeal and hold her tightly to my chest before remembering that I'm still—that's right—totally soaked. "Oh sweetie, I'm sorry I'm all wet! Where's your family? I'll take you to them."

"Wait, *you're* Millie?" The man looks beyond shocked. He's dumbstruck.

"One and the same," I say. What is his issue with me? I try to pull Lottie off me, but she has a vice grip that cannot be loosened. She's crying into my wet hair, and I'm pretty sure they're happy tears, but I'm also aware that toddlers don't know how to process happy tears, so this could get loud fast.

"Here, let go," the man says. He puts his hand on her back, and I back up protectively.

"No, it's fine. I'll take her to her family. I know her."

"Oh, do you, *Millie?*"

I reel. "Are you trying to be this rude? You dump my drink on me, insinuate that even with a hot pink bra, I'm not worth looking at if you're in the room, and now you're insulting my name?" I squeeze Lottie. "Come on, sweetie. Help me find your family."

HotJaw McJagweed snorts. "I can help with that."

"Of course you can. I'm getting the sense there's nothing you can't do." I try to push past him, but he puts one hand on

Lottie's back—she's really crying now—and another on my elbow.

"I'm not saying that as some humble brag." We're so close that I have to crane my neck to look up into his blue eyes. His cologne is subtle, but just rich enough to be smelled over the diner. It's intoxicating, with hints of bergamot, cedar, and vanilla that make me both hungry and lightheaded at the same time. His voice is low and the twitch in his lips tells me he's trying not to laugh. "I'm sayin' it because I'm her dad."

CHAPTER TWO

MILLIE

Surprise hits me at the same time as recognition. I must process the recognition before the surprise, because I blurt out the name I've been trying to remember since I first saw him: "Tom Brady."

The amusement falls from his face as quickly as his shoulders slump. He suddenly looks weary. "Nope. Duke Ogden."

"No, not your name. That's who you look like! I've been racking my brain to think of who you reminded me of, and it's Tom Brady. Has anyone ever told you that?"

He wrenches Lottie from my grasp and she starts screaming and reaching for me. "Real original, *Millie*. I haven't heard that one ten thousand times before, either."

He strides off, holding his sobbing child, and once again, I'm left staring at him. Tia comes to check on me.

"Who on earth does that guy think he is?" I ask her.

We watch him march over to his table, pick up a diaper bag,

and drop a handful of bills on the table. A tall, brunette woman I missed earlier waltzes after him. "That's Duke Ogden."

"Yeah, he told me his name. But where does he get off thinking he's heaven's gift to humanity like that?"

She blinks at me. "Hon, he's *Duke Ogden*. The quarterback? Heir to Tom Brady in looks, skills, and contracts? He has endorsement deals with Mercedes, Under Armour, and like ten other huge companies." She knocks on the side of my head. "He's one of the most famous men in the country. You seriously don't know who he is?"

"Oh, that makes more sense." I feel a bit chastened. I could have been more gracious when he told me the room was probably looking at him. "I just thought he looked like a younger, hotter Tom Brady."

"That he does." Duke has left the building, but that doesn't stop us from standing side by side and looking at the door he exited through. "As long as you don't compare him out loud to Tom Brady, you two will get along just fine."

I grimace. "Why? Is that such a bad thing?"

She looks at me like she's trying to tell if I have a brain in my head. I shrink under her gaze. "I'm guessin' people have compared you to Emma Stone, what, like a thousand times in your life?"

"Give or take."

"Right. And you don't even look that much like her. But now imagine that you were super popular and super talented but no one—and I mean no one—mentioned you without also comparing you to Emma Stone. Would that get old?"

"I see your point."

She pats my back, one of the only parts of me that's dry. "Good. Now go get cleaned up and I'll have your order to go."

"Yes ma'am," I say.

In the bathroom, I see that, in addition to my dress being

dyed brown with soda, I'm still wearing the fuzzy yellow blanket Duke let me borrow. Lottie's blanket. I can't believe I missed the fact that she was right there. The brunette at Duke's table must have been holding her. His estranged wife? Girlfriend? Whoever she is, I can't imagine she's too happy with me and my stupid bra.

I quickly peel off my dress, let the hand dryer dry my bra as well as it can, and then slip into Tia's spare outfit. She's a little shorter, with less curves than I have, but the white shirt and black pencil skirt aren't scandalous on me, at least. You can only see my bra if you're really looking, and I have neither time nor tolerance for anyone who's looking that closely.

After changing, I pay for my order, wave to Tia, and head back to my office for my next appointment.

Forty-five minutes later, I jot down a couple of notes and stand to stretch. With my mind free for ten minutes until my next session, my thoughts instantly go to Lottie.

And her dad.

I hate making people feel bad. I didn't mean to insult him, and I firmly believe that intentions matter, but hurt matters, too. Maybe I should send him a card or flowers, or something. Do football stars like flowers?

I text one of my best friends, the CFO of our company, Parker. At five-feet tall, she has an Ariana Grande vibe that always seems to attract the biggest jock in the room. She thinks tall guys are obsessed with short girls, and maybe some of them are. But I think she intrigues guys of any size, and it's only the bold ones who dare approach her. She can come off as an ice queen, but underneath the frost is a fiercely loyal heart, a razor sharp wit, and a knowledge of sports that could rival a bookie's.

On top of that, her ex played football in college. He plays professionally now, in fact.

. . .

MILLIE: If I inadvertently offended a football player, should I send him flowers?

She's busy at work on a new campaign for Jane & Co., but Parker responds immediately.

PARKER: I don't know a football player famous for his love of flowers. What happened?

PARKER: More importantly, WHO ARE WE TALKING ABOUT?? Should I come up?

I look at the time. Rats. I have four minutes before my next session.

MILLIE: No time. But it's that dude who looks like Gisele's ex-husband. Duke something.

PARKER: DUKE OGDEN?!

Parker's office is almost directly beneath mine, and I'm not imagining her squeal.

PARKER: I KNEW he lived here! I knew it! Tripp and Jane were so dodgy about Tripp's bff who couldn't make the wedding. And

I know Duke grew up here. I'm going to find him. Where does he live? Where did you see him?

MILLIE: Parker Jane, breathe. You swore off tall dudes, remember? AND football players.

PARKER: I just made an exception.

I'm typing the words before I've even processed why they matter, why I can't let her call dibs.

MILLIE: He's Lottie's dad.

Three dots appear, and I sit with the worry of what those dots will become.
I shouldn't have worried.

PARKER: Oh, Millie Vanilli. Are you okay?

Her empathy makes my throat ache.

MILLIE: Meh. Nothing a giant turkey leg at the Pumpkin Patch can't solve. 5:30?

. . .

KATE WATSON

PARKER: You got it.

I stuff my feelings in a box the moment my next client's face appears on my screen

CHAPTER THREE

DUKE

Wanna know what's cool?

Spilling a drink on a gorgeous woman, finding out she's the subject of your three-year-old daughter's most enduring obsession, and then inadvertently offending the woman just to have her blatantly offend you right back.

So cool.

The cherry on top of this poop sundae?

Lottie is crying for her. Crying for Millie. Again.

I will never escape this woman. Especially not now that she's *here*.

Several months ago, I flew out of town for an overnighter and had my best friend, Tripp, watch Lottie. During those two days and a night, Lottie met Millie, and nothing has been the same since.

Tripp and Jane haven't told me anything about her other than that she's one of Jane's best friends. When I asked what her hold on Lottie was, they said she "has a way with people."

Yeah, well, so do cult leaders.

Ugh.

What is she doin' here?

"So you finally met *her*," my sister says, not daring to say Millie's name out loud, because Lottie is already devastated enough as it is. "How'd you screw it up?"

We're standing on the sidewalk next to my Range Rover, a sheen of sweat forming across my forehead while my baby girl's sobs tug at my heart ... and split my ears a little. "Right. I forgot you two became best friends at my best friend's wedding."

"I'm telling you, she was fabulous, Duchess. Kind, funny, super cool."

"And yet she couldn't keep from calling me Tom Brady, so ... clearly not that fabulous."

Reese winces. The wind blows her freshly dyed hair into her face. "That's too bad. I liked her."

"Well, you can dye your hair brown, but you're still a dumb blonde at heart."

Reese's eyes roll in a perfect semicircle, including doing that fluttering thing only actors and over-dramatic little sisters can pull off. "Takes one to know one, you bigger, dumber, blonder Brady."

"You forgot 'hotter.'"

"Did I, though?"

I sigh, swaying Lottie like I did when she was a baby. Sometimes I can't believe my little girl is growing up as fast as she is. She's almost four, and yet it feels like I was shushing and swaddling and all the other S's just last week.

Which I kind of was, less the swaddling.

Lottie's regressed in the last two years.

I blame my ex.

She abandoned us during my cancer treatments when our daughter was almost two. But knowing that Carlie is a blood-sucking harpy doesn't actually help the daughter she quite literally walked out on. Lottie barely remembers Carlie, but lately, I've wondered if she remembers the pain of her leaving.

Somewhere in the recesses of her mind, she seems to know that she had a mother, a woman who should have loved and cared for her, but who just... wouldn't. So while she doesn't cry for Carlie, she clings to me, to Reese, to my parents—to *Millie*—more and more lately. A lot more.

My career makes it hard. I travel for games, for practices. I travel for interviews, contracts, ads, heck, even photo shoots. If it weren't for Reese agreeing to be my nanny over the summer and now through the season, I don't know how I could have managed it all as a single dad with a demanding career.

As it is, I can't deny the fact that my almost four-year-old, who potty trained herself at twenty-one months, needs pull-ups again. Her tantrums are worse now than they were at two. She's become afraid of monsters to a degree that our bedtime routine can take hours, and she still ends up climbing into my bed half the time. It's easier to move her back to her room once she's asleep than it is to get her to fall asleep there in the first place.

And that's to say nothing of Millie.

Millie, who Lottie is once again crying over—screaming for in the middle of the street—no matter how much I shush her. I talked to her pediatrician a couple of months ago after the first Millie-meltdown, and he said that kids Lottie's age can get attached to anyone or anything.

My best friend, Tripp, suggested that maybe Lottie has separation anxiety. I dismissed it at the time, but I asked the doc his thoughts. He just laughed and patted my shoulder like I wasn't half a foot taller than him and told me that I was worrying for nothing. All kids go through separation anxiety, he said. With a schedule like mine, if I were to indulge her worry, I'd reward the very behavior I want to extinguish, he said. I'd never have another minute's peace.

Following that advice has given me less peace than ever.

When I fail to calm Lottie down after several minutes, I have to wrestle her into her car seat. I'm strong, but there's no one stronger than a toddler who doesn't want to get into her car seat. She wriggles and writhes like a greased pig, and I'd be lying if I said her right hook doesn't pack a punch.

Honestly, I'm kind of impressed.

Passersby keep giving me judgmental looks, and I'm feeling worse about my fathering skills by the minute.

I shoot Reese a desperate look, but she just shrugs. And that's when I feel a tap on my shoulder.

It's Nico, who owns the second-hand and vintage shop a dozen feet from me. He has a son my age and coached our soccer team up through ninth grade, when I quit to focus on football. He's a good guy and tough as nails.

Which is why it's uniquely odd to have him push me out of the way while shaking a can of Reddi-Wip. He pops the top off with his thumb and sprays whipped cream into Lottie's screaming mouth before backing up.

She stops instantly. Surprise and confusion make her blink, and she closes her cherub mouth, swallowing and giving me the chance to buckle her five-hundred-point safety harness.

"Thank you," I say to Nico.

He nods wordlessly and returns to his shop.

Once we're home, Lottie has a vulnerable sort of calm that usually follows her tantrums, so I take her swimming in our heated pool instead of reviewing tape. I played last night—a home game—and now the Carolina Waves have a bye week. That means I have two weeks stretching ahead of me to study film and to get healthy.

Physically, I'm okay. I got sacked a few too many times last night, and my back has been spasming ever since, but I'm okay.

Mentally, though? These last two years have felt like memorizing playbooks in different languages while taking too much Benadryl.

The pressure to figure out how to help my little girl is worse than anything I've ever felt on the field. I can't tell if she needs me to be tough or tender, and I worry I'm doing both at the wrong times and in the wrong way.

After swimming, she and Reese settle on the couch with apple slices and peanut butter and watch *Moana*. As soon as Lottie falls asleep on her aunt, I head straight back down to Maple Street, where the brand new Serenity Counseling office is. They're the office that's working with my best friend's farm.

Tripp owns one of the country's biggest orchards and farms, complete with animals of the petting zoo variety. A couple of months ago, he told me they were going full steam ahead on an animal-assisted therapy program with some hotshot therapist. He wouldn't give me more details than that, but in fairness, I've always thought therapy was pretty overhyped, so maybe the sniffs and huffs I threw his way made him hold back a little more than he would have otherwise.

And now he's on his honeymoon, so I can hardly call him and ask him for advice. Or his new wife. She and Tripp had a rocky start, but the rest of us liked her from the beginning. If I hadn't sworn off women after my divorce, I may even have given Tripp a run for his money with Jane.

All right, probably not. She's not quite my type. An image of red hair, flawless ivory skin, and a healthy sprinkling of freckles pops in my head before I can stop it.

No. No way. *Definitely* not my type. I've never dated a redhead before, and more importantly, I have no plans to date *anyone*, let alone someone who compares me to Brady.

Listen, the guy's the GOAT—the greatest of all time. I can't help that I look like him, but our playing styles are nothing alike, and I'm not chasing any of his records.

Newsflash, all y'all armchair experts: I'm a running quarterback. If anything, I'm chasing the records of guys like Cam Newton and Steve Young. I want highest passer rating *and* most rushing touchdowns. If I happen to collect as many Super Bowl rings as Brady along the way, will I be mad about it?

No, I will not.

But as much as I'd love to be thinking about a playoff run this year, I have something more pressing on my mind: working up the nerve to walk into that counseling office. I flex my hands, which have been gripping the steering wheel too tightly. I look at the bare ring finger on my left hand and resentment bubbles in my gut. As angry as I am with my ex, the person I'm more angry with is me.

What is wrong with me that I couldn't even fall in love with the woman I married? If I could have, everything would be okay. *Lottie* would be okay.

This is my fault.

Which is why I need to stop stalling and get myself into that office, already.

Muscle up, Buttercup.

Mustering all my courage, I march back into the Serenity Counseling office. Ms. Angie is sitting at the receptionist desk, looking as calm as a summer's morning. Even though she's a couple of decades older than I am, she looks like she drank from the fountain of youth. She worked in the administrative office at the school when I was a kid, and I had a huge crush on her then. I even gave her a valentine in fourth grade.

Seeing her always makes me feel like a little kid.

"Hiya, Duke. Back so soon?"

I want to grab the back of my neck but I refrain, keeping my hands in my pockets. Any good quarterback has to have an unreadable poker face, but I showed my hand earlier. I won't do that again. My gut is squirming like a bucket of worms, but I don't let it appear on my face.

"I'm not exactly sure what I'm doing here, Ms. Angie."

"The fact that you're here is good enough, sugar. Ms. Campbell is just finishing up a telehealth appointment, so if you can wait a few minutes, I'll send you into her office."

A few minutes later, Angie points me in the direction of the therapist's office. I open the door just to see a presumptuous redhead whip around in her desk chair. The smile drops off her maddeningly appealing face.

You've gotta be kidding me.

CHAPTER FOUR

DUKE

"What are you doing here?" I ask. She's wearing a different outfit than the one I accidentally possibly ruined. This looks more like the kind of outfit the servers over at the diner wear.

Wait. This *is* the outfit the servers at the diner wear. She must have bummed it off Tia. If I weren't so annoyed, I may feel guilty. But she compared me to Tom Brady for a laugh, so I can't bring myself to worry over some stupid dress. Even if she looked gorgeous in it.

"Uh, I work here. Did you come back to get Lottie's blanket?" She leans over and rifles through a big black Tori Birch bag. Then she stands with Lottie's yellow blanket. "I should have considered it might be special to her. Sorry for holding on to it," she says. Pink tinges her ivory cheeks, making her look distractingly glow-y.

Also, does she have to be so gracious given how we ended things? She stands and holds the fleece blanket to me. In truth,

Lottie doesn't give a lick about it. It's one of those blankets that I keep with me to wipe up random kid messes if I run out of baby wipes.

"Uh, yeah, thanks." I reach over her desk and our pointer fingers touch, shooting a bolt of electricity up my arm and straight to my chest. Literally.

"Whoops!" She laughs, shaking out her hand. "Sorry, I must have had a static charge from the fabric. This nylon flooring doesn't do me any favors."

"Heh," I mumble, not quite laughing, not quite grimacing. Not quite *anything*. I'm flustered. I didn't expect to see her here. I didn't expect her to be so calm and … and lovely, frankly. She's funny and self-effacing and just generally not being a jerk, and the combination with her undeniable attractiveness? It's disarming.

I take the blanket because I don't know what else to do. Then I turn for the door. My hand hesitates on the handle, though. And hesitates.

"Was that all you came for?" she asks softly. Her voice isn't as low as it is deep, which doesn't make sense. But it's like it has a sub-tone that only I can hear, and that tone is shaking me to my core. I spin and say the first thing that comes to mind.

"Why did you have to compare me to Brady?"

She screws up her face in a grimace. Her scrunching button nose is a bit too endearing to handle right now. "Can I apologize for that? Because I'm sorry. Tia told me what that must be like for you, but I swear, I had no idea who you were."

I sigh with exhaustion. "Come on."

"No, I promise you, I didn't know," she insists. "I don't really even know Tom Brady, except that he plays football and was married to Gisele Bündchen."

She sounds so earnest, but the words coming out of her mouth are absurd. Gisele is famous, sure, but between the two of them, Brady's fame eclipses hers completely. A total eclipse of the fame. "Why would you know him through her?"

She puts her hand on her hip. "Seriously? That woman is an *icon*. She's one of the richest female entertainers and most powerful women in the world. She's a mom of two, has launched fashion lines, written a bestselling book, and worked her butt off trying to save rain forests. The fact that she married a super hot dude is like a blip on the radar."

I stand a little straighter. She thinks Brady is hot? "That 'super hot dude' is one of the most famous athletes in the world."

"Cool. You know she's worth over four hundred million, right?"

Four hundred—

I open and close my mouth. That can't be true.

Can it?

"You're serious."

"As a cancer scare," she says. I stiffen at her wording, but she's nonplussed. Another thing she appears to be genuinely in the dark about. "Listen, Duke, I know as much about sports as I know about supply chain management. Which is to say that they both exist and are important to people, but I'm not one of them."

I honest-to-goodness snort. She's painting herself as uninformed and frivolous, but there's nothing frivolous about the way she speaks or carries herself or even about her answer. And there's certainly nothing frivolous about her profession. "In that case, your apology is accepted. And I should probably apologize for the way I handled things myself. And for the whole drink incident."

She waves her hand. "It's Diet Coke under the bridge."

I narrow my eyes. She's funny, smart, and a bit eccentric. If I hadn't sworn off women, I'd flirt a little. But I've sworn off women, and the memory of why hits me like a three hundred fifty pound defensive lineman.

"I—" My throat goes dry and I have to clear it to continue. "I didn't actually come to talk about soda and stars."

"Nice alliteration."

I nod in acknowledgment but any lightheartedness in me has evaporated. I guess she can tell, because her arch expression falls and her face becomes open and entreating. I can't explain what that even looks like. Is it how her vivid green eyes narrow a fraction while her eyebrows lift? Or the slight cock of her head that makes it feel like she's trying to listen harder?

"I'm here about Lottie."

Without meaning to, I drop in a loveseat that's so comfortable, I want one for myself. She gets up from her desk and sits in a cozy sage green armchair across from me. The room has a great feel to it—the walls are a creamy white, the natural wood end tables are light and clean. A boxwood wreath on the wall and a large aloe vera plant in the corner remind me to breathe deeper.

And, as cliché as it sounds, the fish tank in the center of the bookshelf is a much-needed distraction. I don't have to stare at my hands or keep my eyes on Millie as I talk. Instead, I can look at the little Nemo-fishes peacefully floating.

"I'm worried about my daughter. She's regressed in almost every way over the last year or two. She's harder now than she's ever been. And I'm drowning."

And just like that, the dam breaks.

With every word, every confession, admitting every time I've given in or lost my temper, I feel more and more like the biggest failure in the world. Millie's face remains earnest, judgment free, and inviting, and I find myself telling her things I haven't even told my parents.

Like how I just want my kid to be normal and how, even

though I blame my ex for breaking my little girl, I worry I'm starting to resent Lottie, too.

As soon as it's out of my mouth, my eyes slam shut and I shake my head, feeling sick. "I didn't mean that. Normal is meaningless and I don't resent her. I could never resent her."

"You don't need to filter yourself, Duke. Parenting is hard, isn't it?" she asks. I nod but feel nauseated doing so. "Minor feelings of resentment are normal for parents. I'm not excusing anything, just putting it into perspective. Kids have a way of throwing chili at you right after you've showered and mopped. That's pretty messed up, if you ask me. Feeling a bit of resentment every now and then is to be expected." Her smile is small but warm. "When the feelings become more intense and frequent, though, that's a sign of a deeper problem."

I bury my face in my hands. "I know. I have to be more patient."

"Maybe. But more than that, you sound like an exhausted, caring dad who needs more resources and education to take care of a sweet girl who's going through something really difficult."

Yes.

My word, yes.

Emotion thickens in my throat so much that it hurts to swallow. "She's been going through this for months and I haven't done anything about it, though. And all I've done is give her more TV time and pray that she'll stop clinging and crying. What kind of father does that?"

"A real one," she says. "She's struggling, and that's making her behavior more erratic and difficult. You've given in *because* you've loved her but didn't know what else to do. If you'd had better options, would you have taken them?"

"Yes!"

"Exactly. You love Lottie, Duke, and she knows that. You are a good dad and she is a good girl, and you're both having a hard time. If you didn't love her so much, you wouldn't be here now."

I sniff, wrinkling my nose. My head shakes back and forth of its own volition, like it's denying Millie's words without my input. "If I'd just been a better dad, none of this would be happening. If I'd have just been a better person ... " My head shakes again.

Millie doesn't respond immediately and I don't have the courage to look up.

"You've mentioned how things have gotten harder since Carlie left. What was going on between you two before that?"

Oof.

Where do I begin? Do I tell her that the one time I got drunk in my whole life ended with me in a chapel o' love with a girl I'd only dated for a couple of months? Carlie was a total jersey chaser, but I was an NFL rookie who got his team to the AFC championship game. Even though we were one game short of the Super Bowl, getting to the playoffs was life changing. It set my trajectory rocketing into space.

I got a little too eager celebrating, and I let her take advantage of the fact. She'd been way more into me than I was ever into her. And that lasted through our whole marriage.

Up until I got cancer.

Do I tell Millie? I can count on my fingers and toes the number of people in the world who know about that, so I'm not eager to bring it up now.

But I need the help.

"I, uh, I got cancer. Hodgkin's Lymphoma. We caught it early. I missed a season doing cancer treatments and told the media that it was a shoulder injury. I guess I wasn't social media worthy anymore because I wouldn't let her use my illness to increase her followers. I was weak and throwing up from chemo, and she left in the middle of the night. Caught a plane to

Europe and hooked up with a soccer player. Either way, her jersey chasing ways took her international."

"She left her baby in the middle of the night while you were in a hospital?" It's the first hint of real emotion I've seen since I sat down.

"They were in a hotel suite with my parents and sister," I say, not sure why I'm defending her.

Maybe because I know that, as much as she wanted to hurt me in the end, she never wanted to hurt Lottie. Lottie was a casualty of war.

"She still abandoned you both." Millie stresses. "Wow. What a betrayal."

Betrayal.

It's not the whole story—evidently my filter isn't entirely broken—but Millie's right. It *was* a betrayal. The lines between Millie's eyebrows show concern, but she doesn't appear to think differently because of it. She doesn't seem like she's judging me. Maybe it's because she's one of the only people in the world who doesn't care that I'm *me*.

Or maybe she's good at her job.

Either way, this is the most exposed I've felt since my first post-game press conference returning from cancer. I'd thrown four interceptions and had looked as wrecked as I felt. No amount of training in the weeks leading up to that game could prepare me after everything my body had been through in the year leading up to it.

I'd been so worried someone would suspect that I'd been through something more than shoulder rehab. My second game wasn't a whole lot better, but a bye week and a blowout against the worst team in the league the following week bought me enough time that I was quickly back on top.

No one except my closest loved ones was the wiser. Also my coach, GM, owner, agent, and ex.

To Carlie's credit, she's never breathed a word about the

cancer.

I'm still surprised about that, honestly.

Maybe this is stuff I should talk to Millie about, but I'll save it for next time. I can't believe I'm even thinking about next time, but just getting everything off my chest without judgment has felt freeing. Maybe Tripp was right about therapy.

"You've had a hard go of things the last two years, Duke. So has Lottie. I'm not surprised you're both struggling. I think you're on the right track to want to get her help. The other therapist in the office is great, but if Lottie doesn't connect with her, I'm happy to give you a referral—"

My eyes snap to hers faster than my center can snap the ball. "Wait, you're not going to see us? Her? Lottie, I mean?"

Millie's neutral expression falters. "No, I'm sorry. I can't. I know you guys."

"What?" My chest roars hot, like someone throwing lighter fluid on my smoker. "Do you mean to tell me that because I dumped Coke on you in a restaurant instead of in your office, you won't help my daughter?"

Her eyebrows raise, but only a fraction of an inch. "No, it has nothing to do with meeting you an hour ago. It's because I *know* Lottie. I know her as the adorable little toddler who likes to squeeze my cheeks, and she knows me as the woman she wishes …" Millie's eyes drop and she clears her throat. What did Lottie wish? Whatever it is, Millie's flustered for the first time. "The point is, I could never be unbiased with her."

"So what? You care about her and she clearly cares about you. I *want* you to be biased." Why can't she understand how perfect this is? The woman Lottie is obsessed with is a child therapist. She'll do anything Millie says!

"I'm not explaining this well. Duke, I care too much about Lottie to be objective. It would be totally unethical for me to attempt to treat someone I could never see clearly. I could lose my license."

I hang my head and grip my hair with both hands, tugging a little too hard. "She'll never connect with another therapist."

Millie's voice is soft and soothing. "You don't know that. She could surprise you."

I lean back in the loveseat, deflated and bitter. "She could *surprise* me? Do you think you know my own daughter better than I do?"

"You know I didn't say that."

"She cried for weeks after she met you. Did you know that? Before every nap, every bedtime, it was nothing but Millie, Millie, Millie. I had to let her sleep in bed with me or neither of us would have had an hour of rest."

She leans back as if recoiling. Or trying to protect herself. "I'm sure that was even harder than it sounds. But I don't see how that's relevant to my following licensing requirements."

Guilt creeps up my throat, but do I stop? No, no I don't. "I just want someone to choose my daughter first for once."

"That is exactly what I'm doing, and the fact that you can't see that tells me it's time for this conversation to end." She stands up and folds her arms. In my profession, I have to be able to read tells, and I'm one of the best. The wrong muscle twitch in a fired up defender is enough to tell me if I should call a different play. But I can't read anything on Millie except the very obvious fact that this conversation is through. "The other clinician in the office will be here Monday, and she has decades of experience treating children. I hope you'll choose to make an appointment with her."

Even though Millie has every right to tell me off, she's still looking for a way to help. A mature part deep in my brain recognizes what a classy move this is.

It's not a move I can reciprocate.

"Gee, Millie," I say in spite of myself. "Thanks a lot."

And then I'm out the door.

CHAPTER FIVE

MILLIE

Throngs of people surround my friends and me at Sugar Maple Farms, the farm we've rebranded. It went from being a sleepy, declining brand to having a huge renaissance. Their jams, jellies, and preserves are cool again, and the farm itself is the talk of the region.

Food Truck Friday at Sugar Maple Farms has become a big deal on its own, too, but combined with a pumpkin patch in mid-October, it's a level of packed I didn't know was possible. Fields have been cleared to make parking space for thousands of cars. If our friend Rusty didn't sneak us in through the employee lot, we'd still be in line for tickets, along with half of South Carolina and Georgia.

But instead, I'm stuffing my face with three of my best friends at one of several dozen picnic tables.

"I hope you told him off," Ash says across the table from me.

"Millie never tells people off," Parker says. "She stays calm and level-headed and lets the other person lose their mind until their own guilt eviscerates them. It's brilliant." She stabs a fry with her fork. Yes, Parker eats fries with a fork. "He's so pretty. Too bad he's a cocky jerk."

"I don't think he's a jerk, I think he's hurting," I say, dipping my pulled pork in a mouth-watering tangy mustard sauce.

"Two things can be true at the same time," Lou points out. "Someone as famous as him, who does what he does, has to have an ego. He's also clearly worried 'bout the impact his ex has had on his daughter."

I would never in a million years breach patient confidentiality. Even though Duke and Lottie aren't my patients, Duke obviously had an expectation of privacy, so I'm careful not to share anything he revealed in my office.

I looked him up after he left, though. His wife's affair and his "shoulder rehab" are widely known. And my friends have seen Lottie's obsession with me firsthand.

I told my friends what happened in the diner, including the whole Brady comparison thing. Parker was both horrified and delighted by my gaffe. I also explained that he found me later, apologized, and then basically demanded that I treat Lottie (who has all the markers of separation anxiety disorder). My friends weren't in the room to see him choked up over his daughter and his own insecurities. The jerky parts of the story are all they have to go on.

"I don't know," Ash says. "We know famous people who aren't jerks. Sonny—" Parker bristles, and Ash changes course mid-sentence. "I mean, look no further than our bestie, Lou. She doesn't have an ego and she's super famous." Her mass of cinnamon brown curls bounce as she points at our other friend.

Lou's pale blue eyes dart around before she leans closer. "Yeah, and that fame is a tightly guarded secret, remember?" she says through gritted teeth.

The nearest picnic table is a few feet away, and with Southern Rock blasting in the background and thousands of people visiting the pumpkin patch, it's not like anyone could hear us, even if they knew exactly who we were talking about.

But we've been on high alert about Lou's identity for a couple of years, so sheer habit makes me glance around the farm to ensure that no one is listening.

"On another note, Jane has known who Lottie's dad is this whole time. Why wouldn't she have told us?" Parker says.

"Because you would have been so chill about that," Ash teases before stuffing fries in her face. Ash looks like Jess from The New Girl but with Felicity's curls. Season one Felicity, to be clear. Her aesthetic is quirky more than nerdy. She likes to match her lipstick to her glasses, whether those glasses are fire engine red, bubblegum pink, or electric blue. She's an advertising genius and is the pizzazz behind our biggest campaigns.

"Excuse me? I'm cool as ice." Parker arches a perfectly manicured black eyebrow and holds her head high. Her high black ponytail doesn't dare even swing.

"Ice ice, baby," I say, holding my Diet Coke out. My friends clink their mason jars into mine.

After dinner, I drag my friends to the animal pens. They pretend it's a hardship, but I know they love them, smell aside. What's not to love about baby llamas, alpacas, and goats? We only have around a dozen animals total, and as friendly and adorable as the goats are, the llamas are my favorite. Not that I have a favorite.

I'm lying. I totally have a favorite, and he's three weeks old and I got to name him, and I named him Louis.

Louis Vuitton Llama, to be precise.

I have no regrets.

Louis the Llama is snow white and has the friendliest, cutest, calmest little soul. He's technically a llapaca—a cross between an alpaca and a llama—which means he's smaller and, well, floofier than a llama. But we all call him Louis the Llama, because few people know the difference between a llama and an alpaca, let alone know that a llapaca exists.

Besides, Louis the Llama rolls off the tongue, doesn't it?

Louis and his pals are kept in a small red barn close enough to the pumpkin patch that we can still hear the happy screams and squeals from the mass of pumpkin patch goers. The barn doors are closed for the night, but there's an attached pen with a secure gate that I have the code to access. The first gate leads to a small enclosure and then a second gate, in case the animals try to escape with one of us.

Once we're in, I call out. "Hi guys! How are my buddies tonight?"

The baby goats run when they hear my voice, and the alpacas and llamas are a beat behind them. The goats are naturally more excited and full of energy than the other animals. Assuming they're treated well, llamas are social, friendly, and gentle. They have an instinctive ability to match a person's energy. I worked with both goats and llamas during my internship. After I got past how hokey it all seemed, it ended up being fascinating and so rewarding. I saw firsthand how topics too difficult to discuss in an office arose more easily when a kid was brushing a goat or cleaning a stall.

I can't wait to do the work I love.

If I can just get a client.

Ash and Lou play with the animals while Parker holds back. She claims she's allergic to pet fur, but what she really means is she's allergic to anything touching her designer clothes.

Yet even she isn't immune to their cuteness. "Oh, look at you and your neck, you fluffy little goof," she says as Louis slowly makes his way to her. She pets him and he pretends he doesn't love it, just like she does. Ash is surrounded by baby goats, letting them climb all over her.

"Watch it with the babies, Ash. They'll eat anything," I warn her.

"Oh, it's fine," she says as a baby goat starts chewing on her hair. "They're just love nibbles." Then Ash gasps and her eyes pop almost comically. She pulls back, and the bright red streak in her hair is noticeably shorter than it used to be. "No! Bad goat! We don't eat hair!"

The goat lunges for more.

Parker laughs while I help get the goats off of Ash—and laugh.

I pick up a squirmy, caramel colored goat named Stella. Her hair is somehow coarse and smooth at the same time, and she's eager to try my big leather teardrop earrings. "I told you last time they'll eat whatever they can get their teeth on," I tell Ash. "Get up!"

She stands and wipes a hand across her butt, removing hay. Then she pulls her curls down to inspect the damage. She's missing easily three inches—curled. Pulled straight, it's almost six. Ash throws her head back, drops to her knees dramatically, and in her best Marlon Brando, cries, "Stellaaaaa!"

"Groan," Lou says.

The goat herself jumps at Ash, and I manage to save my friend's sweater from Stella just in time. "You will never learn."

She springs up, her curls bouncing like a bobble head. "I know."

Before Parker or Lou can comment, we hear voices, and my heart starts to hammer moments before the owners of said voices turn the corner around the barn. A little girl is begging to see the animals, and her dad's voice is placating.

They round the corner, and I almost laugh to see Duke and Lottie.

Again.

CHAPTER SIX

MILLIE

"Miwwie!" Lottie cries. Duke moans like an injured llama before he sees me. "Lottie, please," he pleads. But when she wiggles out of his arms, he puts her down and glances up to see me. Our eyes connect, and he looks about as happy as I feel.

He laughs darkly to himself. I barely hear him over Lottie's squeals, but what I do hear is unmistakable: "I will never escape her."

Lottie launches herself at me, and I pick her up without thinking. "I knew I'd see you again!" she says, hugging me tightly.

She has what I can only describe as kitten breath, and her little arms wrap around my neck so fully that I almost feel complete. My thoughts flash back to the last time my heart seemed to expand like this. The memory of my niece's auburn pigtails against my cheek makes my eyes sting.

"Hi sweetie," I say, blinking back tears. I'm sure everyone

around me thinks this is just about Lottie. Or maybe not, I think, looking at Parker, Ash, and Lou. My friends know how much I miss my niece and they know how badly I want to be a mom. The sympathy on their faces hints at more than the here and now.

The pain deep in my soul does, too.

Ash comes over and squeezes my shoulder. She greets Lottie with the peek-a-boo of a seasoned aunt. Ash has three older brothers, all married, and a handful of nieces and nephews. She doesn't have my burning desire to be a mom, but she loves kids.

Lottie wriggles down and grabs my hand, pulling me close to her dad, who looks like he can't believe his bad luck. He also—and I hate that I'm thinking this—looks gorgeous. I'm a sucker for muscled arms in fitted sweaters, and Duke's are everything I could want and more. He's changed from the v-neck he wore earlier today to a cable knit fisherman's sweater that matches his eyes so perfectly, I have to wonder if he bought it or if a girlfriend did.

You know that old saying, "The clothes make the man"?

The saying is wrong.

This man makes the clothes. He could make a garbage bag look good.

"Duke," I say. "What a surprise seeing you here."

"It's a small world." He sounds equal parts wry and annoyed. "I didn't know you'd be here. Rusty let us in."

Parker clears her throat loudly behind me, which is good, because I've forgotten my manners. "Duke, these are my friends Parker Emerson, Ashley Moore, and Lucy Williams. Ladies, this is Duke Ogden. And of course you remember Lottie from the wedding." I peek at Lottie, who's grinning. She holds me like I'm a prize her dad won for her at a festival booth.

They all say hello, and although Parker is a mega-fan, she plays it as advertised: cool as ice. Lou is as Southern as she is musically gifted, so she's a bit more visibly excited to meet an

NFL star. Meanwhile, Ash is bubbly and friendly, asking questions about his life that he answers more kindly than I expected. And boy does she ask.

He tells us a story about a flight from hell to an away-game, and we're all laughing by the time he gets to the fallout of the bad chicken. He mimes lots of explosions from multiple ends, and Ash is giggling as hard as Lottie is.

Parker shows her knowledge of the game by remembering how abysmally the team played after that incident, and Duke looks impressed.

"You still rushed for almost a hundred yards," she says, sounding dubious rather than fawning, "so it couldn't have been that bad."

"Only because my RB put the *runs* in running back. He was pinching his butt cheeks too tightly to make a good play."

This gets a hard laugh from Parker. "I knew Sonny looked off in that game. He's always had a weak stomach."

"Always ... do you know him?"

Parker's shoulders tense more than shrug. "We dated for a year and a half before he transferred to Clemson."

Duke rears back. "No way. You dated Sonny Luciano?"

Parker's eyebrows raise to points. She loves being challenged, even as innocuously as this. "Ask him what the tattoo on his left delt means. He'll tell you it's the Thai word for faith, because he and his friend got theirs together when they were in Thailand for a humanitarian trip freshman year. What he won't tell you is that when the Thai tattoo artist asked him what he wanted the tattoo to say, Sonny answered, 'Same as his.' So his tattoo in Thai literally says—"

"Same as his!" Duke throws his head back and howls with laughter, and the sight makes me smile even bigger than the story.

He and I didn't get off to the best start, but here I am, holding his daughter, watching him make jokes with my best friends, and admiring his smile. Not how I expected this day to go.

"Ah, man, I cannot wait to bust him over this. The dude lied through his teeth to me." Duke pulls Parker in for a selfie, laughing wickedly while Parker smirks. Then he texts it to Sonny, and shows us the caption: "Same as his? Cool tat, bro."

A moment later, our old friend is face-timing. He's as handsome as ever, with his dark hair cropped close to his head and his piercing turquoise eyes shining bright against his lightly bronzed skin. His brow is sweaty, and when the screen jostles, I see a gym in the background, predictably.

Parker's face comes up on the screen, and Sonny beams like, well, the sun. "Parker Jane Emerson, you dirty dog. You swore you'd never tell the team!"

This is the first time they've spoken since their tragic breakup when Sonny transferred, yet it's like no time has passed.

Except that Parker's ears are red and she's almost vibrating with nervous energy. "Right. At Chicago. I never said anything about future teams."

"Nuh uh uh uh uh. 'The team' is a general term that applies to any and all future teams henceforth and ever. I'm calling Lou so I can sue you for breach of contract."

"I'll have to recuse myself," Lou says, sticking her ethereal face in front of the camera. "Good to see you, Sonny."

"Lou! Hold up, what's all that hair behind you, PJ? Is that Millie? And Ash, too? What in the world are the Janes doing with my QB?"

Duke is so much taller than us that I can't see his face on the screen, even with him crouching, but I hear him say, "The Janes?"

I incline my head toward his and mutter, "We all share a middle name."

His navy blue eyes drop to mine, his gaze way more arresting than it needs to be, thank you very much. "All of you?"

"Well, Jane doesn't have a middle name. But the rest of us, yup. Parker Jane, Ashley Jane, Lucy Jane … "

"And Millie Jane." My name rumbles from his chest and into my body, starting at my torso and sending a shiver all the way down to my toes.

"Miwwie!" Lottie echoes, startling me. Of course I couldn't forget that I was holding the little cherub, but this all feels so natural. So easy.

I'm too concerned about Lottie's emotional state to let myself fully love the feeling, though. And I might be a bit too concerned about my own state, if I'm being honest. It's almost a relief when the little girl jumps down … until she grabs my hand, grabs Duke's, and then starts pulling.

She's surprisingly strong.

Duke tries to snatch his phone from Parker, but she and the others are still chatting it up with Sonny. "Wait, pumpkin," Duke says, but Lottie just keeps tugging us toward the animals. When I see who she's leading us toward, I smile.

She's caught sight of Louis, with his marshmallow white coat of pure, cuddly fluff. And because he's the king of cool, he waits for her to come to him, even though I know how excited he is for cuddles. Lottie squeals and buries her face into his neck the same way she does in mine. "Yyama!"

The way she can't pronounce her l's is probably adorable enough to create world peace.

I crouch beside her and pet Louis' back. His wool is smooth and fluffy, and he's such a perfect cuddle ball that I can almost see the hearts in Lottie's eyes. "Lottie, this is my friend Louis. Do you think you could help me feed him?"

Lottie squeals and hugs him. Then she follows me to the fence, where I scoop some pellets and place them into her hands. Lottie turns purposefully back to Louis, her little chin tucked down and her eyes fixed on the llama. Baby goats and a couple of the alpacas run to her and try to get at her hand, but she's undeterred. "Shoo, shoo. This is for Youis." She rhymes his name with Huey.

She could not be cuter.

As the animals surround her, she jerks her head around, trying to place Duke first and then me. He's only a couple of yards from her, and I'm even closer, but she looks to be reassuring herself that we're here. Judging by her hesitation, she's also unsure what to do now. Duke starts toward her, but I pantomime a hand across my neck, telling him to stop. He does, but he looks as uncertain as she does.

"Daddy?"

He smiles. "You can do this, pumpkin."

She scowls and looks at me, but I reinforce what he said. "You can do it! We'll be right here. Just keep your hand flat to feed him, okay?" I show her what I mean and she nods tentatively. But when she looks back at Louis, her lips are pursed in determination. She holds her hands out flat to the fuzzball and loudly whispers in his ear that she kept this food safe for him because she loves him.

She pronounces "loves" like "yoves."

I put a hand to my chest, and I catch Duke staring. Not at Lottie, but at me. When we make eye contact, his smoldering gaze jumps back to his daughter. Louis slurps up the pellets, and Lottie stiffens. Duke lunges, but I shake my head, stopping him again. When Louis finishes eating, he nuzzles her face, and she visibly relaxes and throws her arms around his neck again.

She beams with pride when she turns to her dad. "I did it! I fed Youis!"

He looks at me for a split second, long enough for me to catch the question in his eyes. I smile. Then he takes two big steps and scoops her up.

"Yeah, you did! That was so brave! I'd be afraid all that llama slobber would turn me into a … slobber monster!" He pretends to eat her neck and cheek, and she giggles uncontrollably. "Oh no! I *am* a slobber monster!" He fakes gobbling her up again, earning more peals of laughter that make my knees weak.

There is nothing more appealing than this playful display of fatherhood. He must have women throwing themselves at him everywhere he goes. I could almost believe him walking down a street with Lottie on his shoulders, women passed out at his feet.

He's catnip.

And I'm starting to purr.

As Duke is slobber-monstering Lottie, Parker, Ash, and Lou end their call with Sonny. Parker has a foreign, wistful look that I haven't seen on her before.

But, then, she hasn't seen Sonny since they broke up at the end of our sophomore year.

Parker and Sonny both were and weren't the best match, what with her being Type A and him being Type … LMNOP? I don't even know. She was always firmly grounded, and he was like a kite in the wind … that someone had let go of. But he was also the funniest, sweetest guy she ever dated and is the only person I've ever seen outside the Janes to crack the Parker code.

They met at the start of our freshman year and broke up at the end of our sophomore year, when he transferred to a bigger school to play football there. He's a huge star now, but he and I have stayed in touch over the years and managed to remain friends outside of Parker. All of us loved him, though not as much as Parker. She hasn't dated a lot since then, but she does better with sunshine than clouds, and no one can outshine Sonny.

Ash practically springs as she walks. "All right, party people," she says, slinging an arm around Parker and another around Lou. "Who's ready for a corn maze?"

Still shining from her victory, Lottie's hand shoots in the air. "Me! Me!"

I can't imagine this is what Duke wants, so it's my turn to send him a questioning look. He has to think about bedtime, and with a child with separation anxiety disorder, which I'm sure she has, routines are even more important than normal.

But Duke's broad shoulders—which currently hold Lottie at an almost impossible height—lift casually. "Let's do it."

"Yes!" Ash runs to tickle a laughing Lottie, while the rest of us follow.

"How was it talking with Sonny?" I ask Parker.

She shakes her head. "Oh, fine. No big deal."

Lou gives me a knowing look before saying, "*That* was no big deal? The part where you looked like you were staring at the sun and loving the burn?"

Parker makes a "pfft" sound. "Stop it. You know I adore Sonny, but that ship sailed years ago."

"Some ships come back to port," I say gently, because I can't help but be loyal to both of them.

During my master's, I had a serious health scare and the worst medical experience of my life. Afterwards, I was diagnosed with PCOS—polycystic ovarian syndrome. Sonny was one of my first calls. His oldest brother is a cell biologist who focuses on fertility disorder research, and Sonny got me in touch with him immediately. They were both so sweet and patient in my hour of need. Their help proved invaluable in getting a hold of my symptoms and keeping myself flare-up free. And he's checked up on me ever since.

I wish Parker could see him as he is now.

But she's Parker, so good luck with that one, Sonny.

"I'm not a port, MJ, and I'm not interested in reigniting a flame that burned out my sophomore year of college."

"So you're not a port, but you're a candle. Got it."

"Shut it or I'll turn all of your stilettos into kitten heels."

I mock gasp and link arms with her. "You wouldn't dare. You love fashion as much as I do."

"Yes, but I also love you not meddling in my romantic life."

"So you admit that you *do* have romantic feelings toward Sonny."

"Say goodbye to the Louboutins."

I really gasp this time. They were a gift from Jane after we got the bonus for the Sugar Maple Farms account, and they're the most beautiful things I've ever seen. I still can't believe I own them in real life. If we didn't already have a security system in our rental house, I'd buy a safe for them. "You're a little bit terrifying sometimes, you know that?"

She bats her long eyelashes prettily. "I try."

CHAPTER SEVEN

DUKE

I'm not sure I've ever seen Lottie this happy.

Her adorable, gap-toothed smile is so big, her cheeks look like crab apples. It almost hurts to see, because that smile has been too rare lately. My baby girl has big feelings and the emotional swings to match. It's getting late, and I know I should get her in bed, but I can't say no to her.

Train rides? Of course. Massive jumping pillows? I'll probably pop it, but okay. Cotton candy? Done. Mini-golf? Naturally. A haunted house?

"I think the haunted house may need to wait till you're older, sweetie. Don't you think, Duke?" Millie says pointedly, just as I was about to start throwing money at the ticket taker.

"Um, right. Millie's right, pumpkin. You have to be—"

"Twelve." Millie gestures to the sign.

"Twelve." I nod, like it was my idea all along.

Lottie pouts, but instead of waiting for the tantrum, Millie just keeps walking. Lottie drags me forward, not willing to miss a moment with her favorite person. We catch up quickly and she takes Millie's hand.

At some point, we got separated from Millie's friends, but because Lottie won't let Millie go, it's just the three of us. More than a handful of locals give me suggestive looks, which I ignore. Let me tell you, there's nothing like being a celebrity in your hometown. It's one of the reasons I had my agent negotiate so hard to renew my contract with the Carolina Waves in the off-season. My contract is already huge, but the chance to be home for the next five years of my career, especially with everything Lottie is going through, is priceless.

"Good game last week, bro!" someone I *don't* know yells, drawing attention to me. In the crowds, people who don't know me haven't seemed to notice me. But now that one person does, a dozen people around us start buzzing. They're pointing and talking about me. And suddenly the swarm shifts. We're not all walking toward a common event, all crushed together; they're all flocking toward *me*.

"I love you!"

"Will you take a selfie with me?"

"Can I have your autograph?"

The more people that gang around us, the more Lottie clings to me. "I'm with my daughter. Please respect our privacy," I tell people, but they don't care. Flashes are going off on phones all around me, and my mood grows darker by the moment.

"Enough," I tell people, picking Lottie up and holding a hand over her face. "You're scaring my daughter. Have some decency!" I bellow.

Lottie just clings tighter.

I've been in a thousand crowds in my day, but this feels different. It's like Lottie's stress and fear are seeping from her rapidly-beating heart into mine, and I grow more panicked by the second. The noise and constant press of humanity is overwhelming. "Stop. Enough!" I shout as more and more people take pictures and videos.

A part of my brain that sounds like my ex tells me to calm down and warns me that I need to think about the optics, think about the impact this will have long term, but it's like I can't stop. The anger is swelling in me, and as another person sticks his face near Lottie's to take a selfie, the pressure is more than I can handle.

I'm about to go Pompei on these fools.

And then I feel a gentle touch on my arm. A thin hand with long fingers rubs circles on Lottie's back. I blink, coming back to myself.

"How can I help?" Millie asks. Her face is right next to Lottie, but her eyes are on me.

She's asking *me*.

A wave of gratitude hits me, almost taking me out at the knees. I give myself a mental shake and pull my emotions back the way Carlie, of all people, always told me to.

I bump my nose against Lottie's forehead and say, "Baby girl, do you think you and Millie could go get me a turkey leg? One as big as my head?"

Lottie's grip only tightens. She recognizes my "pretending I'm not anxiously pleading" voice when she hears it.

Millie's tone is so soft, it barely carries to me. "Lottie, can I show you where we'll be?" She points over my shoulder, so I lift Lottie up enough to see the food carts ten yards away. "Your dad is so tall, you'll be able to see him the whole time, I promise. Besides, if we're going to find a turkey leg as big as your dad's head, I'm going to need help carrying it." Millie says, tickling Lottie's back so that she squirms. I feel rather than see the smile forming on Lottie's face. The movement of her round cheeks is always a dead giveaway.

But Lottie still isn't budging, so Millie tries again, all while people are asking me about last night's game, whining about some stupid throw I missed as if I did it to spite them.

"Okay, come to think of it, do they even make turkey legs as big as your dad's head?" Lottie raises her head from my shoulder. "I think we'd need a Brontosaurus leg."

"We'd need an Uncle Tripp yeg!" she says, and Millie giggles with Lottie.

My best friend is an inch taller than me. An inch and a half, *maybe*, but the rest of the world acts like that inch is a foot. Including, worst of all, my own daughter.

"Ew! Hasn't your dad ever told you we don't eat humans? Especially not stinky ones like Uncle Tripp. Come here, silly billy." Millie takes Lottie from my arms like we've made this trade off a thousand times. She mouths to me, "I've got her," gives me an encouraging smile, and then pushes past obnoxious fans like they're nothing more than stalks of corn. But her smile is enough to remind me of how I need to act with the masses. Respectful. Nice.

Fake.

And I can do it now that I know my daughter is okay.

"Hey guys," I say to the crowd in general and no one in particular. "Sorry for getting a little overwhelmed back there. Sometimes Daddy Bear comes out." I laugh self-deprecatingly, as if I did anything wrong, and then I take dozens of pictures with people. I sign autographs. I leave voicemails for strangers mocking their team. Someone actually hands me his baby *through* another person. Someone gave his baby *to* a stranger to give to me—yet another stranger—for a picture before getting his infant handed back to him.

Sometimes I hate my job.

I charm the pants off people to make up for the negative press I know will come after my momentary freak out. The haters will only watch the first videos and the "Dukedom" will only care about the last. Both will troll each other, and I'll continue to let my social media manager post and respond to comments for me, because I hate it all.

If it were up to me, I would practice my butt off every day, play football every week, and live an otherwise completely anonymous life. Unlike Carlie, I despise fame. I take no joy in being recognized. I don't want to be the face of any brand. I just want to play football and live my life.

Is that so much to ask?

After a half hour, I politely make my excuses, not that the fans who just found me care that I've been doing this shtick for thirty straight minutes. I weave through the crowd to the food trucks, where I see Lottie asleep on Millie's shoulder. Her fist is tightly wrapped around a turkey leg, and the strings of white lights overhead glow against her skin, making her look like a medieval angel. You know, because of the turkey leg.

I see Millie before she sees me. Her heart-shaped face is rested against Lottie's, and she's rocking back and forth like someone who's done this before. I take a moment to really study her—her big green eyes, her rosebud lips, her button nose. My grandma always called freckles "angel kisses," and this woman has been kissed by a lot of angels. Her camel-colored sweater clings to areas I've tried hard to forget since our run-in at the diner.

She's breathtaking.

I can't take my eyes off her. And as if she weren't alluring enough, the way she holds my daughter is like she's been handed a gift. A gift she knows the full worth of.

It's the most attractive thing I've ever seen.

If I hadn't sworn off women altogether, I would get her number based on this moment alone. I would text her tonight, find a way to "run into" her tomorrow. I would take full advantage of my bye week and spend time with her every day until my next game.

If I hadn't sworn off women, I would be fascinated by this

woman who cares too much about my daughter to treat her because she can't be impartial. I think she's wrong, for the record. But the fact that she cares?
Whew.
I could fall hard.

CHAPTER EIGHT

DUKE

When Millie finally catches sight of me, she gives me a once over that lingers on my thighs, biceps, and pecs. She bites her lip in a way that makes me smile. Her eyes jump to mine, and her cheeks flame up.

I stride toward her. "Caught ogling the quarterback, huh?"

"Is that the role you play?" she asks, and I can't tell if she's serious or not, a fact that bugs me more than I care to admit.

"Do you mean the *position*?" I sit next to her and snake the turkey leg from Lottie's hands. "You really don't know anything about sports, do you? How were you even friends with my boy Sonny? He's all football, all the time."

Truth be told, I know exactly how Sonny would have stayed friends with this woman. When football is your whole life, people on the outside can feel like a lifeline.

Also, she's drop dead gorgeous, and Sonny is a man with working eyeballs.

"Is he really?" Millie seems surprised. "He talks more about his radio interviews to me than he does the game."

The smell of the turkey leg pulls my attention off of Millie. I sink my teeth into the meat and moan. I love food. I'm an athlete, so nutrition is essential for my performance, but because of my cancer history, I also avoid sugar and starch in any form. A couple of giant turkey legs is typical fare at my house.

Carlie loathed my diet. She's always eaten whatever she wants and managed to have an amazing body and peak health in spite of it. But that also means she's not understanding of other people's restrictions. Once when we were throwing a dinner party for some friends on the team, she rolled her eyes when I insisted on offering a gluten-free option for one of the wives who has Celiac's disease. People like Carlie don't enjoy eating with people like me. Heck, some of my teammates don't even enjoy eating with people like me.

"How is it?" Millie asks after I take a bite. She stares at it longingly.

"Good, even cold. You wanna try?"

"No, I couldn't," she protests. Still staring.

"Yeah you could. Here." I put it in front of her face and wait for her to give me the obligatory "are you sure" look? She does. I nod. And then she takes a bite.

"Mmm. I love me a good turkey leg."

"Really? Meat on a stick doesn't look like it would be your thing."

"Why, because I'm a girl?"

"No, because you were wearing Louboutins in your office, and in my experience, women who wear Louboutins don't eat carnival food."

"This one does. And I'm so sad for those women. I love meat. It's my jam. More than jam is, in fact, considering that I don't eat jam. Or fruit, really, except strawberries and blackberries, you know, because they have the lowest glycemic index of all fruits, and holy cow, am I still talking?" Her eyes close, as if she's trying to erase the last ten seconds from her memory.

I rest my elbow on my knee and crane my neck to look at her. "When did you get so chatty?"

She covers a yawn. "It's late and I get punch-drunk when I'm tired."

"I'm on a strict sleep schedule and have a toddler, and I assure you, it's not late enough for this."

"It is when you couldn't sleep last night because you were so anxious about your first day in your new office."

I take another bite, savoring the salty dark meat before I respond. "Today was your first day?"

She nods, rocking Lottie along with her. "Yes and no. I've been in contact with Angie and with the other therapist, and I've been doing telehealth appointments out of the office at our rental, but today was my first full day sitting in the practice that I basically talked Tripp into starting. I just don't want it to fail after he invested so much into it."

I scoff. "I don't think you know how much Tripp's worth. I'm not demeaning your practice, but Tripp was already going to die rich *before* he got the inheritance from his grandpa. With that and with how much Sugar Maple Farms has already taken off since y'all finished the rebrand? Shoot. The guy'll be a billionaire by forty."

"That's nice for him, but I need the practice to be a success for me, too. I left my job for this, and I have bills that won't get paid if I don't."

"Now that, I can understand." The look she gives me tells me she doesn't believe me. "No, I do. I'm not like Tripp. My dad was an insurance agent here in Sugar Maple, South Carolina. Funny enough, in a town of a few thousand people, you don't get rich selling insurance. My momma stayed home with Reese and me. She played volleyball at a D3 school in college, so when Reese and I were both in school, she became the high school volleyball coach. They were good with money, though, and they never lived beyond their means. They instilled that in me. When I got my first big contract, I couldn't even pay their house off because they already had. So I bought them one in Hilton Head."

The corner of her mouth lifts in a smile a little too alluring to be sweet. "I bet they loved that."

"They hated it," I say with a laugh. "They were so mad at me for spending that much money when I should have put it in long term savings and never looked at it again. They lectured me about how nothing in life is guaranteed, how I couldn't become one of those professional athletes who went bankrupt with a salary a hundred times more than most people ever make. They threatened to sell the place, so I promised I'd go on a spending hiatus until I had double the amount in the bank."

"That's reasonable."

"Not for them it wasn't. They said I also needed to save half of every paycheck and donate at least 10 percent to charity, or they'd sell the place *and* never accept another gift again. So I promised I would."

"Wow," she says, pensive. "I wish I'd gotten some financial wisdom from my parents. Maybe that would have prevented me from taking out enough in student loans to buy a small island. If not for Jane, I'd probably have used a credit card for my—" She stops herself abruptly, and although the twinkling lights above us make it hard to tell, I think her naturally rosy cheeks are a bit pinker. "Anyway, Jane came into my life at a good time. She's always had a good head for money, and I do not."

I know we just met today, but I'm disappointed that she stopped herself from telling me something. It was clearly personal, maybe even important. Communication is a big deal to me, on the field and off. Misunderstandings and miscommunication make everything worse.

"What were you about to say? About using the credit card

for something?" I ask. I've finished the turkey leg and toss it into the garbage can a few feet from our picnic table. It swishes in. I look back to Millie, and she's screwing up her face. "Need I remind you of my many confessions today?" I ask, bumping her leg with mine. We're both wearing jeans, but our legs touching feels intimate.

"I have PCOS. Polycystic Ovarian Syndrome. Do you know what that is?"

I nod. "It's a fertility disorder, right? With metabolic origins in some women?" She looks surprised. "I follow Sonny's older brother on Instagram, and he talked about it in a video last week," I admit.

"Well, he would know. Mine is one of the metabolic ones, so I have to eat a pretty restrictive diet to keep my symptoms under control."

"What does that have to do with the credit card?"

She blows air out of her mouth in a long puff. "It's a tale as old as time. Medical debt." And then she starts to explain how, the summer before she started her master's program, she started getting stabbing pains in her ovaries. "You can handle me talking about this, right? I mean, you have a child."

"I can handle it. I can even handle discussions about tampons and menstrual discs, if I have to."

This earns a grin and an appraising look from her. "Um, what?"

"I was married, have a younger sister, and was raised by a mother who talked openly about periods."

"I like her already," she says. And then she tells me about finding out that she had an ovarian cyst that required surgery. "The doctors thought it was precancerous and convinced me to do radiation. I was too scared and naïve to ask them to wait to see if it had abnormal cells. I told my parents, and they were convinced that I was going to die if I didn't do it." Her voice catches. "So I got the radiation. And after they were done, they told me that the cyst was benign. I got radiation for nothing." She sounds hurt even more than bitter. My nose stings just looking at the naked pain on her face. "But the worst part is—" she closes her eyes—"that it left me infertile."

I know for a fact that, while radiation isn't painful, the emotional scars of dealing with it are. To say nothing of other physical impacts it can have.

And it's that shared pain more than anything—more than my attraction or fascination or the way she cares for my daughter—that makes me admit something I haven't told another living soul. Something that hurts, considering how much I always wanted a big family.

Something she uniquely, perfectly understands.

I rub Lottie's back and choke back the tightness in my throat. "That makes two of us," I say. "Radiation sucks."

Our eyes meet, and listen, I'm not saying some bolt of electricity shoots from my heart to hers, but dang it if I don't feel something.

"I'm sorry," she whispers.

"Me too," I say. And somehow, just sitting there and sharing my burden with someone who gets it makes it feel lighter. Something she said in her office finally clicks. "So that's why you said you were serious as a cancer scare, isn't it?" I ask. She nods, and now I realize something else, too. If her PCOS is of metabolic origins ... "With your diagnosis, does this mean ... do you ... *do we both eat keto?*" I ask, not the slightest bit embarrassed by how excited I am to find someone else who also eats a low carbohydrate diet.

Her jaw opens. "Yes! You too?" I nod, and she squeezes my shoulder (and yes, I flex. I can't help it.). "Do you know what a relief it is to have someone understand that I don't eat this way to be a buzz kill or to lose weight like a Kardashian?"

"Yes! I literally eat this way to stay healthy!" I say, and Millie nods enthusiastically.

"Seriously, if I have one more person in my life say, 'Just eat the cookie!' I think I'll slap them. My friends never pull that garbage with me, thankfully."

"Same," I say. Millie shifts Lottie in her arms. She's held my thirty-five-pound child for at least an hour. I grab Lottie from her, and she shakes out her arms and rotates her neck. "I would have taken her before this, but you looked so content."

Now that I know about her infertility, I recognize the longing and wistfulness in her face. And something like nostalgia for a time when all of her hopes and dreams were still before her.

Or maybe I'm reading into it. What's that word? Projecting.

Either way, the look on her face is worth a library. "I *was* content. She's a really special little girl."

"A special little girl who needs help." The words slip out before I can stop them. "I know I shouldn't have said that, but I'm desperate. And she would do anything to spend more time with you."

"I *cannot* treat her," she emphasizes, biting the inside of her cheek. "Not formally. But I can give you some practical advice, if you want it."

"I want it. Please. I'm dying here."

"If you're sure."

"I'm sure. Millie. I need you. Your advice, I mean," I add so she doesn't think I'm some creep who would hit on her while holding a child.

Besides, I swore off women, remember?

Millie looks at Lottie with a dreamy expression and smoothes her hair from her sleeping face. When her eyes return to mine, I'm struck once again by how intense they are, how they seem to see past walls and facades to the heart of me.

She takes a deep breath. "Okay."

CHAPTER NINE

DUKE

I'm sitting in my home theater with an ice pack on my back and watching clips of myself while Lottie colors next to me.

This isn't a narcissistic thing—it's film work. During a bye week, players watch film of themselves to assess their weaknesses and strategize how to minimize them.

I've always loved film work.

I'm not one of those guys who can't take criticism. Those types of guys don't last in the pros. They flame out in college when they have a tough coach or a bad season. They're so eager to be liked, to make sure people buy into their self-image that they ignore their actual performance, go on a crazy bender when their competition exceeds their work ethic, and see what a joke they are on Sports Center. Those kinds of guys end up destroying a hotel room after a bad game on the road, get cut from the team, and become cautionary tales to the incoming rookies.

I am not that guy. I value criticism. If my coach, my trainer, my agent, heck, even my friends give me a note on my performance, I take it to heart, study it, and incorporate it into my training.

So why can't I take notes from Millie?

Stop thinking about Millie. Study the film.

I rewind the tape and start over. This is my chance to self-scout, to study my performance and really look at the weaknesses my opponents can exploit.

My footwork needs attention. My release points were sloppy last game.

But all I can think about is what Millie said last night about how my expectations of Lottie are all over the place. I expect her to be able to function like a typical almost four-year-old, while swooping in to protect her from typical things that kids her age can manage. I want her to learn to sleep in her own bed, but I keep her out late so she'll fall asleep in the car and can avoid the fight. By not setting expectations and keeping to a reasonable routine, my inconsistency means that Lottie is often rewarded for throwing a tantrum because I don't stand my ground.

It's not that she went on and on, and she said it all much nicer than this.

But she said it.

The more she shared, the colder I got. I should have stopped myself, should have just listened, but instead, I dropped an, "Oh, is that all?" As if she'd been lecturing me for hours rather than sharing insight for a few minutes. She stopped then, her ample lips pressed into a thin line.

"You begged me for this, Duke. You insisted that I give you advice, but I should have listened to my instincts. You obviously love your daughter. You're also obviously not ready to hear this. At least not from me. I'm going to go now."

I felt too stupid to stop her when she walked away.

Fourteen hours, a restless night, and a distracted workout later, I still feel stupid. And too guilty and preoccupied to even do my job.

Why did I get so upset? Why couldn't I just accept that I should get Lottie on a schedule, brainstorm a couple of simple ways to stand my ground, and thank Millie?

Because I want her to like me. I've never cared much how people feel about me, until now. And the one person whose good opinion I want, knows what a crappy parent I am.

She didn't say that. She told me that I was doing a great job. That Lottie felt loved. That every parent struggles sometimes with giving in. But all I heard was that this is my fault, even if she didn't say it. If I weren't so inconsistent, my daughter would be fine. If I wasn't gone for work so much, she wouldn't have separation anxiety disorder. If I hadn't gotten cancer and been too sick with chemo to hold her. If I hadn't thrown up in front of her and made her cry. If I hadn't driven Carlie away ...

"Wook, Daddy."

Lottie's voice breaks through my spiral. I shake my head, pulling my eyes from the theater screen and my mind from an abyss of shame. She's holding a picture she drew. I'm pretty sure it's two heads with legs popping out of them. The tadpole people have little circles for eyes and rudimentary smiles. "I love it, pumpkin. Tell me about it."

Pro tip: never ask a kid what it is. Ask them to tell you about it. I learned that one the hard way.

She looks so proud of herself, and I'm eager to have her tell me about the picture. When your kid draws a picture of you and her with big smiles, it's hard to feel like you're *that* big a failure.

She curls her arm around my neck and speaks in a singsong voice, going up at the end of each word. "It's meeee and Miwwie! She's my best friend. She should be my mommy."

It's not Lottie and me.

It's Lottie and Millie.

BABY LLAMA DRAMA

My heart shrivels inside of me as the shame returns full force.

As if I don't have enough failings, my child is now drawing pictures of a woman she wishes were her mom, because I'm not enough for her. A lump forms in my throat, and no amount of swallowing can make it go down.

"That's out of my control, kiddo," I croak.

"It's okay. I can ask her. Can I have ice cream now?"

If I weren't so used to the way she can jump from topic to topic, I would be dizzy. "No, but let's go make lunch."

She balls her hands into fists. "But I! Want! Ice cream!"

To add insult to injury, I'm getting a tantrum now? "Lottie, no. You're not having ice cream. You were perfectly content ten seconds ago without ice cream. You don't need it."

"YES I DO!"

Why is this happening? Why does she have to go from zero to sixty about such meaningless things? Why do her tantrums at almost four have to be so much worse than they ever were at two?

I can't do this. I can't be the dad I need to be and the football player I want to be at the same time. There's no way. Of course I had a bad game the other night. I have too much on my mind every minute, even for me, the King of Compartmentalizing. I've always prided myself on my ability to leave my baggage at the door and get my head in the game. Until this season. Now, I feel like I'm constantly being held hostage to the whims of a volatile tyrant ... a tyrant of my own making. I did this to her. I gave in too many times, and now she's drawing pictures of someone else, because giving in only made everything worse. And I'm about to do it again, I can feel it. I drop my head in my hands, wishing she could just accept a simple boundary ...

A boundary ...

Millie's words from last night flood my mind.

"Boundaries are one of the most loving things you can give a child. Kids love them," she told me.

"Ha. Not my kid. She fights 'em tooth and nail."

"I believe it. But healthy boundaries are important. Kids crave them. They thrive on them. Imagine if every time you pushed on a fence, it moved. Sometimes it moved closer, but most of the time, it moved farther back, giving you more and more access to a world of things you thought were inaccessible. What would you do?"

"I'd push the fence."

"Exactly. Even if sometimes the fence moved closer and boxed you in more, it would be worth it to try just in case it moved way farther back, right? Your job is to set a firm, clear boundary so that when she pushes, she knows where the fence stops every time. It's an act of love, a kindness. It lets her relax and be content in the boundary. When you're at the end of your rope, do the kind thing. Show her how much you love her and stay the course."

Do the kind thing.

I'm not naturally nice. My experience with crowds is proof of that.

But for my daughter, I can be kind. I can show her how much I love her.

I hope.

CHAPTER TEN

MILLIE

I know I should listen to my mom's concerns, but I can't stop thinking of how badly things ended with Duke last night.

Again.

I'm walking around the woods outside of our spacious luxury rental (it belonged to Tripp's grandparents). The size of the trees blows me away. I don't know anything about trees, but they're beautiful and fresh and the whole world smells like rain. Talking to my mom is never relaxing, but the warble of birds and the soft babbling of the river a dozen yards away help.

The Janes are all inside occupied with their own activities. Last I saw Parker, she was in the home gym doing a yoga pose that looked more like advanced gymnastics. Ash was redecorating. And Lou was writing a sad, soulful song on her guitar.

But it's my day off, so naturally I'm managing someone else's crisis.

Mom is frustrated with Dad over how he never listens, and

all I can think of is Lizzy Bennet and her parents. Except, instead of feeling like my dad and I are kindred spirits, like we're both escaping Mom's "poor nerves," Dad is complicit in them. I love my dad, but he'd rather debate his friends on Facebook or do a crossword puzzle than talk to his wife. He claims he's "not built for all that talking," and since I was a teen, he's shifted such conversations to me.

Do you know what it's like to be a fourteen-year-old hearing about your mom's anxieties and fears? She set the example for my siblings to follow, and before I could even drive, I was the person everyone in the family came to talk to.

It's as fun as it sounds.

Zero percent fun.

I walk down to a pier, have a seat and kick my shoes off, and dangle my feet over the edge. My toes skim the water as I talk my mom through the latest emergency she refuses to get outside help for. And she pushes back on following any of my suggestions, just like always.

I'm two seconds from throwing myself in the river when another call comes in. It's a local number. Could it be a client inquiry?

"Mom, I have a client calling. I'll talk to you later," I say, and I switch to the other call before she can argue.

"Hello?"

"I did it!" an exultant male voice says.

"I'm sorry, I don't have your number in my phone. Who is this?"

"Oh, sorry, it's Duke." *DUKE?* I'm too busy processing to answer right away, and he continues. "Duke Ogden. Lottie's dad? From last night?"

"I remember you, Duke," I say. As if I could forget him. "I'm surprised you're calling me. Is everything okay?"

"Yes, it's great." He pauses, and when he speaks again, it's with uncertainty. "Sorry, Ms. Angie gave me a business card with your number. Is this okay?"

"Totally okay," I say. *Right?* I've only been thinking about the guy all morning, wishing I had been gentler when he begged me for advice. He cares so much for his daughter, and dealing with her anxiety has taken a toll on him. "You said you did something? Want to tell me about it?"

"It's dumb. You don't have to—"

"It's fine, Duke. I *want* to hear it. I feel bad about how we left things last night." My voice is calm, but I squirm even talking about it.

"I do, too." He doesn't talk as slowly as most of the Southerners I've been around, even less so now. "I'm sorry for how I overreacted. I asked for your help and then threw it in your face."

His apology calms my squirming, restless feeling. "I should have done things differently. You asked for a drink of water and I used a firehose."

"No, I *needed* the firehose. I was on fire."

"I could have used a lower stream—"

"Millie, please. I appreciate you trying to soften this, but I was out of line. You have nothing to apologize for."

Whenever I talk to people outside my inner circle, I feel like I have to wear a calm, confident front. I'm not Millie Campbell, I'm Therapist Millie, and people expect me to have my stuff together so that I can help them.

Duke expected help from me yesterday. Will he expect it again today? I hope not, because I'm having a hard time keeping up my front. I like him. I'm wary, because he's managing a lot of heavy emotions, and that's hardly the best time to enter a relationship, but I like him.

And I think he likes me.

He tells me how he set a boundary with Lottie for lunch—she couldn't have ice cream—and how he sat with her while she threw a tantrum over it. He didn't get mad or bargain. He sat there. It took twenty-five minutes, but eventually, she calmed down and he told her he loved her so he wanted to help her be healthy. They went to the kitchen and he gave her options for lunch that would give her good, lasting energy.

"And it worked! I can't believe it, but it worked!"

"I'm so glad! I bet you feel like you're walking on clouds," I say, looking at the actual clouds rolling in over the river. "And now that you've shown yourself that you can do it once, you'll be that much more prepared to handle it next time."

"Right." He blows air loudly enough that I wince at the sound. "Next time."

"Don't say it like it's a bad thing. You're creating new muscles. It takes time."

"You're right." He sighs. "But here I am acting like I won the game when we're still in the first quarter. Shoot, I just barely won the coin toss."

"Hey, I know less about football than Lottie does, but at least you're playing on the same field now. That matters. It's not the last play that counts, it's the next. Right?"

"You ain't lyin'," he says.

I grin. "That is the most Southern I've heard you sound yet."

He snorts. "My mom grew up out West. She doesn't have an accent, and that rubbed off on us." There's a long pause. "I can do this."

I love his determination. "You can. Consistency is key. Just keep flexing those muscles."

"I will. And I'm going to call Angie and get in touch with the other therapist at your office. I have two weeks until my next game. I'll still have to be at the field a lot for practice and game prep, but I'm going to do everything I can to make sure Lottie's getting the help she needs."

I hiss. "About that…"

"What?" He sounds panicky. "What do you mean?"

Of course the minute Duke's ready to get help, that help isn't available. "Linda—the other therapist—had to delay her move a few weeks. She's still coming, but the moving company she hired canceled this morning, and she's scrambling to find new help. So ... "

"That's just my luck," he mutters.

A bird trills loudly near me, and a moment later, the same song echoes from the phone.

That's weird.

"This is going to sound strange," Duke says, "but where are you?"

"Outside of our rental," I say. "If you're about to ask what I'm wearing, this call's over."

"Ha ha," he says flatly. I hear his breathing change. It sounds like he's on the move. "Is that ... are you renting Tripp's lake house?"

The bird sings again, and the same echo issues from the phone.

I spin around and look behind me, scanning the trees for any sight of him. The foliage is so dense that it's hard to see. I stand to get a better view.

And that's when I see him striding toward me, looking like a man on a mission. A *hot* man. If his football career fizzles out, he should model v-neck cashmere sweaters like this one. Here I am wearing baggy jeans rolled at the cuff, an oversized green cardigan, and my hair up in a messy bun, while he's rocking cashmere like it's his job.

But his eyes rove over me appreciatively, as if the outfit isn't basically loungewear. And he's smiling. Dimples out.

Give me strength.

"What are you doing here?" I ask as he steps on to the dock. He stops next to me.

"I could ask you the same question. You're on my dock."

"What? I thought this was Tripp's."

"Nope. That one's Tripp's." He stands closer than necessary and dips his face next to mine, pointing to another dock a short dozen yards away. His cheek brushes against mine, sparking a million tiny fires on my face.

"You live here?"

He puts an arm across my shoulders and turns me so I'm facing the woods. "That's my house."

I squint and look past the trees, and that's when I see the back of a massive house obscured by thick vegetation.

"I didn't realize I was trespassing," I say, not in the least bit mad about it. Unless he is. But he's smiling and he called me, so he *can't* be mad about it. "You guys really need to thin out these woods if you expect a girl not to wander out onto the wrong dock."

"Sure. We'll chop down hundred year old trees just so you don't miss the clearly worn path from your rental to its accompanying dock."

"Oh good, you'll get right on that, then?"

He sniffs a laugh and stands to his full height. "I'll see what I can do," he teases.

"I knew I could count on you." I pat his arm and then step back when I realize what I've done.

If I didn't know better, I'd think we were flirting. But we can't be flirting. He wants me to help his daughter. That's all this is.

Isn't it?

The dark, rolling clouds move in front of the sun, dropping the temperature instantly. A shiver runs over me, and I wrap my arms around myself. The wind whips some hair out of my bun, and it gets stuck to my lip gloss. Duke reaches a hand to free the lock from my lips and tuck it behind my ear. His finger glides across my cheek, making me shiver even harder.

"Do you want to come over for a minute to warm up?" he asks. "I make a mean cup of herbal tea."

My place is just as close as his. There's no reason for me to go over to get warm, and he knows it.

This can only mean one thing: he's asking me over to spend time with me.

He's flirting.

"Tea? What do I look like, an old English lady?"

"I love tea."

"Oh, I didn't realize you lived at Downton Abbey. Is that why your parents named you Duke?"

He chuckles. "Are you coming, or not?"

"Sorry," I say. "Tea is a hard pass, milord. If you had Diet Coke on hand…"

"Reese has a cache of Diet Dr. Pepper. It's the best I can do," he says, his voice deep and enticing.

"I'll take it."

CHAPTER ELEVEN

MILLIE

*W*hat am I doing?

Oh, that's right, I'm flirting.

I'm flirting with the father of the little girl who captured my heart.

I'm flirting with a man who deeply, personally understands the pain of infertility.

I'm flirting with a man who doesn't think I'm a drama queen for eating a restrictive diet.

And, I cannot overstate this next point: I'm flirting with a man so hot, Ancient Greeks would have knelt down to worship his beauty. Heck, I might do the same.

Also, can we talk about the fact that he is absolutely flirting back with me? Because he is. He smiles and smirks when we talk. He leans in a lot more than he needs to. Yes, the man is unreasonably tall, but I'm five-five, and my throwback Adidas sneakers give me another couple of inches. I'm tall enough to smell his cologne when he leans down.

I love that he cares enough to wear cologne. I like a guy who puts a little effort into his appearance. Not to the point of swapping skin care secrets, but buying clothes he knows look good on him? Yes. Wearing cologne? Double yes. And his scent is spectacular. Intoxicating, manly, sporty, even a bit woodsy ... although that could be the actual woods, come to think of it. I inhale deeply when he reaches around me to turn on a patio heater, and the smell fills my lungs and keeps going until it reaches the tips of my toes.

I can officially confirm that the woodsy smell clings to him like pine to a Christmas tree.

Listen, I'm not some weirdo who's going to kiss his neck when it gets close, but you'd better believe I have to stop myself from fisting his sweater, pulling him against me, and sniffing the devil out of that spot right beneath his perfect jaw.

When he steps away from me, I almost sway in his direction. Instead, I wrap my sweater-covered hands around my perfectly ice cold can of soda and sink into one of the lux Ethan Allen patio chairs that are nicer than any piece of furniture I've ever owned. I tuck my legs under my butt and angle my body so that I'm facing his chair, only a foot from mine. He hands me a sherpa blanket, and I bundle up in it.

"If you want to warm up, you should really try tea instead of ice cold soda," he says, gesturing with his steaming mug.

"You watch your mouth, mister," I say. He chuckles and shakes his head.

We're sitting outside on the wraparound balcony just off of his kitchen and dining room. From what I can see inside, the house is gorgeous. Tasteful, expensive without being decadent. Lots of clean lines, but still warm enough to feel like a real home. It helps that Lottie's scribbles dot the refrigerator.

As much as I'd love to tour his house, I'm glad we're outside. Going in would feel like too big a step. We're already balancing this weird chemistry and our mutual love of his daughter, who asked me to be her new mommy at my best friend's wedding. If I start making myself at home in his actual home, my heart is going to go places my mind can't pull us back from.

Besides, the dude is hot, but I barely know him.

I want to get to know him.

Cool it, Millie, I tell myself as I take a drink of my soda. *Attraction isn't enough to build a relationship on, let alone a life.*

Even if he is an adorable, devoted, loving dad to a little girl you already love and *he understands your health history and sorrow in a way no one else ever has* and *he's best friends with your best friend's husband, so you already know he's quality.*

Okay, my self-talk isn't helping.

"So, uh, we've established that I don't know anything about football. You said something about a ... " I scramble to think of anything to say ... "buy week? What is that? Shopping around for new players, or something?"

His eyes widen. "Buy, as in b-u-y? Is that what you think it is?" He laughs so loud, an animal skitters from the forest floor below. Then he spells it out. "B-y-e. Bye, as in goodbye, I'm taking a freaking vacation and praying my back spasms will stop."

I'm surprised to learn how busy football players are between games. I assumed they'd work out and practice, but as I ask him questions, he tells me about reviewing film from past games, both as a team and for individual weaknesses, learning an extensive new playbook every week, team events with VIPs, interviews with the press, volunteering, and more. We talk about the mental component of juggling so much in his life, and he admits that being a single parent with sole custody is hard, but he refuses to keep her home unless he has to.

"Did Carlie want shared custody, if you don't mind me asking?" I keep my voice gentle, knowing what a sensitive topic this is, but his face hardens anyway.

"She asked about it at first, but my lawyer said she proved

herself unreliable when she abandoned us. He also stressed to her lawyer how Carlie's commitment to her public life as an influencer would have exposed Lottie to danger." He's trying to sound steady, but his nostrils are flaring like he's trying to keep his breathing under control.

I'm a big proponent of shared custody when the child's safety isn't at risk. If we were in my office, I'd talk through a lot of that, but as it is, my heart hammers in my chest just imagining Lottie being abandoned like that. Rage makes my vision feel almost foggy. "How did Lottie handle that?"

"Not as bad as you'd think. Carlie wasn't the best mom. She was on her phone constantly, obsessed with her social media following. Have you—do you—?"

"No. I have no clue who she is and no interest in looking her up." And I mean it. I don't want the algorithm to put her garbage into my feed, and I don't want it sending anyone else to her, either.

Even if I'm curious.

"She wasn't all bad, but she never cared about being a mom. We had a nanny even though Carlie talked all the time online about how she was a full-time mom. She made it big selling pictures of our perfect family to desperate women on the internet. Do you think she ever once talked about the nanny?"

I shake my head. "So did Lottie miss her?"

"The nanny or Carlie? Yes and no. My parents moved in while I was going through my treatments. Mom helped me all last season. And then Reese moved in this past summer. Lottie knew Carlie was missing, and she cried for her sometimes, but she was so showered with love that I think it distracted her. Until it didn't."

I put my hand over my chest and exhale a bundle of worry. I'm emotional imagining Lottie's fear and confusion. How traumatizing was it for Lottie to wake up to her mom abandoning her when her dad was in the hospital? She couldn't have understood Duke's condition, but on some level, she would have understood that he was weak, tired, gone a lot, and probably too fragile to hold her or play with her. How could she not have separation anxiety disorder after so much trauma? The fact that she's holding up as well as she is tells me that she's a remarkable, strong little girl who knows deep down that her daddy loves her more than anything.

"What about you?"

Duke takes a long sip of tea. "I don't miss her. We didn't have a happy marriage."

I want to pry, but a muscle in his jaw tenses, enhancing his cheekbones even more, and suddenly, I don't want to talk about his ex-wife.

Good riddance.

The glow from the patio heater glints in his deep blue eyes, and without thinking, I squeeze his arm. This is my go-to show of support, but with him, it feels flirty. I tried to play it cool down by the dock, but now that he's invited me over, I let my natural reaction come out. "Is this fake?" I knock, half-expecting a gong of metal beneath the cashmere.

He flashes me a smile I'm sure thousands of women have fallen for in the past. Smart, smart women. "You're one to talk," he says. "I caught a glimpse of your delts."

"You know, Duke, those things women keep under their Diet Coke-saturated hot pink bras aren't called delts, they're called breasts."

He laughs hard again, and I find that I could get used to watching this man laugh. The way his Adam's apple bobs when he throws his head back makes me want to revisit my stance on not kissing the man's neck next time it gets near me.

"You little minx. You just can't stop talking about those things, can you?" It's my turn to laugh. He mirrors my earlier move, squeezing my shoulder muscle. I'm no waif. I work hard to keep this ship right and tight, thank you very much. So when

I feel his firm grip on my right deltoid, I flex a little, hoping it'll keep his hand on me longer. It does. "Shoot, girl. You legitimately work out." He massages my shoulder muscles. "Do you do CrossFit?"

"No, I'm a HIIT girl," I say. High intensity interval training is my favorite kind of workout. Flipping tires doesn't appeal to me, although I admire the heck out of people who do it.

"Then you need to come over to work out with me." The gleam in his eyes sparks something deep inside my chest. "I have a gym in the fourth car garage downstairs. Come over tomorrow morning and I'll show you around."

My eyes drop to the half-curve of his lips. I'm not even trying to hide my attraction anymore, but neither is he. His hand is still on my shoulder. I'm furious at my cardigan for getting in the way of him being able to touch my neck. I'm about to say yes when a scream from inside the house shatters my heart like crystal.

CHAPTER TWELVE

MILLIE

Duke bolts into the house before I can even kick the blanket to the ground, but once I do, I dart right behind him. I don't even bother closing the sliding glass door; I'm too worried about Lottie. When I reach them, Duke is on his knees, cradling Lottie to his chest while fat tears roll down her face.

"I thought you ... were ... gone!" She sobs, gasping between words. "I thought ... a monster ... took you ... like Momma."

Duke makes a loud shushing sound as he rubs her back. "Shh, sweetie. It's okay. Don't even think about that. I'll *never* leave you."

Lottie keeps crying, and Duke keeps shushing, and the moment is so heart wrenching, I find it hard to swallow. Promises like the one Duke is making are dangerous. I should know. I promised my niece that I would never let anything happen to her.

But some things can't be controlled.

Some things can't be promised.

So even though this moment has nothing to do with me, the thickness in my throat compels me forward. I crouch down behind Lottie so she can't see me, but I make eye contact with Duke. The worry lines in his forehead are settling in deeper than any wrinkles will ever show. I put my hand on his forearm and give him a questioning look. He nods almost pleadingly.

I'm relieved that he's going to allow me to help, but this won't be pretty for him. I hope he'll trust me. I wait for Lottie to be calm enough to talk. I want her in her emotions but not so deep that she can't communicate. When she's stopped crying, Duke looks at me. "Lottie, Millie's here. Do you think we could talk with her?"

Lottie peeks at me from where her face is tucked into her dad's chest and nods. I have Duke turn her outward, and he wraps his arms around her tiny chest protectively once she's facing out.

I kneel in front of her and put my hands on both of her knees. Then I start tapping one side at a time. It's called bilateral stimulation, an essential part of a therapy known as Eye Movement Desensitization and Reprocessing. I can't do actual EMDR therapy on her—I'm not her therapist. EMDR is extremely effective for people with PTSD and trauma histories, and it's intense. I'm planning to just give her a taste of it—EMDR Lite.

As I tap, I drop my voice to its most soothing possible tone and ask her to close her eyes and tell me about what happened to her mom. Duke hisses, but I give him a sharp look that stops him in his tracks. He must avoid talking about his ex with her, but she needs to process the pain and fear of it. She's stuck in it.

So I ask her to tell me about it.

She doesn't seem to remember an actual moment, but she's made up a story in her mind of what happened that's every bit as powerful. Her dad was "sick of work," she says, and she tried to find her mom, but a monster took her.

I ask her how she felt when she couldn't find her mom. I ask her to think about that fear and I try to keep her in it. It sounds cruel, but by pausing her here, tapping bilaterally, and leading her through what comes next, I'm going to help her brain reprocess the moment so it can become manageable.

The words she uses are simple but powerful. Scared. Alone. Left. By myself. She doesn't have the vocabulary or awareness to expand on what these words mean to her, but they're enough.

Next, I ask her to tell me how she *wanted* to feel in that moment. I have to guide her a bit to understand, but she tells me that she wished her daddy had been there to hug her and hold her. She doesn't mention Carlie again.

"Focus on what you wish happened, okay? Imagine waking up and your daddy being there. He's smiling and picking you up and holding you so tightly. How does it feel?"

"Happy. He's squeezing me so tight! He's warm and *so* happy to see me. He's kissing my cheek and says he yoves me *so so so so* much."

"Do you feel safe?"

She nods and smiles. "Mm-hmm. I yove him."

I hear a sniff and look up to see Duke crying softly, and the sight makes my own eyes water. I'm a sympathetic crier in the silliest of circumstances. The fact that I'm not outright weeping right now is a testament to my training, because nothing else could keep me from falling to pieces. Lottie's eyes are still squeezed closed as she tells me all about the amazing bear hug she's imagining with her dad. When she starts talking about his scratchy beard, I know it's time to transition her out.

All the while, I keep tapping and tapping. My forearms are tired from moving my hands for even these few minutes. It feels like it's been ages, but I know from experience that it's probably only been five minutes.

"How are you feeling now, Lottie?" I ask, and she nods her head, opening her eyes.

Duke spins her around and hugs her tightly, telling her how proud he is of her and how much he loves her. She's not crying anymore, but he is. I feel both full and wrung out at the same time. I'm half tempted to leave, but after that mini-session, I don't really want to.

Especially not when Duke grabs my hand in his, looks at me like I'm his refuge in a storm, and whispers, "Thank you."

CHAPTER THIRTEEN

MILLIE

*M*y phone is blowing up.

I escaped to the (super swanky) bathroom for a few minutes after the cry-fest was over and answered my friends "Where are you??" texts by saying, "I'm at Duke's! Next door!!" and now I'm trying to ignore the five million texts making my butt buzz as I help Lottie and Duke make keto pizza for us and naan bread pizza for Lottie.

Lottie is sitting on the huge marble island, putting one piece of shredded mozzarella at a time on her pizza. Duke has an eclectic playlist going in the background, ranging from blues to '80s metal to indie to classic country. Every minute or two, thunder booms in the background and lightning flashes into the already lighted room. When the storm first hit, Lottie and I ran to the huge windows to watch the lighting while Duke hung back. He started the music right when the thunder began, and I have to wonder if he isn't secretly afraid of thunder.

The very possibility makes my knees weak. Tough but tender? Strong but vulnerable?

Stick a fork in me. I'm done.

"Do you need to answer those texts?" Duke points a spatula at my butt pocket.

I pile prosciutto and salami onto my pizza. "Nah. It's just going to be a lot of GIFs and punctuation."

His grin is so big, he could sell toothpaste. "Really? What will those GIFs be of, pray tell?"

Women fanning themselves, no doubt, but no way I'm telling him that. "Tom Brady."

He throws a handful of shredded cheese at me.

I dodge it and laugh. "You are a child, sir."

"You just had to bring up Brady, didn't you?"

"Yes, yes I did."

"Well, at least tell your friends that I haven't abducted you and then stow that thing, will you? Grown ups aren't allowed devices at the table." He winks.

"Okay, give me a sec."

I tell Lottie that I'm going to step out onto the deck. I make sure she acknowledges me before I leave. By the cocking of his head, Duke takes notice of the way I do it. I'm going to have to give him a whole host of disclaimers that not everything I do is because of clinical insight. I mean, this was, but at some point, I'll do something weird or stupid, and I don't want him thinking that it has some deeper meaning.

"At some point"? Getting a little ahead of yourself, aren't you?

I am. I really am.

Out on the deck, the fire has burned out in the covered pit. The rain is falling hard, but I don't want to risk Duke hearing me in the house. I call Parker, simply because she's the most invested in anything related to Duke.

"Please tell me that you're currently holding his Heisman." Parker blurts.

"Ew! No, you creep!"

Parker's laugh is like a tinkle. She has a naturally high voice, which I never notice when we're in person. Her presence is so much bigger than she is. "It's not an innuendo, you dork. The Heisman Trophy? It's the award given to the best college football player? He won it his junior year."

"Wait, isn't that the award Sonny was up for after he transferred?" I only vaguely remember this detail, but I mention Sonny more to see how she responds.

"Good memory. He had twenty-two rushing touchdowns and tied the conference's single-season rushing record that year, and he totally should have won."

Hmm. She's gushing about his accomplishments and annoyed on his behalf. Interesting. Also, the number talk is boring. "Wow. Cool story, Hansel."

"Oh, hush." She asks me what we're doing, and I give her the Cliff's Notes version. "So you're both pretending that you're helping Lottie, but you're both really flirting your McLadypants off? Got it."

McLadyPants are the maker of the world's best underwear. We did their rebrand, and they've skyrocketed in popularity since then. Their "Blanche Knows Best" line of comfy, sexy, wedgie-proof granny underwear is a game changer every woman should know.

"I don't think he wears McLadyPants."

"Ugh. Men and their non-wedgie underwear." she says.

"Don't forget how all their clothes have pockets."

"Don't get me started on pockets," she says. "Just so you know, I approve of this union, and I expect a signed football for my silence."

"Pfft. What silence? You took the conversation to 'the Janes' thread to make sure everyone knew every detail. I have the GIFs to prove it."

"Girl, everyone deserves to know that you're hanging out with Duke Freaking Ogden. What I mean is that I won't tell anyone how totally smitten you sound. I'll let them figure it out themselves."

My neck feels hot, and I don't think it's just the scarf or the space heater. "Whatever." I should say something more. I should protest more. But for all of her bluntness, Parker's wit is a precision instrument. She's smart, observant, and hides her layers behind a veneer of carbon black mascara and even darker humor. "Anyway, I need to get back in before they think I've bounced on dinner. I'll be home ... later, I guess?"

"I'll see you when I see you, Sport."

When my phone is safely stuffed in my back pocket, I look out from Duke's deck and breathe in deeply. Humidity aside, the air here is nothing like in Chicago, where we all moved from. It's fresh and fills my lungs with the promise of rain, and, although I know I should get back inside, I pause and breathe it in.

The last several years haven't been easy. Everything with my niece, my health scare and diagnosis, the subsequent medical bills. A difficult Master's program. Going into business with my friends and seeing the toll it took on everyone as we struggled to make ends meet. It's been one thing after another for a long time. Landing the Sugar Maple Farms account was the best thing that could have happened to us, and I feel like I'm on the verge of more "best things" just by being here. In Sugar Maple, not at Duke's house, to be clear.

At least that's what I'm telling myself.

Another text comes in, and I expect it to be from my friends, but it's from my sister Brianna. I unlock my phone to see the details, and when I do, I almost drop the phone.

Shock runs through me. I feel like I've just been electrocuted. Or struck by lightning, maybe.

Brianna's text is a picture.

Of a pregnancy test.

And it's positive.

I instantly try to call her, but she responds with a preprogrammed, "Can I call you later?" She and her new husband, Greg, are probably celebrating the crap out of this. But I know it's bittersweet for Brianna, too. She has to be thinking of little Sophie. Missing her even more than I do.

My phone buzzes again, and this time it's my mom calling.

I'm not going to answer, and that means I'll have a text from my older brother in five minutes and one from my dad shortly thereafter.

I can't.

The sliding glass door opens, and I dash tears from my cheeks before spinning around and pasting a false smile on my face. "Hey!"

Duke's holding Lottie. "Pizza's ready," he says. Then his eyes narrow. "Are you okay?"

"Great! I just found out my sister's pregnant!" I say it too brightly and start bouncing toward them. Of course I'm happy for my sister, but I'm acting *too* bright. Almost manic. Duke grabs my arm when I reach them.

"Are you sure?"

I shrug so falsely, only Shakespeare would have words to adequately describe the move. My chest feels tight, my throat aches, my nose stings.

I want to sob.

Duke looks behind him, and I see that his sister, Reese, is sitting at the huge dining room table. I almost forgot that she's nannying for him. Duke bumps his forehead against his daughter's. "Pumpkin, go start eating with Auntie Reese, okay? I'm going to talk with Miss Millie for just a sec."

"She's not Miss Miwwie, she's *my* Miwwie," Lottie says. She grabs her dad's cheeks and kisses his nose before wiggling down and running into the house.

Thunder shakes the house, and the rain intensifies as if on cue. The deck is a huge wrap-around one that extends past the kitchen and dining room and over to the family room. Duke pulls me away from the window and around the corner, presumably away from prying eyes. Then he puts his hands on my shoulders. His touch is strong, warm, and reassuring.

"I can tell you're upset, Millie. Is your sister in a bad relationship, or something? She already has a daughter, right? Your niece?"

The emotion inside of me bubbles below the surface, staying lodged in my throat until the ache is almost too intense to bear. "No, my sister's in a good situation. And, yes, she had a daughter. Sophie. She was the cutest, funniest, most precocious girl in the world."

Duke makes a quiet "oh" of understanding.

"She died of a congenital heart defect just before she turned four. I'm happy for my sister, I swear. It just hurts remembering my niece. Thinking about how she'll never get to be a big sister. Thinking about how this new baby will never know her. Thinking about how exciting but hard this must be for my sister. And then that makes me feel guilty for my future niece or nephew, because I'm putting all this baggage on an unborn child, and I don't want a baby to grow up in the shadow of an older sibling who passed away, and my whole family wants to process this right now, and I'm the person everyone processes to, and ... it's a lot. It's just a lot."

Duke pulls me into a hug, and I don't fight it for a second. His big arms wrap around my shoulders and back, and I reach mine around his waist. I press my cheek to his chest. Tears stream down my face as fast as the rain. I don't let myself full-on ugly cry (and you've never seen ugly crying until you've seen a redhead ugly cry), but I get close. My chest shakes and I can feel his sweater getting more and more soaked, but I can't stop myself. Duke smoothes my hair down and rests his chin on the top of my head.

When the worst of my tears have shed, I'm hollowed out but better. I haven't had someone hold me while I cried in a long time. I'm usually the one doing the holding. But Duke is good at this. Better than good. He could go pro.

"I'm sorry, Millie," he says. "This would be a lot for anyone, and you're more empathetic than the average bear."

I snort and then wish I hadn't, because I'm worried I just got snot on his sweater, and if I did, I'll have to go into hiding to escape the shame. I sniff. "Average bear? What are you talking about?"

"You know, Yogi Bear, the old cartoon. 'He's smarter than the average bear,'" he sings quietly, and I laugh into his muscled chest.

"Did you just sing? What is going on here?"

Duke's arms tighten in a playful squeeze. "I didn't realize what an uninitiated rube you are. You don't know *anything* about pop culture. You must be so embarrassed."

"Pop culture? I'm pretty sure this bear of yours existed before our parents did. Besides, I know who *you* are, so how uninitiated could I really be?"

"I'm not trying to be a diva, but I'm actually kind of a big deal and you still had to Google me. But Yogi Bear? That guy is international. You're an uninitiated rube, and I stand by it."

"You live in the sticks, and I moved here from Chicago."

"Don't you make fun of the sticks, you urbanite."

I've gone from shaking crying to shaking laughing in a minute, and it's making me buoyant. I feel like a weighted balloon that's been cut free, and I'm at risk of floating away if he lets go. "Wow, yesterday you splash Diet Coke on my favorite dress, and now you escalate to name calling? You've got game, buddy. I can't wait to see where we go from here."

He stiffens and releases me. "We'll see." He says, shooting finger guns in a way that feels suddenly chummy rather than flirty. "We should probably head back inside before the pizza gets cold."

Talk about getting cold. "Yeah, good thinking. Thanks for the talk."

"Anytime."

He says this casually as he opens the door for me to go inside, and I'm too busy reeling over his total one-eighty to remember to school my features for Lottie and Reese. Naturally Reese asks me what's wrong when I get inside. I tell her it's nothing, that I got some news from home, and she studies me with the same intensity her brother did.

I eat pizza in a fog, and when Reese mentions playing Candyland, I bow out as graciously as I can with Lottie pleading. Duke doesn't protest, though, and I don't know what to make of it. Of *any* of it.

He called me today. He actively sought me out. He invited me to his house and insisted I stay for dinner. He initiated some legit physical contact. He bantered. He flirted—big, real, delicious flirting.

And then he retreated.

Understanding gurgles in my intestines like bad takeout.

He's an international super star and apparently one of the most eligible bachelors in America. He's got women knocking down his door—flirting is probably just his default mode.

Maybe he's not the kind to take his flirtations to an intimate level, but I showed him my hand when I talked about what comes next for us, when I mentioned the future.

He knew he won, and he dropped me when the thrill of the chase was over.

I walk home in the rain with an umbrella Reese pushed on me, and I head straight for my room rather than checking to see where my friends are.

I've known him for less than forty-eight hours, and already the rejection hurts. All the more so because of Lottie. I love that little girl fiercely, and I let myself get swept up in the fairytale of a readymade family.

Now that I know the truth, though, my guard is up.

CHAPTER FOURTEEN

DUKE

"What did you do?" Reese asks when Lottie is in bed. Lottie fought to sleep in my room, so we compromised with me bringing her bed into my room, because even though I know Millie told me to draw a line, I can't draw that many at once. I'm not Super Dad.

Plus, I'm feeling guilty.

"What do you mean?" I'm loading dishes as my sister shoots lasers from her eyes across the island.

"Millie ran out of here so fast, she made Deion's combine forty look like a Sunday stroll. So I repeat, what did you do?"

"I liked you better blonde. You were dumber."

"You want to play with fire, Scarecrow? Light a match," she dares.

"That's some quality smack talk, sis."

She does a full eye roll from one side all the way to the other. "Duke."

"I didn't do anything," I lie. "She lost her niece to a congenital heart defect a few years ago, and now her sister is pregnant. Millie just had a range of emotions about it."

"That explains the fact that she'd cried her waterproof mascara into clumps, but it doesn't explain the way you were avoiding her gaze and the way she looked like you slapped her." She grabs a dishcloth and starts wiping the counters. Her phone rings, and she stops.

"Hey, Mom. How's the cruise? What? Wait, slow down." She presses the speaker button and holds the phone out for both of us to hear. "What's going on?"

"Honey, it's Gramma Hazel. She's had a nasty fall and needs someone to help her."

"Okay, where is she? Can we get a home health nurse over there?"

"Oh, you know how crotchety she is."

"That's my mother," Dad says in the background.

"Then you know better than anyone how she refuses to let strangers into her house, let alone to help her," Mom says.

"What do you need us to do, Momma?" I ask.

"I know this is a big ask, but Reese, is there any chance you could stay with her for a couple of days until we get back? We'll fly out from the port when we get to Greece."

Reese looks at me with a drawn brow. "Mom, don't leave early. Y'all just disembarked, and it's only a two-week cruise. Reese can stay as long as Gramma Hazel needs her."

"Why don't we bring Gramma Hazel here?" Reese asks. "Myrtle Beach is close enough that I can have her back tomorrow."

Lottie would lose it if she saw Gramma Hazel. If she even hears me complain of a headache, she gets upset.

Subconsciously, she must remember visiting me in the hospital, seeing me weak in bed following chemo. I shaved my head beforehand so the hair loss wouldn't upset her or Carlie, but the nausea and bone-deep exhaustion weren't things I could hide. My case was minor comparatively. I only needed four rounds of chemo with immunotherapy and radiation, but it was enough to drive my wife away and break my daughter.

She's not broken. She's hurting, I chide myself. *And we can thank Carlie for that more than cancer.*

Right now would be a pretty handy time for my ex to be in the picture. But she didn't push for custody at all after her inquiry. She didn't even care enough to fight.

Of all the unforgivable things she did, that ties for first.

"But what about Lottie?" Mom asks.

"I'll have Rusty come play nanny. Lottie knows and loves him. Reese can leave tonight. Lottie and I will be fine."

"Are you sure?" Reese mouths.

"Are you sure?" Mom asks.

"Positive." I've used up so much of my family's hospitality over the last two years that I owe them this. If my grandma needs help, I won't stand in the way of her getting it.

Even if I need help, too.

"Enjoy yourself, Mom. Go kick Dad's butt at minigolf and get a sunburn. You deserve it."

Mom hems but finally agrees. We say goodbye, and Reese holds the phone thoughtfully.

"Are you really sure about this, Duchess?" my sister asks.

"Of course, sis. Are *you* sure you can handle Gramma Hazel for a couple of weeks?"

"That ol' bird is a softy. We'll have a great time," Reese says. She means it, too. Reese loves old people. She's floundered since college, moving from one job to the next. But she goes out to Myrtle Beach and stays at our grandma's condo a few times a year, and she always comes home happier.

Reese kisses my cheek and runs to her room to start packing. Gramma is in the hospital tonight, but she'll be released tomorrow, so Reese will leave in the morning.

True to my word, I call Rusty and make a soft inquiry about his schedule the next couple of weeks.

Good heavens, the man is busy. He's busier than I am. Not only is he running the fruit stands for the farm, he's filling in for Tripp while our friend is on his honeymoon. He's busier than I am.

What am I going to do?

I need someone who Lottie knows and loves and someone who knows and loves her in return. I need someone who can handle her tantrums and mood swings without losing it themselves. I need someone I can trust, someone *she* can trust.

And I need that someone by tomorrow. Because yes, I have a bye week, but if Lottie isn't used to her new babysitter by next week when my intense schedule resumes, things are about to go from bad to worse.

The list of available *someones* is tiny.

I know I shouldn't bug him, but I call my best friend. He answers on the fourth ring, but he doesn't say hello right away. Instead, I hear him whispering something to Jane that sounds like, "then throw me my shirt."

"Uh, hey buddy. You there?" I say.

"Yeah, gimme a sec. Jane thinks it's weird for me to video chat without a shirt on."

"We're not video chatting."

"She's about to change that. Once she takes off my shirt so I can put it on." I can hear the grin in his face, and a stab of envy pierces my heart. Even when I was newly married, I was never this happy. Shoot, Tripp and Jane looked happier fighting than I ever felt when I was with Carlie. She and I were never electric like that, and as much as I blame her for the way it ended, I can't help but wonder what was wrong with me that I couldn't connect with her the way she clearly wanted to from our first date.

In truth, I've never connected with *anyone*.

But Millie came dangerously close.

And I still don't know how I feel about that.

We swore off women, remember?

I don't know if it's the fact that I've been part of a team for as long as I can remember, or what, but my inner voice is plural. Us. We.

It's not weird.

The call switches to video, and I accept their request just to see Jane wearing a hotel bathrobe and Tripp wearing the t-shirt Jane must have thrown to him. They're sitting on the edge of an unmade bed, the morning sun streaming in behind them. They both look stupidly happy. Glowy and smug, too, like they just discovered the secrets of the universe.

Freaking newlyweds.

Tripp's light brown hair is standing up and Jane's long, dark blonde hair is in a loose side braid.

"Now what's so important that you had to interrupt our honeymoon?" Tripp asks.

I tell them.

And the truth is, I'm not even sure why I'm telling them. I know they're on their honeymoon, and I know what people do on honeymoons. But I also know that I have no one else I can talk to right now who won't feel obligated to do something about it, which will make me feel guilty. Jane and Tripp are on a tiny island on the other side of the world. They literally *can't* do anything about it. In fact, I'm surprised they have such good reception.

When I'm finished explaining my sticky situation, Tripp looks sympathetic while Jane looks ... suspicious. Shrewd.

"I don't know, man," Tripp says. "Anita and Booker could probably help, but I'm not sure how Lottie would handle that." Anita is Tripp's farm manager and the older sister of Millie's receptionist, Angie. She's an old friend, but Tripp is right: as much as Lottie loves Anita and Booker, she doesn't know them well enough to stay with them, and they certainly couldn't travel with me to the training facility every day or stay in my loft downtown with us when team meetings go late.

"You should ask Millie," Jane says. A current of electricity runs through me. "She'll have some telehealth clients, but she has the most flexible schedule, she's incredible with kids, and we all know how much Lottie loves her already."

And now I know exactly why I called, and I'm furious with myself.

Because I realize a small part of me—a part I'm barely acknowledging exists—hoped Jane would suggest this very thing.

That same small part also knows that if Jane hadn't suggested it, I probably would have asked her what she thought about the idea.

I am such a jerk.

I'm attracted to Millie. Okay, I'm *wildly* attracted to her. My body has an almost chemical reaction every time I think about her, let alone see her. People talk about how they can't think straight when they're around the person they're interested in, but it's not that I can't think straight, it's that I can't *see* straight. The perfectly steady, undeviating course I had in my head is suddenly littered with forks and off ramps I never noticed before.

I'm not taking any of them, but for the first time since Carlie left, I see them.

And all roads lead to Millie.

No no no. I can't think like that. I'm not planning to date the woman. I need her to watch my kid for a couple of weeks. That's all. If I were planning to date her, I'd have kissed her on the balcony instead of shutting down and shutting her out. I know that's why she was different over dinner. We were like magnets being drawn closer and closer together up until the moment when, bam, I flipped polarity and pushed her away. Reese picked up on it, too.

If I hadn't gone so cold so fast, I would have been able to ask Millie myself. Shoot, she'd have probably still been in the kitchen with me when my mom called. Knowing Millie, she probably would have offered to help.

And now, it's anyone's guess what she'll say if I ask.

Which is why I'm not planning to ask. This has to come from Jane.

I wrinkle my forehead. "I don't know, Jane. Do you actually think she'd agree to it?" I make my voice as hesitant as I can.

Tripp's eyes pop. "Wait, you'd let a woman you don't know babysit Lottie? Even if Lottie's obsessed with her?"

"I met her," I say vaguely. "She's really nice." The amused look on Jane's face tells me she knows a lot more than her husband does. "And y'all could've told me that Millie is the hotshot therapist you hired, by the way."

"You've known for months that Millie was Jane's friend, but you've never met any of them. There was no context. Also, you think therapy's a joke," he reminds me. "Why are you being so weird about this?"

He's right, but I'm annoyed anyway.

"I think he means that you could have told him how hot she is," Jane says, nudging Tripp's ribs. I don't deny it. "Call Millie. Or … did you need me to?" Her dark blue eyes flash a knowing challenge.

I keep my expression neutral, even if she sees through me like a window. "Would you mind?"

"Do you *promise* not to hurt her?"

Tripp gives his wife a confused look. I narrow my eyes, looking at the far-too perceptive face on the screen. I have no intention of hurting Millie. So why can't I promise her best friend that I won't? "I don't want to hurt her."

"That's not what I asked, Ogden."

Jane has become like a second sister to me, and it's as annoying as one sister is. "I promise."

"Then I'll call her, and I'll even swear it was all my idea."

"Wasn't it?" I ask.

"Goodbye, Duke." She winks, stands up with phone in hand, and walks out of view.

Tripp grabs the phone, bringing his face clearer into view. "You gonna tell me about this later?"

"Maybe. Enjoy the honeymoon, pal. I hope I didn't wake you two."

Tripp grins like a fool. "No, no you did not."

"Dude, happiness is obnoxious on you."

Tripp laughs and hangs up.

An hour later, I have a text from Jane. "She's in. You'd better keep your promise."

CHAPTER FIFTEEN

MILLIE

"I am such a sucker," I tell Louis the next day. I'm brushing him while baby animals run around us. I nudge the goats away from eating my palazzo pants. But Louis stays cool, letting me go at my own pace. Louis's mom is a certified therapy animal, and soon we'll have Louis and a few others trained to get certified, as well. Then if my practice doesn't start filling up soon, Linda and I will still be able to take the animals into nursing and foster homes in the area.

And in the meantime, I'm having Duke and Lottie meet me here today on neutral ground. Because, while I am sympathetic to Duke's plight and I definitely don't want his grandmother to go without help or his parents to fly home from a vacation early, I need to exert some control before I let him be my boss for two weeks.

I take a deep breath and then make a face. I love animal stench about as much as anyone whose first job was the makeup counter at Sephora. Which is to say not at all. But I do love animals. Every stroke of the brush down Louis's fluffy wool pulls stress from me. I can almost see the knots of anxiety waft away on the cool breeze.

"You seem to be enjoyin' yourself." I look up to see Rusty enter the pen. His boots crunch on the hay as he sidesteps some droppings. Rusty is as handsome as he is wholesome, with his wavy dirty blond hair, deeply tanned skin, and hazel eyes. In jeans and a long sleeve waffle crew pulled up his forearms, he looks like he was born for this life.

Yet I suspect his passion lies beyond the farm. Over the last few months, Rusty's also freelanced for Jane & Co., using his graphic design degree and working with Ash on ad campaigns. I don't know how he can do so much and still find time to drop off boxes of produce, jams, salsas, and fresh baked bread for us every couple of days.

I know *why* he does it, though. He's in love with Ash.

She couldn't be more oblivious to the fact; she friendzoned him the second she laid eyes on him. Ash has always had a thing for ... how do I put this nicely?

Oh, right: tools. Emotionally stunted, narcissistic tools.

Rusty's as far from that as they come.

I ache for him, knowing a bit of what it's like to want someone who doesn't see you that way. Most everyone has had an unrequited crush before. I mean, I have one right now.

Had one, that is.

"I am enjoying myself," I say as Rusty sits on a hay bale next to mine. "Louis will be the king of therapy animals. Can you believe this chill?"

Three baby goats are jumping at Rusty's knees, and he scoops the most excited one up onto his lap.

"Louis is pretty cool," he drawls, "but give me a baby goat any day. They're so playful and adorable. Their energy makes me feel like nothing is as dire as I think it is." I bite back a smile. I'm pretty sure Ash's patronus is a baby goat. With glasses.

"Anyway, how's the practice comin' along? Any new clients yet?"

"A few inquiries, but no one's on the books."

"Give 'em time," he says. The baby animals are swarming Rusty now, which doesn't surprise me. Animals are great judges of character, and each is clamoring for his attention. He pets them all as they bleat (goats) and let out high-pitched neighs (llamas). "Small town and mental health awareness don't always go hand-in-hand, but everyone wants someone to talk to. Just show them you can do that and they'll come around."

"Thanks for the advice," I say. "Now do you have any ideas for how I'm going to handle Duke while I'm babysitting Lottie?"

He chuckles and shakes his head. "He's the one who should be worried."

"Why do you say that?"

He gestures with his head before standing up, alerting me to someone's presence. "There's my favorite girl!" he says. A moment later, Lottie launches into his arms. Louis the Llama nuzzles my hand, sensing the shift in my energy. I smile at Lottie and Duke but stay sitting, grateful for the llama's calming presence.

After a moment, Duke comes to me. My hands are warmer than they would normally be in the morning chill, but Louis is a good space heater. That doesn't do anything for my nose, though, which is cold enough that I'm sniffing. And if my nose is this cold, it's also purple.

It's a super attractive look, I know from experience. Super. Attractive.

Good thing I don't care about attracting Duke anymore.

"Hey, so, uh, thanks for helpin' us out," Duke says. He takes Rusty's seat on the bale beside me. He looks nervous, wringing his hands. The walls guarding my heart tremble but stay firm. "I never intended for you to get this involved in our lives when I came into your office the other day."

Oh, I believe that. He made clear last night that he doesn't want me involved in his life at all. He had his flirtation, won, and can move on now. If I didn't adore his daughter and worry far too much about her well-being, I'd have laughed in Jane's virtual face when she called last night. I just nod at Duke. I don't even know what to say.

So he continues. "I'll pay, of course. Whatever you want."

"Jane said fifteen thousand a week."

"*Fifteen thousand a week?*" He closes his eyes for a long moment. "Um, yeah, okay. That's more than the minimum base salary in the NFL, but sure." The war between sarcasm and desperation is playing out on his face, and I'm glad I'm wearing sunglasses so the sparks in my eyes don't incinerate him.

Fun fact: Jane said nothing of the sort. I plucked this number out of thin air for two reasons: I'm still hurt and this is an absolutely monumental request. It may have been Jane's idea and he's in a real bind, but he's still the one asking. This two-week babysitting job will finally pay off that "medically unnecessary" radiation so I can start paying down my student loans.

But first I have to put the pinch on Duke and his sticker shock.

"Then maybe you should have one of your little rookie pals help, instead. I'm sure they'll do a great job caring for your only child, and I have it on good authority that it'll save you some money." I'm up and already walking away when he grabs my hand. I hate how my body responds to him, how my mind tells me to shake him off but my hand wants to wrap around his. I hate how everything from my toes to my nose warms at his touch. I hate how much I don't hate any of this.

And boy, does that annoy me.

"Millie, stop," he grumbles. "I was being a jerk. Of course I'll pay. I'll pay you ten times that if it means you'll help. Lottie loves you, and I need you. I'm not too proud to beg."

"Fine. But I have some ground rules if this is going to work."

"Of course."

"First, I have clients who rely on me. I'll move my appointments to nighttime so Lottie's in bed, but I cannot miss a session. That means that you'll have to cancel any meetings or events to make sure you're able to be with your daughter during those times."

I only have eight weekly clients right now and a couple of biweekly ones, so I'm making this sound more urgent than it will be. But hopefully I'll have at least a couple of new client inquiries, too, and I'll take those seriously. If I don't make my career and my clients a priority, no one will.

"Second, you are not allowed to flirt with me."

"Pardon me?" he asks as if he's never even considered the idea, as if he's utterly flabbergasted that I would even suggest something so off the wall.

I lean down so my face is close to his. Close enough to see just how thick his light brown eyelashes actually are. Close enough to see the stubble on his cheeks and that cleft chin I want to press my lips into.

Yeah, this rule is for me at least as much as it is for him.

"I'm simply asking that you treat me as you would any of Lottie's nannies. Unless you make it a habit of flirting with them too? If you have any ideas about winning me and then dropping me at the end of this little game, erase them from your mind now. This is a professional arrangement and I expect us both to behave like professionals."

His nostrils flare. "Anything else?"

I pause. "Not off hand. But I reserve the right to add to or amend these rules at any time."

"Do I get to respond before you seal this pact in blood?" He's still sitting on the hay bale, and I'm still standing in front of him, but the power dynamic is shifting, and I'm powerless to stop it.

"Yes ... "

"If I'm paying you thirty K for two weeks of work, then you

can't just have any evening off. I understand that you have clients, but I'll need your help some nights. I have unbreakable commitments, too, you know."

"What, some football pals need help picking out lingerie models?"

"Try a charity event for foster kids," he says coolly.

I bite the inside of my cheek, studying him. "Fine."

"Second, you and Lottie will have to come to everything you can. She's going to love the idea of you babysitting, but the reality will rock her world. I'll need you to bring her to practice, to the charity event, to everything she can reasonably attend so she knows that I'm safe and she's safe. If that's a problem, then this isn't going to work." He stands, but I'm already so close that his chest bumps against me as he rises, pressing against my arm and reminding me just how rock solid he really is. "Third." He stares down his perfect nose at me. My neck almost hurts from craning up to look at him.

"Oh, you get three rules?"

"No. This isn't a rule, it's a statement." His voice is low enough that it reverberates in my chest. "I'm a single dad, Millie. I'm navigating a lot of firsts, and I'm messing them up, along with about everything else in my life. But you need to know I'm not interested in games. I'm not looking to *win* you or *drop* you." I lower my head, feeling a bit chastened, until his finger raises my chin and I'm peering into his eyes. "But if I did get in the game again? You should know that I play for keeps."

His gaze could vaporize me for how it burns past my angry facade and into my fleshy, vulnerable heart.

"Now if you'll excuse me, my daughter is currently trying to sit on a baby goat, so I'm gonna save that poor creature from Lottie's cute aggression."

As I watch Duke pull his daughter away, the power of his words hits me hard.

This job is going to be a lot more drama than I anticipated.

CHAPTER SIXTEEN

MILLIE

That evening, Parker, Ash, and Lou insist on driving me to Duke's on their way to the diner. The house itself is absurdly close, but the driveways are a couple of hundred yards away because each mini mansion sits on a dozen or so acres. I tell them I can just walk through the forest and be there in two minutes, but they refuse to take no for an answer.

Duke doesn't "need" me until next week, but he insists that Lottie's going to need the time acclimating to me. He even wanted me to come tonight rather than tomorrow so I could watch their evening routine.

Is this all a ploy? Are his reasons as hollow as they sound? Why does he need me to stay at the house rather than be there during her waking hours?

I have no good answers to these questions, but I'm getting paid an astronomical sum, so I'm letting it slide. I've erected a fortress around my heart, and I will *not* let Duke breach it again.

"You really don't need to do this," I say to my friends.

"Like we'd miss seeing you off on your first day of family camp?" Ash says from the driver's seat of her Subaru Outback. She buckles up and adjusts her mirror so she can see me in the back. Ash's car is ten years old, and she loves it like a cowboy loves a pickup."Never! Besides, Duke is hot, and I believe firmly in my right to ogle hot men."

"No touching," Parker says from the passenger seat at the same time I do.

"I'm not going to touch him." Ash adjusts her sunglasses. "Man, you touch a man's abs one time—"

"One time?" Lou laughs beside me. "Ash, need we remind you of sophomore year? We all had to stop bringing dates back to the apartment to prevent you from creepin' out on them."

She gasps dramatically as she pulls out onto the main road from our long, winding driveway. "Creeping out? Not even! I made those dudes famous with my abs page. Besides, I never showed their faces."

"It was objectifying," I say.

"If it was so objectifying," Ash says, "Why did they agree to do it? They signed four-page waivers, gang."

Ash has a point.

She started her "Abs of Chicago" page for her Psychology of Social Media class sophomore year. It made her quite popular with the hyper-fit men of the University of Chicago, to say nothing of the hundred thousand followers the page gained that semester thanks to her captions. Her very first picture was of a guy with a glistening fake tan. She photoshopped a pat of butter in the middle of his stomach and a bottle of syrup next to it.

"Ordered pancakes and got waffles. Still waiting to talk to the manager. 1/10 for the butter. #tummywaffles."

(Yes, that's right: Ash invented the #tummywaffles trend.)

The guys who let her post their picture didn't date any of us for long. When a guy laughed and said no, we knew he was quality.

Sonny never let Ash put his pic up. I'm sure Parker's remembering that right now.

"Besides, I deleted the page," Ash continues, turning into Duke's driveway. Overgrown trees surround us, some branches dipping down almost to the car.

"And an entire generation of gym rats had to go back to posting workout selfies to get the adulation their six and eight packs rightly deserved," Lou says pityingly.

We all tsk.

"Well, here we are, sweetie," Ash parks the Outback in front of Duke's gorgeous rustic contemporary lake house. She shifts in her seat, her curls bouncing and her Jackie O sunglasses reflecting my image. I look ... nervous.

I am.

"Make good choices," Parker says, getting in on the game. "And remember who you are."

"We love you," Lou says, fake tearing up.

With a small laugh, I grab my bags, head up to the door, and try to wave them away. But Lottie is too quick on the uptake. The door is open before I can even ring the doorbell.

"Miwwie!" She throws herself at me before I've put my bags down, and the two of us stumble backwards toward the stairs. I brace myself for the tumble when a pair of strong hands grabs my arms before we can fall.

"Whoa, easy there," Duke says, pulling us back upright. Lottie squeezes me with all her might as Duke puts his hand on my back to usher me into his house.

"Aw, that is the cutest," Ash says out her rolled down window. Her phone is out and she's taking pictures of us. "I'm going to sell these to TMZ and get rich, gang. RICH!"

Duke looks beyond alarmed, but I shake my head and say loudly, "She's *teasing*, right Ash?"

"I make no promises." She blows us a kiss. "Have fun! Don't do anything I wouldn't do!"

With that, my cackling friend peels out, leaving me with the insta family of my dreams.

As the nanny.

Duke's hand is still between my shoulder blades, something I vehemently tell my body to ignore, in spite of the delicious sensation it spreads through the muscles and nerves of my back.

"Can I get your bags?"

"Sure, thanks. Should we go in, Lottie?" I ask, and she squeals in the affirmative. I walk her into the house and try not to gasp at the incredible entrance. I've seen the kitchen, family room, and dining room, and they were all so tastefully done that I could forget how stupid rich Duke actually is. But this entrance? The chandelier hanging down from what's probably a twenty-foot ceiling? The marble floor, the entrance table, the artwork...

I have to stop myself from gasping.

"Is everything okay?" Duke asks, closing and locking the door behind me.

"Yes, totally. It's just... your house is stunning, Duke."

His face twists a little, and I get the feeling that there's a story here. "Thanks," he says. "It's a bit much. Rusty's gonna help me redo the entrance in the off season. Make it a little more down to earth."

Oh. His ex must have put this together. I've purposefully avoided looking for Carlie on social media. From everything I've heard of her, I've gotten *tacky* vibes more than something that could create this. The kind of woman who would rather post a picture of her kid than actually play with her. This ornate, elegant entry isn't tacky. Not at all.

But it isn't warm. Not like the kitchen and dining room are. They're beautiful, but they're made for real people.

"It's lovely, but of course you should change it if you want to," I say.

I put Lottie down and let her drag me through a tour of the house. Her room, the theater room, her playroom, complete with a rock wall, a trampoline, and gymnastics mats. The house has three guest rooms, all with their own bathrooms, and a full mother-in-law suite with a sitting room and kitchenette. There's a small library with hundreds of books, including a kid's section. Duke even has a soundproof music room with a dozen guitars on the wall and a full drum set.

I thought Tripp's rental was nice, and it is. More than.

But this house is bonkers.

MTV Cribs style.

When Lottie opens a pair of double doors, I enter without thinking. Then I abruptly stop.

It's the master bedroom.

Lottie pulls me in, and I go without protest. The king size bed rests in the middle of the room. The bed is made, but there's no decorative pillows or fancy duvet covers. There is, however, a litter of stuffed animals and a little pink and gray blanket on it. Duke has a custom made dresser, and his massive walk-in closet is less than half full. His wardrobe is largely designer but without being flashy. No gold-threaded smoking jackets or weird dragon designs, or anything. Not that Lottie lets me peek for long before she pulls me further in. I spot a spa-worthy bathroom before we reach the center of the room. I feel stupid being this close to his bed, but Lottie jumps up on it to roll around with her stuffed animals, so I glance around a bit more. His nightstand has a stack of books, including Malala's autobiography, a Jim Gaffigan book, the Bible, and two parenting books.

The room is clean, tidy, and impersonal. Unlike the rest of the house, there are no pictures, no artwork, no plants. It's like a blank slate. I wonder if it's unintentional, like he hasn't had the time to think about his own space, or if it's purposeful. Maybe he wants something ultra-zen to keep his mind uncluttered when his life is so messy. On the opposite side of the bed, there's a valet stand with Duke's pajama bottoms...

Bottoms only. No top. Oh my heavens, does he not wear a shirt to bed?

Stop thinking about his abs. Stop thinking about his abs.

"Do you yike it?" Lottie asks, standing on the bed with her arms outstretched. Fortunately, she doesn't notice that I've broken out into a sweat thinking of her dad without his shirt. "This is my other room!"

"I love it. But I like your first room even better."

She grabs my cheeks so our noses are touching, one of her signature moves. Her brown eyes are pools of innocence. "My room has monsters," she whispers loudly. "You don't want to go in my room."

"You already showed me your room, silly billy. I didn't see any monsters." I pick her up and start taking her out.

"There *are* monsters," she insists, not hugging me the way she normally does. Her arms are in front of her chest, and without her holding on, she's much harder to carry. She's tall for her age, lanky, like her aunt, but with full, round cheeks and a cherubic pout.

I close the door behind us and start to carry her upstairs. Duke is grilling steaks outside, but he's roasting veggies, too, Brussels sprouts and asparagus. I love them both, but I'll have to make sure I don't use a bathroom anyone else will use. Newsflash: asparagus pee is not the smell I want Duke associating with me.

Maybe I just won't eat it.

"Why do you think your room has monsters?"

"Because Momma Doggy is gone," she says, a frown tugging the sides of her lips downward. "And the monster took it."

At the top of the stairs, we see Duke coming in the sliding glass door with a tray of steaks in one hand and utensils in the other. The door slides closed behind him. "Why would a monster want Momma Doggy?" I ask Lottie.

Duke's head snaps over to mine, and his eyes are round in alarm. He gives a hard shake of his head, but I don't know what he's warning me against. A monster? Momma Doggy? I try to send him a "What do you mean?" look with my eyes.

"Lottie, remember, we lost Momma Doggy at the airport and they couldn't find her."

Lottie goes from sullen to raging in a millisecond. "No! We! Didn't! She was in my bed and a monster took her!"

Duke puts the tray and utensils down and comes over to take Lottie from me. I roll my shoulders out—I'm not used to carrying kids.

"Baby girl, there is no monster. Monsters aren't real. You've gotta let this go."

"There is a monster," she screams, hitting his chest with her little fists and crying. "It took Momma Doggy!"

"Lottie, no hitting," he says, but she keeps slamming her fists into his chest. He's strong enough to tolerate it, but she's putting increasingly more force into her movements. "Stop it, Lottie. You're going to lose TV time if you hit me again. Lottie, I mean it!" He keeps escalating his consequences, even as she keeps hitting him and screaming louder until her shrieks are ear-splitting. I actually wince. "Lottie, enough! Don't make me take away *Bluey*!"

I want to step in, tell him that he's threatened ten times now to take away TV, but I also see the pain on both their faces, and any sort of barrier melts away as emotion fills me. What am I supposed to do? I'm not the mom. I'm not the therapist. I'm not even the actual nanny. I'm a woman who cares way too much and is helpless to do anything about it.

The oven dings, and I use that as an excuse to walk away

from the painful scene. I go through the steps of taking the food out and dressing it with everything Duke laid out, and Lottie is still raging.

After getting everything else ready, I set the table and serve myself. The act of normalcy distracts Lottie. Red faced and sweating, she pushes her hair from her eyes and comes over to the table. She sits on my lap instead of in her chair.

"Sweetie, I won't be able to eat if you're sitting on my lap. Can you sit right beside me?" I ask.

"No. I need to sit with you."

"Lottie, please?"

"No! I want to sit with you," she insists.

Duke flashes me a "been there" look.

What am I supposed to do? Do I just let her sit here? Is this a hill worth dying for? Is this a boundary that shifts a lot?

"Do you normally sit on someone's lap when you eat?" I ask, because nothing else is coming to me.

"No. But I want to sit on your yap." She takes my napkin and drapes it across her legs.

The irony of her using manners...

Duke watches with an amused look on his face. It's not petty, but I interpret it as a challenge, anyway. And that helps me shift my mindset back to work mode for just long enough to think of what to say.

"You want to sit on my lap, huh? I get it. Sitting together is fun." She nods. "You're going to need to sit in your own chair so we can both eat, but which spot do you want to sit at? My spot with the boring utensils and glass plate or yours with the super fun utensils and pink and awesome blue plate?" I phrase my question so over the top, I already know how she's going to answer.

"Your spot!" she says. She giggles maniacally when I move to her chair and hold her plastic utensils.

Duke looks at me admiringly, but it's a look he doesn't get to give me. I feel his eyes on me throughout the rest of the night and I see them in my mind when I try to fall asleep.

Yup. This is going to be a *lot* more drama than I expected.

CHAPTER SEVENTEEN

MILLIE

A few days into this temporary nanny gig, and Duke and I have mastered the art of communicating without talking to each other. When he's not working out, studying film, talking to his agent or coach or an organization of one kind or another, he's talking to Lottie. When either of us needs to relay a message, we talk through Lottie, send texts the second we're out of range, or, most recently, talk through Louis. The llama.

Lottie and I have spent time with the animals everyday this week. Four of our adult animals—two llamas, a goat, and an alpaca—are already certified therapy animals, and last month, my co-worker Linda and I completed the training to be certified with each of them. When their babies are all a year old, we'll certify a few of them, too. But even without certification, all of the animals in this pen have proven friendly and safe around people.

I would never treat Lottie, but I can and do use what I know.

Being around animals releases chemicals that improve moods and help alleviate anxiety, so the mere act of spending time in the barn or pen is helping. Additionally, though, I give her jobs that I hope will show her how capable she really is.

I'm starting slow. This week is just brushing the animals and talking to them. Lottie tells them elaborate stories that don't always make a lot of sense, but she's already a verbal kid, and her vocabulary explodes with the animals. She talks to them differently. She tries to calm the jittery, excited goats, and she tries to soothe Louis, assuming that his calm demeanor is hiding a secret sorrow that only she sees.

"I know, Youis. It's okay," she says as she brushes him. "You miss your daddy. It's okay. He woves you." Her l sounds vary between y- and w-, and both variations prick at my heart.

While Lottie brushes Louis, I say, "Lottie, sweetie, I'm going to go into the barn to get Louis some food."

Lottie narrows her eyes to see where I'm pointing. We're outside in the pen, and the bins are just a few feet into the barn, but it's around the corner. Over the last few days, I've learned that Lottie doesn't like losing sight of people, especially if it'll mean that she's alone. Lottie could handle Duke and me stepping out of view the other night because she was with Reese and, I'm sure, because she's seen her dad go out to the deck and reappear a hundred times.

She doesn't have the same confidence with me, and it's worse since Reese left for her grandma's house. I can't even go to the bathroom without Lottie crying. She lays down on the floor, reaches her fingers beneath the door, and waits there, talking or crying until I'm done.

It's like she thinks if she closes her eyes, I'll disappear.

It's also making it really hard for me to go to the bathroom or shower properly. My body may be clean, but I have enough dry shampoo in my hair to play Mrs. Doubtfire.

I'm sensitive to her fears, but avoiding triggers only heightens the anxiety around them. Duke's habit of constantly keeping Lottie in eyeshot or earshot means that her very natural fear of separation has only increased. She needs exposure therapy.

And unfortunately, I'm finding it a lot harder to execute than expected.

Hence the dry shampoo.

But I'm determined to take what steps I can, even if they're baby steps.

"Just keep petting Louis, and I'm going to sing a song the whole time so you can still hear me, okay?" Lottie's eyes narrow further, so I add in some bribery. It's therapy, not desperation, I tell myself. "And I'll even get you cotton candy."

The pros of exposure trump the cons of a sugar rush. Right?

They do for now. Lottie's expression goes from scared to elated to uncertain, so I sing the Paw Patrol theme, which I know by heart, and walk into the barn to scoop pellets into a Ziploc bag. I go more slowly than necessary, trying to draw out my absence while singing about Marshall, Rubble, Chase, Rocky, Zuma, and Skye at the top of my lungs. When I've delayed as long as I can, I come out of the barn, belting out the last line. "Paw Patrol, whoa oh oh oh oh—Oh!"

Duke is standing with Lottie on his shoulders, a paper bag with food in his hand and a wide, cheeky grin spread across his face. He had a Zoom call about a potential endorsement deal earlier today, so he's wearing a button down with a cardigan, jeans that accentuate his glorious thighs, and a pair of Vans. His thick blond hair is high and styled a little to the side, and he has a few days' worth of growth that is so scruffy, I want to feel it underneath my fingernails. At least until he opens his mouth.

"Wow. I didn't know what a singer you were."

If Lottie weren't in hearing distance, I would tell him to shut up. But she's beaming. "Miwwie is the best singer in the universe! She sings to me when she goes to the bathroom, Daddy."

Heat creeps up my chest and neck. "So she knows I'm there, not for, you know, fun," I explain.

"No, of course not. Why would singing while … evacuating your bladder be fun for anyone?"

I fake a smile for Lottie's sake but mutter, "Zip it," as I pass. He chuckles.

After I give Louis and the others one last snuggle, the three of us leave the pen and wash up at the hand washing station just outside the barn. We head over to a picnic table beneath a sugar maple with deep red leaves.

The air is crisp, and on this side of the farm, the smell of the apples in the orchard is strong enough to make my stomach growl.

Duke pulls out a couple of turkey legs and some collard greens and gives Lottie chicken strips with ranch, which she immediately digs into. "Miwwie p-omise cuh-un can-y," she says unintelligibly after taking a huge bite.

Turns out Duke speaks *unintelligible* fluently. "Don't speak with your mouth full, pumpkin," he says. He looks at me crossly, but his words are sugary sweet. "And Millie should have checked with me first, because tomorrow is our Halloween party, and I don't want you sugared out two nights straight." With his daughter on the same side of the table as him, she can't see annoyance flashing on his face like a neon sign.

But she can see my face, so I smile warmly. "I'm sorry for not checking with you. It was a reward for Lottie doing something brave. She let me walk into the barn out of view while she brushed Louis."

His smile matches mine, down to the falseness. "That's great! In the future, I'd appreciate it if you keep in mind that I don't believe in celebrating behaviors that meet baseline expectations."

He's using bigger words so she can't pick up on what we're saying. I do the same. "I'm sympathetic to that point of view, but in my *vast experience*, incentivizing desired behaviors leads to better adoption of those behaviors."

His nostrils flare as he keeps up the charade. "Still, as someone with a unique health history and awareness of the negative effects of pure glucose, I would think you would be more careful about picking incentives and could, perhaps, be more creative next time."

I can't let my irritation show, so I fake a laugh. Lottie is digging into her food and doesn't seem to care what we're talking about, but I'm not going to be the one to screw this up. Especially not when he's being a hypocritical jagweed. "You bring up a good point, and I'll take that under consideration. But I remind the pot to think twice before calling the kettle black, considering what prompted your initial phone call to me last weekend."

He glares at me over his smile, and I blink prettily back. We got us a good ol' fashioned Sugar Maple Standoff.

"Point taken," he says. He takes a massive bite of his turkey leg.

"Ditto." I say before taking one of mine.

"Get a room," Lottie says, and Duke and I both choke on our food.

Duke spits turkey leg onto the table in front of us, while I try to keep mine in my mouth through my laugh-cough. "What does that mean?"

"I heard someone yeww it at you and Miwwie at the Ha-yo-ween party at the park yast night." I snort and swallow at the same time, but the bite of turkey gets lodged in my throat. I swallow again, but the food just stays there. I try to cough, but it won't budge, and when I try to breathe in, nothing happens.

Oh my gosh.

I can't breathe.

I'm choking.

I grab my neck. Panic rises in me, stopping in my throat with the turkey. I wave my hands at Duke, but he's busy telling Lottie something about how she shouldn't repeat words when she doesn't know what they mean. I slam my hands on the table, and he ignores me while he finishes his lecture, so I stand up, still slamming my hands to get his attention. His head jerks to mine, and instantly, irritation is replaced by fear.

"Are you—?" He doesn't say the word, but I nod and point to my throat.

He runs around the table and throws his hands around my waist. His fingers crawl up my ribs while I fight to gasp, cough, breathe, anything!

Duke puts his fist right where my ribs meet below the middle of my chest. He thrusts his fist into my upper abdomen in a J-motion over and over and over. Why is it taking so long? Seconds turn into hours as spots form in my vision. Duke lets go of me with one hand, pounds his palm into my back several times, and then returns to do more j-thrusts, all while I feel increasingly dizzy and panicked.

He gives the hardest thrust yet to my abdomen.

The food dislodges and flies out of my gaping mouth.

And

I

can

breathe.

Tears stream down my face as I greedily guzzle in air. Duke's arms stay around me, holding me up so I don't collapse to the ground. I'm facing away from Lottie, and in the background, I hear her ask what we're doing, but I don't hear Duke's low voice over the sound of blood rushing in my ears. I don't want to scare her, but I can't spare an ounce of energy for anything except breathing.

And breathing.

And breathing.

Slowly, I regain strength and can stand on my own, and Duke's hands shift. One hand stays on my waist while the other rubs circles on my back the way I've seen him do to Lottie a dozen times already. His hand is so big, strong, and steady, and it makes me feel anchored to the ground when I was scared I was sinking into an abyss.

I was so scared.

When I've finally managed to calm down, I turn around and toss my arms around his neck, my eyes still wet.

"You saved my life," I whisper, unable to hold back emotion. He's bending down so my face is against his. His whiskers poke into my cheek and neck, and the prickly feeling is another reminder that I'm alive because of him.

"I thought I lost you." His whisper is harsh and urgent, and his words send shockwaves through the walls of my heart.

I don't know what to say. I should let go, but I can't. And Duke doesn't seem eager to let go, either.

A moment later, Lottie's arm wraps around my leg. I peek down to see that she's hugging Duke's leg with her other arm, and her smile stretches from ear to ear. "I yove you Dad. I yove you Momma Miwwie."

We both put a hand on Lottie's back, but as much as I know one of us should correct her, I don't.

Neither does Duke.

"We love you, too, sweetie," Duke says. We release each other, but Lottie instantly grabs both of our hands.

"And now, cotton candy!" she declares.

Duke's gaze burrows into me over Lottie. And it's then that I notice that his eyes are wet. The creases of a deeply furrowed brow remain in his head like pencil marks an eraser couldn't completely remove. Concern bounces off of him like an echo, and by holding my eye, I gather he's not afraid to let me see it.

What does he see in my face? How terrified I was that I

would lose him and Lottie? How grateful I am to be here with them? How deeply I feel for them, in spite of these last few days?

"If Millie said you get cotton candy, let's get you cotton candy." His eyes pull from mine, and part of my heart follows.

And no amount of warning bells can stop it.

CHAPTER EIGHTEEN

DUKE

I hate fame.
    I hate it.
  The tabloids are all in a tizzy over a picture that was released of me and Millie hugging, with Lottie at our feet. The picture tells a compelling story. We look like a happy family.
  A very happy family.
  I keep pulling up the picture while I should be suiting up. My mind won't stop returning to the debilitating fear I felt seconds before that picture was taken. The fear that I was going to lose Millie.
  And someone was watching? Not calling 911, not rushing to help, just ... watching?
  Whoever took that picture cared more about cashing in on my life than saving Millie's.
  Let me say it louder for y'all in the back: I HATE FAME.
  Carlie suggested that we take CPR and child safety classes

before Lottie was born because it was, and I quote, "trending on momstagram."

I've never been so glad she was an influencer.

The feeling of Millie's unmoving rib cage haunted me all last night. I couldn't sleep thinking about how close I was to losing her, and the thought of losing her made me want to kick myself, because I don't *have* her. I've made such a point of staying away from her, keeping things surface level, treating her like the nanny-slash-therapist rather than the brilliant, stunning woman I'm painfully attracted to, I've taken to using my ice barrel to manage my feelings.

Cold immersion therapy for the win.

I've told myself for almost two years that I will never marry again. But honestly, a big part of that promise came from a deep-seated fear that there's something broken in me.

Because I've been married, but I've never been in love.

I never dated seriously in high school or college because I was never interested in anyone for more than a couple of weeks. I don't know if Millie's right, that it was the thrill of the chase, but whatever it was, I could never see myself with anyone long term, and it felt like a waste of time pursuing something with someone I saw no future with.

I dated Carlie for six months. It was my longest relationship, and a big part of that was because I was in training camp and then traveling with the team. I wasn't tired of her, but I didn't love her, either. She was fun and beautiful and she laughed at everything I said while still challenging me enough that I didn't feel like I was being catered to. And Carlie was strong in her own right. When a much more famous player on the team hit on her my rookie year, she slapped his face and asked him if he'd kiss his mother with that mouth.

Carlie's loyalty was one of the best parts about her. So while I was never in love with her, I did love a lot of things about her. I had a deep affection and concern for her.

Yet I already feel more intensely for Millie than I felt for the woman I shared a life with for almost five years.

Somehow it's only been a week since we met, but we've shared twenty dates' worth of information and experiences during that time. Shoot, we've spent more time together than couples on the Bachelor spend before getting engaged. (I blame Reese for that errant thought. Reese and her cheesy-romance-loving-heart and contractual stipulation that "On Monday nights, we watch *The Bachelor*.")

But while I may not be ready to dive in head first, I'm also keenly aware that watching Millie's cheeks go purple and ashen was enough to make me question everything.

"Bro, you've been staring at that pic on TMZ for five minutes," Sonny says, slapping my bare back. "And your pants are still around your ankles."

I toss my phone into my locker, pull up my pants, and throw a fake punch at his gut. "Shut up."

Sonny throws his head back and laughs. "Looks like a certain redheaded friend of mine has you wrapped around her manicured finger, doesn't she?"

"Nah, it's nothing like that," I lie.

Sonny's locker is only a few down from mine, and he strips down to his boxer briefs. Other players file in around us, slapping hands and butts, talking smack. A few of them ask me about Millie, even as Sonny pulls on his uniform. When it's over his head, he shoots me an expectant look.

"She's a good friend. That's all," I lie again. At this rate, my pants may start on fire.

"For now, maybe. But I know Millie. She's as good a catch as they come, and you're too smart not to notice."

I don't deny this, and Sonny's smile somehow gets toothier. "Just get changed," I grumble.

"Whatever you say, Loverboy."

I pointedly ignore all of Sonny's remaining innuendo and

finish suiting up. Then I rush out of the locker room and up the ramp, taking bigger strides than normal. Loud noise echoes in my ears, and all over the field, I see chaos and opportunity. A spotlight shines in my eyes. Adrenalin courses through me, and I feel revitalized, in spite of the shock of emotions I've experienced over the last week. It's like all of that frenetic mental energy has faded away and distilled into a single focus.

I'm always like this before a big game.

And, evidently, before the team's Foster Family Fall Festival.

On one half of the field are hundreds of makeshift "houses" (really booths with a roof) where most of the team will go trick or treating. On the other half are bounce houses, games, swag booths, and more. The team partners with foster agencies throughout the state of South Carolina, and every year, we hold the Foster Family Fall Festival, my favorite team event. With thousands of kids in foster care in South Carolina, the event lasts up to eight hours. The team foots all travel expenses and we always get a great turnout.

Not everyone's religious beliefs accommodate Halloween celebrations, so we have options available so anyone can come and have a good time. Also, to make the event friendlier to those with mobility or other issues, the team members and our families are the ones who dress up and "trick or treat" to the kids and families, not the other way around. The team provides each family with the candy, along with jerseys.

As each of us come out of the tunnel with our pumpkins, we look around for our families. Everyone brings their kids or nieces and nephews or even friends' kids. A Fourth of July's worth of fireworks sets off in my gut when I see Millie and Lottie holding hands, dressed up in adorable dog costumes like mine. When Millie spots me, she puts on a thick Australian accent that is scary good.

"Look, Bingo, it's your dad."

If you haven't heard of the TV show "Bluey," you're missing

out. Yes, it's a kid's show about a cartoon dog family, but it always makes me want to be a better dad with only minimal shame that I can't compare to Bandit Heeler, the undisputed best dad on TV.

And I tell you what, the costume may be a literal dog onesie, but Millie looks straight up sexy as the mom, Chilli Heeler.

She's always so put together that seeing her hair flattened under the hood, an errant red lock sticking out ... it's hot. Not in a creepy way, just in the way that any single dad assesses any woman. She looks like she could be a *mom*. Like she could be my daughter's mom.

Where's my ice barrel when I need it?

When Millie and Lottie get to me, I pick Lottie up and swing her high into the air before putting her down and taking her hand. Without thinking, without being able to stop myself, I put my free arm around Millie.

It's the friendly thing to do, okay? The woman is taking care of my child, after all.

She hesitates at first—she's seen the same tabloid speculation I have, even if we haven't done more than acknowledge it, and there are plenty of people here who could post to social media—but Lottie is staring up at us with heart eyes, and it's enough to make Millie hug me back.

Oh, this feeling. Like drinking a cup of hot tea on a winter's day, feeling the warmth spread through my body, bringing my cold heart back to life. I could get used to this. No, I could become *addicted* to this.

"Ooh," Lottie says like Bluey or Bingo would, "You're in *love*."

Millie responds with that same Australian accent that is way too good. "If you ask me to smoochy kiss him," she says, referring to Lottie's favorite episode, "you're going to have to give me all of your chocolate."

I laugh, even though I definitely wouldn't mind if Lottie

asked Millie to smoochy kiss me. "Yeah kid," I say in my best Bandit Heeler voice. "Now run along. It's candy time."

Lottie bounces as she walks with her candy-collecting pumpkin dangling around her elbow so she can hold both our hands.

Millie smirks at me. "What was that?"

"What was what?" I hope she's not talking about how affectionately I squeezed her arm when she hugged me. I knew it was a risk, but it was worth it to feel the muscles tense as she leaned into me.

"Your accent. Was that Irish? Or Eastern Canadian, maybe?"

"What? Of course not. That was Australian." Our starting row of booths is coming close.

"Not even close, pal. Your voice lilted. Is that what you think Australian accents sound like? Do you think Irish and Australian accents sound the same?"

She's being so delightfully saucy, flapping that big, beautiful mouth of hers, that I want to take a bite out of that bottom lip and—

Whoa.

I forcefully push the thought from my head.

I haven't wanted to kiss anyone in years. And I've never wanted to kiss someone with that kind of emotion behind it.

It doesn't matter. We've sworn off women, remember?

Shut up, I tell the team inside my head. Or maybe they tell me.

I'm not her boyfriend. I don't want to date her. I don't want to growl and kiss her and maybe nibble at her neck a bit.

I don't, okay?

Okay or not, my mind is going places my body is not allowed to follow.

We're at my "street," and at the very first makeshift house, where three boys are standing with their foster mom. She smiles when she sees me, making the dark, umber skin around her eyes crinkle. The boys are maybe ages ten through twelve and are standing together with identical looks of awe on their faces.

My first couple of years in the league were a PR mess. I'm not one to suffer fools gladly, as the Good Book says, and because I got my team to the playoffs as a rookie, I've received veteran press coverage since the beginning.

Need I remind you how much I hate fame?

I didn't know how to deal with the crowd. I was never *trying* to be a jerk, but I genuinely didn't understand why it all mattered to anyone. Who could care about my head space during a certain moment on field or if I thought my coach was right to call a specific play? It happened. Add to that the constant Brady comparisons, on and off the field, and I wasn't the happiest camper.

Carlie always told me to act my brand in these moments. Who do I want people to see when they see me? She would prepare me to project that image into my head so I could let it guide me. It helped me manage media and fan interactions a lot, even if it's not natural for me. But nothing off the field is natural for me. I just want to play football and never have a stranger acknowledge my existence.

Is that so wrong?

Still, I don't mind it from these kids as much as from middle-aged men too fixated on their fantasy football teams.

"Trick or treat!" Lottie says, holding out her pumpkin.

"Bro, your dad is Tom Brady?" the youngest kid says to Lottie.

Millie snorts and then coughs into her arm to hide it, and I war between annoyance and laughter with her.

Lottie looks at the youngest kid in confusion. "My daddy is Duke. What's a bro?"

One of the other kids elbows the youngest. "Bruh, that's Duke Ogden!"

CHAPTER NINETEEN

DUKE

I never realized how emotional trick-or-treating could be.

Making the simple switch to asking questions has had two effects: first, I'm taking way longer at each makeshift house (and I'm forcing the players behind me to slow down, too). Second, what I've seen as a feel good activity has become deeper.

A lot deeper.

I've always congratulated myself on being part of something that brings joy to these kids, and I still think it does. But I'm humbled to realize that I didn't want to look at the children beneath the costumes or makeup. Honestly, it's hard, even with Millie here, and especially with Lottie. She's eager to move from place to place, but the foster parents are having fun with her while Millie and I talk to the children in their charge. Some of them are infants while others look like they're about to graduate high school. Both extremes form a lump in my throat, and each new interaction adds something to that lump, either in size or in texture. The thing lodged in my throat is making my nose itch and the back of my eyes sting.

A few of the kids don't want to answer questions. They either want selfies and signed swag now, thank you very much (which I get), or they look like trapped animals when I ask them anything. Through a series of glances or touches to my forearm, Millie tries to help me navigate which ones to engage with on a deeper level.

I don't actually need the help, but I don't tell her that. Reading people is my thing. I get the sense she likes being helpful, though, and if it means that she keeps her hand on my forearm or, better yet, grabs my hand for a quick squeeze, I'll pretend I need all the help she has to give.

I get to learn something about Millie during all of this, too. She's comfortable enough if the spotlight shines on her, but she doesn't seek it out. Whenever the conversation turns to her, she can make small talk or go deeper, depending. I like it all. Plenty of the tween girls are under the impression that Millie's my girlfriend, so they ask her about herself. And while I know some deeply personal things about her, her quirky confessions capture my attention. Like how her favorite holiday is Christmas, but she prefers decorating for Halloween. Her favorite colors are red and hot pink, but she mourns not being able to wear them because of her hair.

"You could totally wear red," one gushing teen girl says to her. "It would look amazing with your skin tone."

"You think?" Millie asks. "What would you suggest?"

The girl's eyes widen with excitement, and she and Millie spend the next few minutes looking at clothes online.

I call the girl's tween sister over on the sly, and we watch Millie and the older girl over their shoulders. The sister helps me find the same sites and I order each of the tops Millie likes.

The younger sister is elated.

"Okay," Millie says. "You've convinced me. I typically save

BABY LLAMA DRAMA

I give him a fist bump while the kids give us all candy (which we'll put back into a donation pile for the kids to take home at the end of the night) and ask for selfies with me. The kids all got to pick out player jerseys; two of them have Sonny's, and ironically, the youngest one has mine. I sign each of them. They'll collect as many signatures as they can throughout the day. The nostalgic ones will keep the jerseys. The enterprising ones will sell them on eBay. I have respect for both.

I answer the questions the boys pose to me, smile, and we're on our way to the next booth, where it's more of the same. After several booths, Millie leans in close to me. I'm hoping she's going to get cuddly, but instead, she says, "You know, you're really nice to answer the kids' questions."

I shrug. "It's what they expect."

"But it's not what you like, right?"

"I don't mind it with them, but otherwise, I despise it," I say quietly. She nods, telling me to go on. "I just want to play the game I love and not have everyone care so much about me, you know?"

"You just want to do your job," she says with an understanding tone.

"Exactly!"

"But you can only do your job *because* of them," she says in that same tone, like she's acknowledging how much the fact sucks instead of condemning me for forgetting it.

Mostly.

"I know I only have a job because of fans."

She pats my cheek. "Smart boy."

I huff a laugh. "Out with it."

"Have you considered asking *them* something?"

"No ... "

"You don't like people paying attention to you off the field, right? Prying into your life? And who would? So why not pay attention to them, instead? You might like how it mixes things up for you to get to know fans rather than having them try to get sound bites out of you. It could also make *them* feel special. Besides, we're moving fast, and we have a couple of hours to get through our booths. Could be worth a shot."

I wait to feel a sting of criticism, but it's more of an elbow to the side than a jab. She's right to nudge me like this. And I bet asking questions would be a heck of a lot more enjoyable than answering them.

"Thanks for the idea. I'll try it."

the garish colors for my shoes, but dang it, sometimes a girl's just gotta wear hot pink."

"That explains the bra," I mumble to her. Her eyes go wide and a smirk plays on her lips, but she doesn't acknowledge me until we leave the booth.

And when she does acknowledge me, it's with an elbow to my gut.

I learn that she's from Ohio, that her first job was at Sephora, that her older sister and brother both still live in the town where they grew up. I discover that her parents are both retired school teachers, and that she's never been outside of the country, let alone to the West Coast.

I eat it all up.

Not all of the conversations stay surface level, though. Millie is normally solid as a rock when we hear stories of heartbreak, but one particularly difficult conversation makes her fists ball up with emotion. I grab her hand and wrap it in mine, and Millie doesn't let go.

A twelve year-old girl named Bailey tells us how her dad and little brother died of different illnesses one after the other and how her mom had a nervous breakdown right after. Her mom is in a facility and she lives with her uncle and his family now. The girl's uncle and aunt have a fierce love on their face as they both put an arm around the girl's shoulders.

I don't know what to say. It's too unreal. I can't understand how Bailey is even standing, let alone sharing all of this. I wait for Millie to answer, but she's overcome with emotion, so I say the only thing I can.

"That is so much, Bailey. I'm sorry. Thanks for trusting us with your story."

She's so matter of fact that she doesn't even have tears in her eyes while the rest of us are either weeping (her foster parents) or trying hard not to (Millie and me). Lottie is holding me close, and it hits me that she's been clinging to my leg this whole conversation, paying attention to Bailey's story in a way she hasn't with the others. Maybe I shouldn't have asked so many questions or allowed the conversation to go this direction with my sensitive, anxious little girl listening. How many nightmares will she have over Bailey's story?

Bailey's aunt and uncle are talking, and I pull my thoughts from my own worries. "We love her mama," the girl's aunt is saying. "We're hopin' and prayin' she gets healthy. Until then, we'll love Bailey with our whole hearts."

"And we will after, too, to be clear," Bailey's uncle says. Bailey rolls her eyes at the dad joke and teases him about his beef jerky consumption, and I have a moment of thinking how normal they're acting in the face of all this grief and trauma. There's no way Bailey's not deeply wounded by the loss of her dad, brother, and now her mom in such rapid succession. But her resilience is something I can hardly wrap my head around.

It's painful and inspiring and makes me want to go into a closet and cry. I don't let myself do anything other than talk, though. When the time comes, I ask Bailey and her uncle and aunt for a picture, not to post it (though she's free to), but to remember this teenage girl who has become my hero.

After Bailey, I don't have it in me to dig so deep again, and Millie doesn't push me. If anything, she holds my hand harder and stays closer to me, even as Lottie does the same. I feel the muscles in my back tense, not with my usual spasms, but with a primal need to protect them. It's like the very coding in my DNA is pulsing to make me do everything in my power to keep my family safe from anything like that ever happening to them.

I'm acutely aware of how my brain has lumped Millie into the same category as Lottie.

Family.

I take a chance adjusting the hand that holds hers so that our fingers are interlaced instead of hands clutching, trying to shift our energy from life-preservation to affection. I hold my breath, hoping this doesn't scare her off, even as my fingers memorize the feel of hers. Her hand is delicate, her fingers long and thin, and her skin is so smooth, I want to revel in every inch of it.

From the corner of my eye, I notice when she looks up at me. I meet her gaze, and she gives me a small smile that makes me feel like I've grown another foot in height. And when she presses her head against my shoulder for a brief moment at the next booth, I grow big enough to fill the stadium.

It feels different going through the rest of the line. Lottie isn't the same eager beaver she was at the beginning, but she isn't an emotional wreck, either. She gets in between us and holds both of our hands, breaking the contact that Millie and I had. We make up for it in long, lingering glances, arched brows, and tender smiles.

We finish the last of our "streets" and I'm about to suggest that we take a break when a voice yells Millie's name behind us.

"Milli Vanilli, is that you?" I turn to see Sonny running through crowds of curious foster families. Sonny is dressed in a cheerleader uniform that shows a bit too much of his thighs and biceps, if you ask me. I swing Lottie up onto my shoulders while Sonny rushes over. He instantly throws Millie over his shoulder and starts parading around, saying, "This is my girl, y'all! Mine!"

"Santino Luciano, you put me down this instant!" Millie laughs, beating her fists against his back. He complies, but the moment her feet touch the ground, she throws her arms around his neck. He lifts her off the ground, and they're laughing like old friends always do when they see each other after long separations and definitely not because there's anything else going on there.

Definitely not.

Yet they're doing that thing people do where they study each other's faces. Her eyes are roving over his features, and he's holding her hair and keeping his hands on her arms and commenting on her costume, and it strikes me suddenly that Sonny is better looking than I am.

I'm not being self-deprecating. I know I'm an attractive guy. I've done an interview with GQ, with the accompanying photo shoot.

Sonny, meanwhile, has also had a GQ spread, *and* is the new face of a men's skin care line, *and* he was ranked hottest player in football last year and I was number four.

Number four.

Sonny is saying something to me about Millie, and I don't know what it is, because all I know is that she's smiling at him. I have an overwhelming urge to pick him up and throw him into a dunk tank so he stops hitting on my girl, but I can't, because she's not my girl.

There is a dunk tank, though.

No, we do not throw grown men into dunk tanks for having a relationship with the girl we're avoiding a relationship with.

If we're in a relationship with her, though ...

That's it.

I walk over to them, Lottie firmly on my shoulders, and I put my arm around Millie.

Sonny eyes me shrewdly, but he doesn't comment on my obviously territorial move. "Who's a good dog?" he says, scratching behind my costume's ear. He looks up to Lottie. "Are you teaching your doggy any tricks, baby girl?"

"He's not my doggy, he's my daddy!" Lottie giggles. She knows Sonny well enough to laugh at his jokes. "You look so siwwy, Sonny Bunny," she adds.

Laughter explodes out of Millie. "Sunny Bunny? Lottie, how are you so smart and funny?"

"She's almost four," he says, tickling Lottie's foot. "She's a genius." She shimmies on my shoulders and laughs. "So ... uh ... did the rest of the Janes come, by any chance?" Sonny asks, looking around casually.

Millie shakes her head. "No, but did Duke tell you we're all here in South Carolina now?"

"You are?" he blurts. Then he looks away with a fake shrug. Sonny is the happiest guy I know, and he's never met an emotion he wasn't proud to wear. Right now, though, he looks like he's trying to hide something rather than feel it. "Nah, we aren't close like that."

"You could change that, you know," Millie says softly.

"Maybe, maybe not," he says.

Lottie tells me she needs to go potty, so I tell them I'll be right back and rush her to the nearest restroom. The last thing I need is her peeing on my shoulders.

Yes, that has happened before.

When we're in the family restroom, number one becomes number two, and she asks me to tell her a story while she poops, but because she also wants privacy, I have to stare at the wall while I tell her the story. If my fans could only see me now.

Ten minutes and two stories later, I'm helping Lottie wash her hands when she looks at me in the mirror.

"Daddy, do mommies and daddies sometimes die?"

The lump from talking to Bailey returns in full force. I want to lie and say no, never, but I know without having to ask that Millie would tell me not to. "Yeah, they do," I say.

"But then they come back as ghosts on Hayyoween?" She's thinking of a Disney movie, with a few of the details wrong. "Is that what happened to my mommy?"

"Your mommy?"

"Yeah, did she die and that's why she's not here anymore?"

I crouch down and turn Lottie to face me on the child step. "Do you remember her? Your mom?"

"She sang that song about the moon, and then the monster took her and Momma Doggy, and they never came back. Did they die?"

I pull Lottie in for a hug and swallow hard. Carlie used to

sing "Moon River" to her before bed. "Your momma didn't die. She ... she had to go away for a while."

Her mouth is right next to my ear because of how tightly I'm holding her. "Like Baiwey's mom had to go away?"

She heard that? "Kind of."

"Is she coming back some day?"

Unbidden, a tear forms in the corner of my eyes, blurring my vision. "I don't think so, Pumpkin."

"Will Miwwie be my new mommy?"

The tear falls. "You'd really like that, wouldn't you?"

"Yes. She's nice and gives me hugs and she sounds like Bingo's mommy and I yove her and she yoves me. Can you marry her?"

I chuckle and wipe the tear before letting Lottie go. I bump my forehead against hers. "I can't control Millie's choices, but I like her a lot, too."

"Then you should marry her, okay? Okay."

"I'll see what I can do."

We leave the bathroom and walk hand-in-hand through the field. Lottie gets jostled by another kid, and she panics and reaches for me to pick her up. I comply gladly, feeling more tender than tough after the emotional afternoon. Lottie stays in my arms the rest of the night. As much as I want to flirt with Millie and wrap her in an embrace, Lottie comes first. She and I carve pumpkins with other kids and families. We throw balls at Sonny and some of the other guys at the dunk tank (Lottie misses; Millie does not). She holds my leg when I take selfies with fans and shifts to my other arm when I sign autographs.

Near the end of the event, she sees Bailey walking around with her uncle and his family. Lottie insists I put her down, and then she runs to the girl and hugs her.

"My mommy had to go away, too," Lottie cries, grabbing Bailey's legs.

And Bailey's tough facade breaks. She drops to her knees

and hugs Lottie, and suddenly the two girls are sobbing for their moms, ignoring the people all around them. Bailey's uncle and aunt and I rush over and crouch down to hug the two crying girls. Someone's missing, though. I look up with my tear-filled eyes and see Millie standing a few steps back, silently crying and covering her mouth. I reach a hand to her, and she extends hers to me. With a tug, I pull her down to the ground with us, and the six of us hug and cry together.

Hours later—after Lottie has fallen asleep on the drive home and Millie and I have held hands the whole way, after I transfer Lottie to bed *and* brush her teeth without her rousing, after Millie and I share a good night hug so electric, it could power a city—I know.

I'm done with my rules. I'm done shutting this dream of a woman out. I am open for business, and I'm open for one person only. Since Carlie left, I've adhered to my path like a tightrope walker. I've focused everything on being the best dad and NFL player.

I've seen where this path leads, though. Lottie and I aren't thriving on the journey the way I intended. I love her, and she's enough for me, but now that we both have an option for more, I want it.

I've reached the offramp, and I'm taking this exit as far as it goes.

It's Millie or bust.

CHAPTER TWENTY

MILLIE

"So Duke's back at work this week, getting ready for Thursday's game?" Parker asks, though she knows his schedule as well as I do.

"Yes ma'am," I say, yawning in her office. Lottie is spinning around in Ash's chair in the office next to us.

I'm exhausted. I had three telehealth clients last night, starting the second Duke got home, and then my brother-in-law, Greg, called just before six in the morning because Bri has restless leg syndrome now that she's pregnant, and she was crying.

"Your pregnant, sleep-deprived wife is crying?" I asked him. "Greg, I think that's pretty normal."

"But not for her. You know what a good sleeper she's always been. We're still in the first trimester. How are we going to survive this if it gets worse?" Greg and Bri just got married last year. He never knew Sophie, and Sophie's dad bounced the second Bri peed on that stick. But Greg is a good guy—even if he's a perpetually anxious worrier who thinks the sun rises and sets on Bri.

"Have you tried calling her doctor to see if he can give her something for sleep?"

"Oh, that's a great idea. I'll do that and call you back."

"You don't need to—"

But he'd already hung up. I'm still waiting for that call back.

Parker glances away from her computer to look at me. "Duke better have his head in the game this week if the Waves are going to have a shot at the playoffs."

"Yeah, he told me he was off last game. He got sacked hard enough that he's had to rehab his back ever since."

"*Sacked? Rehab?* Who are you, and what have you done with my friend?" Parker sounds more smug than surprised, though, and the implication couldn't be clearer: you like Duke.

"Workplace hazard," I say.

"And how are things going at *work?*" Parker asks. Her eyebrows ask a lot more.

I drop my head to the desk. "I don't know. PJ, he's so hot and cold. I know he likes me. I know it. But he was never in love with his own wife! I don't think he's *ever* been in love."

"So?"

"So, that's a giant red flag. What's wrong with him that—"

"Nope."

"What do you mean, *nope?*"

"I mean what I said. Nothing is wrong with him. Carlie tricked him into getting married. He's a God-fearing Southern Gentleman who took the commitment seriously, so he stayed married."

"But how did he not fall in love with her? People in arranged marriages fall in love *all the time*. Especially after five years!"

Parker's head shakes impatiently. "But this wasn't an arranged marriage built on mutual values. This was a step away from coercion. I don't understand why he didn't get it annulled."

She must read the hesitation on my face, because she asks, "MJ, have you ever actually been in love? And don't try to tell me you loved that dork, Derek."

I think about my most recent ex, a guy who decided to end our relationship when I told him I was infertile.

No, I didn't love him, not before the breakup and certainly not after.

I think of every other guy I've dated, some for a couple of months, some for a few more than that.

"No," I admit. "I liked some of them enough to keep dating them, but there was always something missing."

"Is there something missing now?"

I eye Parker suspiciously. "What are you doing?"

"Dropping truth bombs."

"Well, stop. I don't like it."

"I won't stop, and you love it. Like you love Duke."

I tsk and look around to make sure Lottie didn't hear. "It's been five seconds. I don't *love* him."

"Tell that to your face. You blush every time you talk about him."

Two can play at this game.

"Hey, I forgot to mention, but I ran into Sonny at the team's fall festival. I think half the women there were trailing him around with drool on their faces. He looks *so good*, PJ. And he's matured, too."

"I hate how much I love you."

"Back at you," I say.

I say goodbye to my friends, grab Lottie, and we walk outside. The weather is mild, but Lottie runs cold, like I do, so she insists we go into Nico's second-hand shop to find hats.

"Sweetie, I'm not sure he's going to have what you're looking for," I say, even though there's a decent chance he will. The truth is that I don't like being disliked. I don't need him to adore me, but I'd settle for him not cursing at me in his native tongue every time I step inside.

"Pwease!" She bats her doe eyes at me, and I'm powerless to refuse.

"Okay."

I push the door open, and the bell rings, Nico sees me from behind the counter, and his expression goes flat. He mutters something when he notices the little girl attached to me and stops. He looks at our clasped hands, smiles at Lottie, and suddenly, he's a different man. He stands and walks over to us, holding his hand out for Lottie. She grins and lets him shake it, but she squeezes my hand tighter.

He seems to notice, because he doesn't glare at me.

"There's my favorite customer," Nico says in his mild Greek accent. "What can I do for you?"

"Do you have any hats for me and Miwwie?"

"And a pea coat," I whisper to Lottie.

"And a pee-pee coat?" Lottie says, laughing hysterically.

Nico gives a gruff laugh before looking at me knowingly. But still, he shows us around.

We leave twenty minutes later with matching hats.

And the Burberry pea coat of my dreams.

Listen, I'm tired and haven't had a chance to shower yet today, and Lottie's fingers under that bathroom door every time I have to *go* are seriously cramping my style, but I've searched for that coat for years and have finally caught my white whale.

Things are looking up.

Or not.

Because when we get to the diner for brunch, Tia grabs something from behind the counter. Then she hands me a bib and a soda in a kiddie cup.

"What's this?" I ask, glancing at Lottie. But a dozen pairs of eyes are fixed on me, almost in suspense.

"We all saw what happened last time you came in, sugar," Tia says. "I thought I'd Millie-proof you."

And then everyone laughs, from the regulars to the servers.

"Hardy har har," I say. "Can you seat us, already?"

"Right this way, y'all," Tia says with a laugh.

Once Lottie and I are seated, Mr. and Mrs. Beaty shuffle over.

"You shouldn't wear red," Mrs. Beaty says. "It's the wrong color with your hair."

I blush, but not because of Mrs. Beaty's comment.

Duke bought me this shirt. He bought me every top the delightful young woman picked out for me. He gave them to me a couple of days ago, and I've made a point of wearing them, because as much as I'm denying it to Parker, she's absolutely right.

I'm falling for Duke.

Not that I'll tell Mrs. Beaty that.

If I were alone, I know exactly what I'd say, but I have Lottie to think of now. What message do I want to send her: how to graciously let things go? How to advocate for yourself?

"I wove your shirt, Miwwie," Lottie says, showing me she doesn't need either lesson. Then to Mrs. Beaty, she says, "Anyone can wear any cowor."

"I stand corrected," Mrs. Beaty says wryly. "Now listen here, Ms. Campbell, my grandson says he's too depressed to get out of bed, and I told him laziness isn't a mental health problem, and I need you to call him and tell him that."

Well, then.

It's going to be that kind of lunch.

An hour later, a handful of locals have moved their chairs around my table.

The Beatys believe in depression but don't think their grandson has it because he was "such a happy baby."

Principal Hicken thinks social media is the root of all evil.

He wants me to do a workshop at the school about the mental health dangers of social media (for free).

The pastor wants to meet with me to understand the difference between anxiety and guilt.

And the whole time, Lottie just eats her chicken strips, drinks her root beer, and cuddles under my arm. So I can't even pretend she needs help to get out of here.

Fortunately, the lunch rush starts and Tia tells us to clear out because she needs the space. But on the way out, I ask another server for a to-go cup. When she brings it to me, she asks if we can meet later to talk about her boyfriend, but "not, like, as a client, or nothin'. Just to chat."

And I'm officially exhausted.

Once we're out in front of Duke's Range Rover, I set my drink on the roof and buckle Lottie up.

The second I reverse, I hear a thump. Then the contents of my soda spill all over the windshield.

"Crap," I whisper. I park the SUV, pick up the now empty cup, pull Lottie out of her carseat, head back into the diner, and ask for another refill.

"Can't Millie-proof everything." Tia laughs, but at least she doesn't make me pay for it.

We get back to the car when Lottie tells me she has to pee.

I take her into the Jane & Co. offices. I'm not sure I'll ever go into the diner again.

* * *

After lunch, a quick TV show, and her nap, we make it over to the farm. I need this as badly as I imagine Lottie does after the morning we've had.

I love my job, but people have a tendency to demand treatment for themselves or their loved ones on the spot, and I've yet to create a comfortable boundary around it. Compounding the problem is the fact that I'm trying to establish a new business in a new town. I need the positive press and word of mouth, but I also need to set a precedent about how people can interact with me.

So when someone from the diner texts me for advice, I choose avoidance. I shove my phone deep into my pocket and turn to Lottie and Louis.

She handled the crowds at the diner well this morning, but it seems to have worn her out, because when a farm worker comes into the stalls, she glues herself to my side. Even when the worker leaves, though, Lottie stays next to me.

All afternoon, we remove rocks from the animals' hooves, feed them, and change the hay in their beds. When Lottie starts brushing them, it leads to more play than anything, but it also allows her to take a few steps away from me, even if she constantly glances behind her to check where I am.

When my brother calls, I take it without thinking.

"Hey bro."

"Hey, Mill. You gotta do something about the Momster," he says. Jason launches into an explanation about how Greg called Mom this morning and how Mom's nerves are shot since finding out about Brianna's pregnancy. Mom and Greg are talking on the phone every day, recounting their every possible fear and worst-case scenario.

"What are you and Dad doing about it?"

"Having them talk to you, obviously. What the crap could we add to the conversation?"

"You could listen. You could validate their fears—"

"Come on, like I know anything about *validating someone's fears*," he says, as if it's technical jargon instead of a normal part of having loved ones.

While we're talking, I keep an eye on Lottie, noticing how she's slowly allowed a bit more distance between us. She doesn't mind walking a few feet away from me, but she looks over her shoulder constantly to make sure I'm there. Talking to my brother means Lottie can hear me even if I'm not in arm's reach.

After a few minutes, Lottie tries to get my attention, but I smile at her and point to the phone. I hope this is a gentle way to help her tolerate not having constant attention. I pace around the animal's stall for a moment before I hear Lottie call for me just out of eyesight.

"Hey, Jason, I need to run," I say.

"What could be more important than helping your own family?"

I bite back a million retorts. My family is great. I love them. But they all have the same modus operandi: if it's broke and it talks, have Millie fix it.

Jason is there with our family. He lives a mile from the house where we grew up and three miles from our sister. He's a single guy with a cushy bank job and plenty of time on his hands. He brags about those facts often.

Would it kill him to let Mom vent her concerns? To encourage Dad to stop being such a Mr. Bennett all the time and actually get involved? To talk to our sister and see how she's doing rather than telling me to do it?

Lottie calls my name again, and I have to keep myself from snapping.

"Jason, I have a job, and right now, I'm needed. You know, you could talk to Mom and Greg about your concerns, right?"

"Come on, Mill. You know I can't handle all that emotional stuff. That's why we have you."

"That's not fair. I'm thousands of miles away and you're practically next door."

"Well, that's convenient. I never pegged you as the person who'd run away rather than get involved with her family's problems."

Emotional manipulation from the guy who doesn't do emotional stuff. The irony! "Gotta go. Bye, Jason." I hang up.

And then I scream.

It's a quiet scream. The kind you keep pent up in your throat so you don't scare children or animals. But my fingernails are digging half moons into my palms, and I want to scream for real. At the top of my lungs.

I love my job. I love my job. I love my job.

This overload of people expecting me to handle their problems is *not* my job.

After taking a deep breath, I step out of the barn and look for Lottie.

Except, there is no Lottie.

I spin around, hay and dirt crunching under my boots. "Lottie?" I call. "Lottie, sweetie? Where are you?" I try to keep my voice calm, but fear makes my heart hammer. My gut clenches and panic rises as I move faster and faster around the pen, looking behind hay bales. The barn and pen are supposed to be ultra secure because little kids will be treated here.

But if they're so secure, where is she?

Blood rushes in my ears as I call for her again and again.

"Rusty?" I yell, hoping maybe he's around and took her for a ride on the tractor, or something, but there's no way he would do that without telling me. He's too responsible and smart for something so thoughtless.

Of course, I thought I was too smart and thoughtless to lose her.

"Lottie? Lottie, please sweetie, where are you?" The acid in my stomach rises into my throat, burning my racing heart as it passes. I'm normally so cool in a crisis, but right now, I can't process. I can't think. I can hardly breathe.

Where is she?

I spin around the pen futilely and run into the barn, calling Lottie's name as I go. The goats and llamas are chasing after me, thinking I'm playing some kind of game, but this is no game. This is my worst nightmare. This is every possible version of hell that I could ever imagine. Lottie has captured my heart completely. I love her more than I love myself, and I've done something unthinkable in losing her.

If something has happened to her, how will I ever recover? *Please, I beg. Please don't let anything have happened to her. Please help me find her.*

My phone buzzes, and habit makes me look down at the screen.

It's Duke.

I don't even think or pause, I just answer the call and blurt out: "I can't find Lottie!"

"What? What do you mean? Where are you?"

"We're at the farm! Duke, I don't know how it happened! We were in the pen with the animals, and I was talking on the phone so she could hear me while she was brushing Louis, and then I stepped into the barn but when I came back into the pen, she was gone!" A frantic sob tears from my throat. I'm terrified thinking of where Lottie could be, of wondering if she's okay, of not knowing what to do or where to go. And beyond the clutter of desperate fear and emotions is another fear, smaller but just as vulnerable.

Duke will never forgive me.

I brace myself for his freak out, but instead he's quiet and calm.

"Millie, that's an anti-climb fence and no one could enter the barn without you noticing. Besides, she'd have screamed and run for you the second she heard or saw anyone. She's either fallen asleep somewhere in the barn or ... wait, when was the last time you took her to the bathroom?"

"Um ... before we got to the farm. About an hour and a half ago."

"She's hidin' in the barn."

I'm too scared to believe him, no matter how badly I want to. "What? How can you be so sure?"

Hints of his accent come through the more confident he sounds. "Because I know her, I know how careful you are with her, and I know how seriously Tripp takes this animal therapy. Everything is top of the line there. The barn and pen are secure, which means Lottie is still inside. I'm going to guarantee right now that she peed her pants and is too embarrassed to let you find out about it."

Hope grips my heart in a tight squeeze. "What do I do?"

"You're not gonna like it ... "

"I don't care what it is. Tell me," I beg.

Thirty seconds later, I'm sitting on a hay bale in the middle of the barn, the baby llamas and goats scampering, humming, and bleating around me. Duke told me I needed to show her that peeing her pants isn't a big deal.

So I've poured Diet Coke in my lap to mimic pee.

You read that right.

Do you know how uncomfortable sitting in cold Diet Coke is? It's something I know intimately. Twice over, thanks to Duke.

I would do it two million times over for Lottie.

I don't know how to bring it up naturally, so I talk to the goats. "Gerald, Stella, can I tell you something?" I say loudly. "I peed my pants, and I feel embarrassed. Do you think Lottie will still like me?"

A rustle sounds from the farthest corner of the barn from the pen. Louis trots over to the corner, and I see his long neck bend low until his head is out of sight.

I choke back a sob of relief. She's here! I continue. "Is that silly? Stella, will Lottie still be my friend? I hope she knows that I'll always be her friend even if she does something like I did."

Another rustle sounds, and this time I hear boots on the wooden floor.

"I miss Lottie." I project my voice to the farthest reaches of the big barn. "And I don't know where the bathroom is. I wish I could find her so she could show me where to go to clean my pants. I'm getting cold."

I'm laying it on thick right now, partially because my McLadyPants are wet and my butt is cold but also because ... okay, no, that's pretty much it. Now that I know Lottie is safe, I can appreciate just how awful having a wet crotch on a cool autumn day is. Poor Lottie must be miserable. She also must feel really embarrassed if she hasn't come out yet. It's time to pull out the big guns.

"Lottie, hon, if you're in here, do you think we could go shopping for new pants together? Maybe we could run over to Palmetto Paws and find some matching outfits. We could be twins."

Palmetto Paws is a mommy-and-me store in the neighboring town that is ... there's no other way to put this ... tacky as all get out.

But it does the trick.

"Yes! Let's be twins!" Lottie runs out to me, beaming. She rounds a hay bale and launches herself into my arms. I grab her to my chest, holding her close. Her urine-soaked pants press against the Tory Burch cardigan I found at Last Chance before we moved. I had to basically fight three other women for this sweater, and because it's dry clean only, there's a decent chance this pee-stain will be the end of it.

I couldn't possibly care less.

I wrangle up some towels from a farm worker and lay them down in the seats of Duke's Range Rover. We sing the gummy bear song all the way to Palmetto Paws, and we walk proudly through the store hand-in-hand. When Lottie picks out two matching tulle skirts for us, I glance around and see matching t-shirts. T-shirts we can't leave without.

Ten minutes later, Lottie and I march out of the store together, swinging our clasped hands as we walk. Our wet, stinky clothes are in the shopping bag and we have on our new shirts and skirts with our boots. As we drive back to the house, I sing along with Lottie and smile at her in the rearview mirror, but something heavy settles in my heart.

For three minutes today, I thought I lost her. It was three of the worst minutes of my life, every bit as painful as watching my niece in that hospital room before she was wheeled into surgery. I can't tolerate the idea of something happening to Lottie. I can't handle the thought of not being with her now that she's in my life.

Duke has been pretty obvious about his interest in me since the Fall Festival, but what does that actually mean? Is he looking for something short-term? Am I a seat-filler for him? A babysitter? A real love-interest?

I glance in the rearview mirror at Lottie, who is singing and chomping with her hands like a baby shark, and love fills me from head to toe.

That's it.

I need to know Duke's intentions, and I need to know them now.

CHAPTER TWENTY-ONE

DUKE

*A*fter a long day of film review, treatment and lifting, and a correction period on the field, I'm tired but excited to be walking into my house. I drop my keys and wallet in a bowl in the entry and walk into the house, which smells like all my favorite things: meat, garlic, and butter. The Spice Girls blare over the surround-sound speakers, so Millie and Lottie don't hear the beep of the alarm or my footsteps as I walk into the kitchen.

I stop in my tracks.

Lottie is sitting on the counter with a mixing bowl in her lap, stirring while Millie is searing steaks in a cast iron skillet on the stove. They're wearing identical outfits: gold tutus with teal t-shirts, and they have their hair up in matching buns on top of their heads.

They're singing along to "Wannabe," but Lottie is saying, "If you wanna be my *mother*," and every remnant of a wall inside of me cracks and crumbles to the ground at the sight.

I pull out my phone and press record just in time to capture Millie bringing her face close to Lottie's as they sing the chorus. The joy on Lottie's face is like nothing I've ever seen. It's not just happiness, it's love. It's *trust*.

And Millie? She keeps her hand outstretched toward Lottie as she takes the pan off the heat with her other hand. Protective but not overbearing. Then she moves the bowl from Lottie's lap, picks up my little girl, and spins her around before setting her down. I catch an unobscured glimpse of the front of their t-shirts, and my heart stutters.

They're fan club shirts from *my* fan club, the Dukedom. Both shirts read "Duchess" with my number—8—beneath.

Duchess.

Millie and Lottie are wearing Carolina Waves colors and they're wearing a shirt about me, singing together in my kitchen as they make dinner, and it is without a doubt the most beautiful sight I've ever seen.

I could watch them forever, but as much as I'm enjoying this, I want to be *with* them. I back up into the hallway, blink emotion from my eyes, and stomp a little.

"I'm home!" I call. The quick patter of bare feet tells me that Lottie is running, so I crouch down as I jump out from behind the corner.

The stance is defensive as much as affectionate. Yes, it allows me to pick her up and swing her high overhead, but it also allows me to not get … *sacked*, if you know what I mean. Lottie doesn't have many special skills yet, but one area she excels at is accidentally smacking me in the crotch. It's bad anytime it happens, but I refuse to let it happen in front of Millie.

Speaking of Millie, she's biting her lip, staring at me like I'm a ribeye steak she can't wait to sink her teeth into, and I have never in my life been so torn. I want to spin Lottie around and hold her close, but I also want to do something about that look on Millie's face. I want to pull the elastic from around her top knot and run my hands through her hair. I want to take her into the hallway and press her against the wall and—

We don't get to think those thoughts, I remind the team in my head. *She's not even our girlfriend, let alone our wife.*

So let's fix that, shall we?

With Lottie safely secured in my arms, I stride over to Millie, my smile stretching further the closer I get. She looks so hot. So utterly, alluringly feminine.

She's barefoot, and I don't know why this feels so intimate except for the fact that she's always worn socks until right now. Her feet are downright cute, especially with that skirt. And Millie's penchant for wearing hot pink extends to her toenails.

Why are her feet so bewitching? And her ankles. I've seen ankles before. But now I feel like some weird puritan fascinated by every glimpse of skin.

She tucks one foot behind the other as I get close. "Sorry, should I have put socks on?"

I put my arm around her and speak into the hair at the top of her head. "No, you definitely shouldn't have."

She peers up at me, confusion tugging her eyebrows together. "Huh?"

"You have cute feet." I almost flush saying it, because it sounds stupid. What, do I have a foot fetish, or something?

No, I do not have a foot fetish, to be absolutely, totally clear.

"You look … " I sigh, giving in to what my heart is saying instead of warring with it. "You look amazing. You always look amazing, but maybe especially right now."

Pink tinges her cheeks, and she looks down at her t-shirt, which is knotted in the middle, barely revealing the waistband of her fluffy golden skirt. "Seriously? You're not … it's not too much?"

I close my eyes for a second longer than normal, but I need it to gain my composure. "You're wearing *my* shirt and matching *my* daughter. It's perfect, Millie."

You're perfect.

My fingers splay across the muscles in her back, and she wraps her arms around my waist, not even shy about how she's feeling my muscles the same way I am hers.

Lottie rests her head on my other shoulder, and with my arms around both of them, I know without a shadow of a doubt that I am in love with Millie Campbell. I want to stretch this moment as long as I possibly can, because this ... this is what happiness feels like. This is everything I've ever wanted. This feeling is what I hoped could develop with Carlie for years. Having it now is beyond what I imagined possible.

Our eyes stay fixed on each other's, and something unspoken passes between us, something important. It's like we're having a conversation without saying anything at all. This isn't a moment between me, my daughter, and the babysitter-slash-therapist-slash-friend.

This is my family.

I lean down to kiss her, and she raises up on her tiptoes so her lips can reach mine.

Her breath puffs against my lips, sending shockwaves through me. Then comes the barest graze of lips—hardly even contact—but it's earth-shattering.

Life-changing.

It's not a kiss, it's a promise, one I intend to keep ... right after I go in for more.

The clicking of heels in the foyer pulls my attention, and my eyes open in time to see Tripp and Jane grinning like fools.

"Well, if this ain't the sweetest thing I've ever seen." Tripp says. "Say cheese!"

"Uncle Tripp!" Lottie shoves herself out of my arms to run to my mountain man of a best friend. Millie shifts, and for a second, I'm afraid she's going to bolt from my arms. But instead, she tucks her head against me. I can actually feel the heat from her face radiating into my chest. I tighten my arm around her and kiss her forehead. A current of warmth passes from her head all the way through me.

"Your timing is impeccable," I say sarcastically.

"You know what they say about payback, don't you?" Tripp says. And okay, he has a point. I may have interrupted him and Jane a time or two, but this is different.

Don't ask me why. It just is.

Jane breaks from Tripp and Lottie and gives Millie a hug. Then she shoots me a sly smile.

"I guess babysitting worked out for you?"

I blink innocently. "I can't imagine what you mean."

"Remember what I said, bucko."

She holds my eyes for a beat longer than necessary, but I'm confident in my motives. I'm captivated by Millie. No question. I'm more attracted to her than any woman I've ever met. But it's so much more than that. No part of her is impressed by my fame. None.

Seeing as I've been a big deal in the football world since high school, that's beyond novel.

But that's not all it is.

Millie is fascinating. She's intelligent and funny and pushes me in a way no one ever has before. Something tells me I will never grow tired of talking with her, of learning about her, of sharing a life with her.

So when I nod at Jane, I know the full weight of what that signifies. Her smile in return is a relief. I don't need any of the Janes working against me.

Because I want to impress Millie, I graciously invite our best friends to stay for dinner. And I graciously let them occupy her attention all meal long when all I want to do is talk with her, myself. And after dinner and a rousing game of Candyland, I not-so-graciously ask them to put Lottie to bed so I can get some alone time with Millie. I make a point of confirming with Lottie that she can handle it and explain that Millie and I will be outside on the deck. She hugs Millie and me extra long, but she mercifully doesn't fight me.

And then, finally, the time has come.

We are alone.

I stop myself from throwing Millie over my shoulder, but only barely. We hold hands with a wordless intensity and make our way upstairs, where I press a button to turn the switchable glass in the windows to private.

Being rich has its perks. I'm not ashamed to admit it. I'm also grateful that my desire for privacy from the outside world also serves to give me privacy from my *inner* world.

Millie looks at the glass change appreciatively, and then it's almost like her eyes go dark, like her pupils are eclipsing the sea green. The urgency we've shared kicks up a notch, but seeing that same need reflected in her, my self-restraint almost crumbles.

I don't throw her over my shoulder, but I do scoop her up.

She squeals and then covers her mouth as I throw the door open and closed behind us.

The second that door shuts, I set Millie down, but she's not having it. Sure, her feet may be touching the ground, but every other part of her is touching me.

Including her mouth.

That mouth.

Her lips taste like peach lip gloss, but her mouth tastes like steak and garlic, and garlic has never been so sexy. Everything about this woman is sexy. Her t-shirt and skirt, the goose bumps up and down those toned arms that are wrapped around my neck. Heck, even her deodorant is sexy.

But nothing compares to her lips. Her big, full lips that I want to chew like bubble gum.

My hand shoots for her thick, fiery red hair while the other is on her upper back, trying to keep her as close as physically possible. Millie's arms are wrapped so closely around my neck that I can tell she feels the same.

This is it.

I feel like an explorer who just found a new world, like Neil Armstrong stepping foot on the moon. I'm Magellan sailing around the globe, Captain Kirk going where no man has gone before.

For the first time in my life, I understand why newlyweds always act like they've discovered the secrets of the universe.

It's not about sex. It's about *love*.

Okay, those are probably not mutually exclusive. I'm a dad. I know how the birds and the bees work.

But as much as I truly cared for Carlie and even felt love for her, our most intimate acts didn't feel as intimate as this kiss.

Tasting Millie's breath and intertwining our limbs makes this kiss hot enough to scorch the surface of the earth, but the emotion behind it is so much deeper than that. It's tectonic plates shifting, taking disparate landmasses and pushing them into one super continent.

So as our kisses slow, the heat shifts all the way down to the molten core of who I am. Our breath that was so hot and heavy slows to something calm and steadying. Our hands move from clutches to caresses, and finally, our lips part. I feel her chest rise slowly and fall against me as she takes a deep breath. I bend my head as low as I can, kissing her forehead as she rests her cheek against my chest.

"Wow," she whispers.

"Wow," I agree.

A shiver runs through Millie, so I scoop her up again and sit us both on one of the oversized deck chairs. She snuggles into my chest, and I pull a blanket from behind the chair and drape it around her. Then I rub her arms beneath the blanket. They're freezing.

"How are you so warm?" she asks with another shiver.

"You get my blood boiling. Is that what you want to hear?"

She shakes with laughter against me. "Groan," she says. "That was so cheesy, it was keto-approved."

I snort. "You're one to talk. *That* was painful."

"You loved it."

"Yeah. I did."

I close my eyes, my cheek resting against hers, feeling the rise and fall of her chest against mine. I know we should talk about that kiss, about the tension that's been bursting at the seams lately, but it feels like we're so far past that. In my mind, it's already settled. She's it. She's my family. The rest is details.

"So ... are we ... " she says.

"Yup."

"And do we need to talk about this?"

"Only if you do," I say. She lifts her head, and I smooth a stray hair behind her ear.

"I do," she says. "As much as I want to keep kissing you, you've been hot and cold with me, and I need to know what this is. I'm not looking for something temporary."

When my fingers touch her cheek, her eyelids flutter slightly and her neck bends toward my hand, as if involuntarily. Yet she's clearly trying *not* to respond, and that only makes me happier. I cup her cheek, rubbing my thumb across her velvety smooth skin.

"Getting married to Carlie was never my plan, but it happened, and I did the best I could. It didn't matter if it wasn't the life I'd always dreamed of for myself. I'd made a commitment, and I would honor it forever. And then we had Lottie. Becoming a dad was the best thing to ever happen to me. It gave me so much more to live and work for. Lottie was like a missing piece of my heart being clicked into place.

"After Carlie left, I adjusted my plans and could only envision one road from here to the end of my life: football and being a single dad. That's it. I didn't even want to look at another woman again, because I knew they would just be detours. I thought I wasn't cut out for marriage. I wasn't made to love anyone except my daughter, so I kept my eyes on the road in front of me." I breathe in, my heart swelling with contentment as foreign as it is full. "But then I met you."

I put my other hand on Millie's cheek now, willing her to understand not just what I'm saying, but what I'm feeling. Her big green eyes peer into mine. My chest expands at her expression, and my heart swells just looking at her.

"The day I met you, that road started to look bleak. Every day since, I've realized just how much my path has lacked. You're it for me, Millie. You are my exit."

Her mouth falls open, and I know I'm not imagining the wetness in her eyes. "Uh, sir, this is a Wendy's."

I laugh and pull her close. "How did I fall in love with such a brat?"

She kisses my neck, giggling against me. "That's just how they make them in Millieville," she says.

"Millieville, huh? Tell me more about this place."

"Well, there's a Wendy's, as you already know."

"Uh huh," I say, my jaw tingling at the feeling of her lips as she progresses from my neck up to my ear.

"It's a small town," she says, still kissing slowly—so slowly—up to my earlobe. "But our population has recently tripled."

"Has it?" I ask, my eyes closing as her breath puffs against my ear, driving me absolutely crazy.

"Yes. A family has moved in, including an adorable, heart-stealing little girl and her insanely hot, funny, surprisingly deep father." Her kisses move back across my cheek now, going faster and faster as she works her way to my mouth.

"And how does the existing resident feel about this new family?"

"Oh, she's a big fan."

"How big?" I ask. Her lips are teasing the corner of my

mouth, but I'm not kissing her until I get a confession out of her.

"Huge," she whispers. "She's the president of the fan club. The Duchess of the Dukedom."

"And … ?" I prompt. Her lips brush against mine so softly, I could almost think I was imagining them. The need to kiss her is overpowering, but I just told this woman I love her, and I get the feeling she's teasing me, and although I don't *need* her to tell me she loves me back, a little acknowledgment wouldn't hurt.

"And … " She sucks my bottom lip into her mouth, and my willpower starts to crumble. I'm about to give up on waiting and kiss her into mindless oblivion when she releases my lips and bumps her nose against mine. "And she loves them. I love you. Duh."

When my mouth meets hers, we're both grinning.

CHAPTER TWENTY-TWO

MILLIE

"I am a grown woman. I don't need an armed escort to walk next door to my boyfriend's house," I remind my friends as they march me up our driveway.

"But you're glowing with new love," Ash says as she twirls a large, red licorice, "and I'm pretty sure that us basking in your glow is the equivalent of an old, ugly witch bathing in a young woman's blood to steal her hotness, or something."

We all stop.

Ash gets two steps past us and turns around. She takes a bite of licorice.

"Um, what?" Parker asks.

Ash puts a hand on her hip. "Like you of all people don't know what I'm talking about."

We all cackle like old, ugly witches. Even Parker.

"Are you saying I drink the blood of teen girls to look like this?" Parker asks. Ash shrugs. "Girl, please. If anything, they're after my blood. I'm freaking fabulous," Parker says.

Lou fist bumps her. "You ain't lyin.'"

We could walk through the woods to Duke's and save a mile, but I think all of us sense that change is in the air, and we're clinging to our time together.

In the two weeks since Duke told me he loved me, a lot has changed. Reese got back from helping Gramma Hazel, who is moving in with Duke's parents for the time being. I returned to my house (after refusing Duke's very generous offer to pay me what I originally demanded. I did accept a more reasonable amount, though, because while it was a labor of love, I wasn't able to work for Jane & Co. or recruit many clients during that time, and I'm not made of money).

But things keep looking up. For all of us. I've taken on three in person clients since talking at the school on mental health (thank you, Principal Hicken). Jane & Co. has secured another big account. Ash and Rusty met with the mayor about adopting a unified theme in the commercial district. Lou released another massive viral hit.

And Duke and I started making plans. *Long term* plans.

Okay, mostly plans that involve football. Now that clients are coming in, I'm scheduling them around his games, events, and practices, and I'm lucky to have a job that allows me so much flexibility to do it.

The plan for today is a flight to New York, because the Carolina Waves are playing the New York Jets tomorrow, and Reese, Lottie, and I are going to watch. This will be my first time watching Duke play, live or otherwise. I've watched clips because I'm trying to learn the sport, but I scheduled a new client intake before Duke and I made it official, so I missed the game.

And I did miss it.

I missed him and Lottie so badly, it felt like my insides were withering like a pulled weed. The game was in Columbia, so I didn't see them at all that day, and I felt homesick the whole time.

And now, I feel homesick whenever I'm not with them. After only two full weeks of dating, being away from Duke and Lottie feels like being away from my limbs. They've become essential parts of me, and I love it. I love the feeling of having people to miss.

The actual missing part, on the other hand...

"She has the dreamy face on again," Parker says, her impeccably glossed lips twisting into a smug smile.

Ash cranes her neck to see, and a wave of curls falls into her face. She flaps the hair away. "Yup. That's the one."

"You sure?" Lou asks. "It looks like her longing face."

"No," Ash says. "The eyebrows on her *longing face* are more pulled in."

Lou nods. "Oh, yeah, I know what you mean."

"*Et tu*, Lucy Jane?" I ask with a glare. We're all wearing jackets, scarves, and hats, and I'm pulling my small suitcase behind me up our long, winding driveway. Honestly, I'm a little offended that no one has commented on how small my suitcase is for a two-day trip when we all know that I wouldn't be the lowest maintenance person on the set of Project Runway. But no. Everyone's too fixated on the fact that I miss my boyfriend to talk about much bigger deals. Like Lou's mysterious call this morning...

"Lou," I say slyly, "You disappeared out of the blue for an hour this morning to take a phone call. Yet you've been tight-lipped ever since. What's the sitch?"

Parker's gaze flits past me to Lou. "You know, she has a point. We've gotten so used to not talking about your career in public that we've forgotten that it's a free for all when we're at home."

"We're not at home," Lou says.

"Semantics. Spill it, LJ."

Lou can't keep a smile from jumping at the corner of her mouth. "Okay, but I swear I'm not tryin' to steal Millie's thunder."

"No stealing required. It's yours," I say.

"Third Street Records offered me a recording contract—"

"What?!" Ash cries. Ash and Lou are both music snobs, and Third Street Records is to them what the world famous Dubai Mall would be to me.

"I know!" Lou says. "They want me to do a Southern states music tour with the last stop at Hot Strings Hall—"

"What?!" Ash shrieks. Her hair jumps higher than she does.

"And perform there with Connor Nash!"

Ash doesn't verbalize her exclamation. Instead, she grabs Lou's arms and screams in her face. Parker and I gush and congratulate her, because even though we don't know as much about music as they do, anybody with ears knows Connor Nash is where it's at. He started out ten years ago in an alt-country group that crossed over to huge commercial success—a duo named Duncan and Nash. Evidently, his partner was a nightmare to work with, and Connor went solo after their first album went Gold. The next album hit Platinum. He's only released two albums since that one, and although they lost some of the soul and gained some twang compared to that first solo album, the guy's still a legend. Performing at the famed Hot Strings Hall in Memphis will launch Lou from YouTube Star "Lucy Jane" to a global star in a hot second.

I just hope it's everything she dreams it'll be.

When we get to Duke's house, I hoist my bag up the stairs to the front door and knock before opening. "Hi honey, I'm home!" I yell.

Lottie comes running from the kitchen. "Mama Millie!"

My jaw drops. "Did you just say your l's? Who did this?" I tease with a bittersweet pang. I pick her up and demand that she let me look in her mouth for the little fairy who sprinkled alphabet dust on her, and she giggles. I know Reese is responsible for this travesty. Yes, I should be happy that Lottie is progressing and can say her l's now, but her saying Miwwie is my favorite. How can she grow in front of my eyes? "You must have worked so hard, you brilliant girl," I say, putting her back down.

"I did! La la la la la," she says proudly.

"Can you show me how to do that?" Ash says, crouching down.

Lottie looks past me to my friends, whom she knows fairly well by now. Ash crosses her eyes, Lou scrunches her nose and smiles, and Parker winks and reaches a hand out for Lottie to high five. Lottie puts her arm around my leg first, but then she gives Parker a high five and waves to the others.

I bring my friends into the kitchen, which is the central gathering place of the Dukedom. They all take seats around the enormous gourmet kitchen island while I plop Lottie on the counter and get us all drinks. It's funny how grand the kitchen looked the first time I saw it. Now, it feels like my domain. A natural consequence of cooking a metric ton of steaks in the short ten days I stayed here.

"So, where's your dad, sweetie?" I ask Lottie.

"Just finished packin'," Duke calls from the stairs. A moment later, he appears with a grin and a suitcase.

Oh, and did I mention that he's wearing a suit?

I go weak in the knees.

Duke must see the lust all over my face, because he cocks one eyebrow in a way that makes me desperately want to be alone with this man. How does he just walk around looking like this without passersby spontaneously combusting?

"All hail the Duke," Ash jokes. "Hey, out of curiosity, how are your abs—"

Parker claps a hand over Ash's mouth. "No."

A flitter of confusion crosses Duke's face, but he saunters

over to me and pulls me into a kiss that is far too PG for my liking, if wholly appropriate for present company.

Duke and my friends start talking like they've done this for years instead of weeks. Lottie makes faces with Ash while Parker and Lou talk football like it's a second language (Lou is Southern, after all). The collective comfort is like warming myself by the fire on a cold Chicago night.

A buzz from my phone catches my attention. It's my brother-in-law. I'm too used to Greg's panicked calls to think much of this one, but I excuse myself and take it in Duke's office just beyond the formal dining room.

"Hey Greg," I say. "What's going on?"

"Millie, she's spotting."

"What? Who?"

He sounds like he's out of breath. "Brianna. She's spotting, Millie. What am I supposed to do?"

The floor falls out beneath me. "Greg, is Brianna there right now? Where are you?"

"She just went to the bathroom and now she's leaving a message for her doctor to call her. What if something happens?"

I'm spiraling down an endless abyss of fear right with him, but I don't have the luxury of emoting. I'm expected to be everyone's rock. I have to hold all of my family's fear and emotion and help them process without ever wavering or wobbling under the pressure and without expecting anyone to do the same for me.

When I'm on the clock, I have almost boundless energy for this kind of thing. But when it crosses into my personal life, no one has any idea the toll it takes on me, especially my family.

Especially right now.

Sweat breaks out across my forehead. My pulse rushes in my ears.

"You have to be calm, Greg. I know you're freaked out, but you need to stay calm for her. She's not the first woman to ever spot." Is she? I don't know why a pregnant woman would spot! It has to be bad, right? "While you're waiting for the doctor, take her to the ER. Don't wait. If her doctor calls you on the way and says it's nothing to worry about, turn around, grab a burger, and go home. But if it is something, you don't want to live with any possible regret."

"Yeah, maybe you're right. I don't know how to be—"

"Greg, you're allowed to feel terrified right now, but you are *not* allowed to let it control you. Hang up the phone now and take Brianna to the hospital. Then call me the second you guys know something."

"Okay. Okay, I will. Thanks, Millie. I don't know what—"

"*Go*, Greg. Now!" I hang up the phone and wipe both hands over my face. I'm a sweaty, nervous wreck. My heart is racing a thousand miles an hour. I feel nauseated and lightheaded.

This can't be happening. She has to be okay. This baby *has* to be okay.

They both have to.

I pinch the bridge of my nose and breathe as calmly as I can, trying to quell the panic storming inside.

"Hey, the car's just about … Millie?" Duke is standing in front of me in an instant, his hands on both shoulders and concern tugging his eyebrows down. "What happened? What's going on?"

I shake my head, not wanting to alarm him. I don't know much about sports, but I took a class on sports psychology. So much of their jobs depend on them being able to get out of their heads and into the game. And a "How to Support Your NFL Husband" guide I found online told me that an NFL wife should never, ever unburden herself to him before a game. There's a time and a place to share concerns with your partner, and that's not the time. And yes, I know we're not married. But if that's not the direction we're headed, we're both wasting our time, and he already said he plays for keeps.

So when he asks me again what's wrong, I put on a fake smile and say, "Oh, just something with my sister. It's not a big deal. I'll tell you about it later."

"You wouldn't have looked that upset if it was nothing. You know you can tell me anything, right?"

I exhale loudly but keep my smile on. "I know." I reach up to my tiptoes and give him a peck. "I'll tell you about it on Monday, promise."

He backs up and appraises me. "You read the NFL Wife guidebook, didn't you?"

My face gets hotter than a flat iron. "Umm … "

"Listen, I'm not that guy. I'm going to be more preoccupied during the game if I think you're holding something back than I will if you tell me. I've gone pro in compartmentalizing, but I can't compartmentalize something I don't understand. *That's* when I worry. The whole world saw that a couple of weeks ago."

The game that led to him finally realizing he needed to get Lottie help. I've watched clips from it. He got sacked five times, hence his newfound back spasms.

I hold him to his word, but I don't let him see the terror I feel. I don't want to put my own emotional burdens on him: "That was Greg. Brianna's spotting, and they haven't been able to get a hold of their doctor yet."

He grimaces. "That's scary. Carlie spotted early on, and I about lost my mind. Is he taking her to the ER?"

"That's what I told him to do."

"Smart woman." Duke wraps me in his arms and kisses my head. "But why did he call *you?*"

I shrug, and the action has little effect on his muscular arms. "Because."

"Because you're the family therapist," he intuits.

I nod against his chest.

"I'm not okay with him using you as his emotional support dog."

I snort, because of course Duke would figure out what's going on. It's one of the reasons I love him. He doesn't just know me, he gets me. "Thanks for understanding."

"That's what I do. I eat steaks and I know you."

"Are you trying to riff on the whole 'I drink and I know things?' meme?"

"Yes, and I crushed it."

I laugh and sigh in immediate succession. "I love you. Thanks for listening."

"Always."

Twenty minutes later, my friends see us off, and I smile and pretend I'm not worried sick about my sister and her baby.

CHAPTER TWENTY-THREE

MILLIE

We're in New York early enough for Reese, Lottie, and me to do some sightseeing, so sightseeing we do. Reese insists that there is shopping to be done on Duke's dime. And although I won't buy anything on his dime, I will gladly look with his sister and daughter, who will.

In between awe at the glorious shops around me, I check my phone for updates on my sister. We're in the middle of Louis Vuitton when my phone buzzes. Lottie pulls on my hand to show me a matching set of Mom and Me bags. If this were Target, I'd snap them up in a second. But Louis Vuitton bags are a different matter, altogether. Even with all the windfalls I've had of late, I can't afford one LV bag, let alone two.

I pull my phone out. It's Greg.

"What is it?" I demand, not able to hold my fear in for another moment.

"It's all fine," he says with an exhale. I hear my sister shouting at me in the background.

"Greg, what are you doing? I told you I'd call her." Brianna says. A second later, my sister takes over her husband's phone. "Sorry, you know how he worries," Brianna says in a voice that sounds apologetic but is really doting to the point of being a bit gag-worthy. Something I truly appreciate for the first time in my life. "It was just a yeast infection. Isn't that crazy? Who knew all that itching wasn't a normal sign of pregnancy?"

"Ew, Bri." I laugh, but I'm so relieved, my throat is sore with a desire to cry. "So you're really okay? You'd tell me, right?"

"Mills, we both know that if I didn't, Greg would," she says. He agrees in the background, and I laugh. "Did you guys get to New York safely? Will you even see Duke tonight?"

"Yes, we did. No, we won't. The NFL has a strict 'no canoodling before games' rule. He's not even in the same hotel as us, and they'll fly home immediately tomorrow after the press conference."

"What was it you said about *canoodling*? Is that what the kids call it these days?"

"Shut it," I say with a laugh.

"We don't say shut up!" Lottie tells me with a look of horror on her face.

I boop her nose. "Thanks for the reminder, sweetie."

"Okay, go have fun with your glorious insta-fam. And send pics. Love you!"

"Love you, too."

When we hang up, I'm so relieved, I splurge and buy myself a bag.

And a matching one for Lottie.

No one said I had to pay *all* my bills down right away, right?

I feel lighter than air leaving. I float as we walk from store to store. Having lived in Chicago for years means I'm sophisticated enough not to gape at the display of wealth and excess all around me, but a part of me is still overwhelmed by the sheer enormity and hustle of the city itself. The streets are tighter, the sidewalks narrower, the sky rises higher, and the press of people is just *more*.

Reese's shopping bag collection is also *more*.

Lottie is getting pretty overwhelmed, so I suggest to Reese that we take a break, and she guides us over to the American Girl store further down Fifth Avenue. Lottie is extra cuddly and delicate throughout dinner, so we take it as slowly as we can and let her watch Bluey on my phone until she's recharged enough.

Then we shop for dolls. Lottie is every bit as talented as her aunt at shopping.

She chooses one doll that looks like me—red hair, freckles, ivory skin, and all—and one with black hair, dark brown eyes, and tan skin. The doll doesn't look like Lottie, but for some reason she doesn't bother to explain, Lottie loves it. A dozen outfits and accessories later, and Lottie is holding both dolls under her arms, and wearing her new Louis Vuitton backpack on her back when we head outside to wait for our driver.

And that's when I see Reese visibly jolt.

Lottie bumps into her aunt's legs, and I almost say something when I see Reese's face. She looks like she's in shock. I follow her gaze to see an absolutely stunning woman with long black hair, dark eyes, and tan skin. Every item she's wearing is designer. Her lashes are long and dark, and just full enough that I can't tell if they're fake or if she hit the genetic lottery in every way possible. Her cheekbones could cut glass, and her full, pouty lips belong in a lipstick commercial.

She's the embodiment of every man's dream. She's my best friend Jane's level of unachievable, impossible gorgeous.

And I know to my soul without ever having seen a picture that Reese knows her.

This woman is the reason Lottie picked out the other doll.

This woman is the reason for Lottie's abandonment issues.

This woman is the reason Duke erected walls around his heart.

She's Duke's ex-wife.

Lottie's mom.

Carlie.

My pulse beats so hard, I go lightheaded. My arms and fingers start to tingle, and not from the frigid cold. It's from knowing that Duke went from this vision of perfection to *me*.

I will never be able to compete with her.

You're not competing with her. He divorced her. He never loved her like he loves you. He told you that, I remind myself. And I keep reminding myself and grounding myself with every technique under the sun as I watch Carlie's Disney Princess eyes go round when she sees Reese and then ... and then her own daughter.

She drops her Anthropologie bags and throws both hands over her mouth. Tears roll out of the corner of her eyes. A man is with her—a handsome, posh, obviously European man who darts to Carlie immediately, doting with concern. He says something in what I think is French, and I remember that Carlie had an affair with a European soccer player. And my self-consciousness morphs to fury, thinking of the pain she caused to the people I love.

People she loved first ...

One person she clearly still loves, based on the pain in her face.

All of this jealousy and rage and sympathy swirl in my brain in the span of two blinks, and Lottie is totally clueless that anything's happening at all. She's also over-stimulated, in an intense new place, and missing her dad. We've made a lot of progress in only a few weeks, but even a kid without separation anxiety disorder would have a hard time with a day like today. Add in the mom who abandoned you into the mix? Meltdown city for anyone.

I both wish Duke were here and am relieved he's not. It isn't fair to either Carlie or Lottie to see each other with no preparation, no processing time. It isn't fair to anyone not to have Duke be part of this decision.

I look at Reese, trying to tell her with my eyes to go talk to Carlie while I take Lottie into the car, but Reese doesn't speak the language of my looks like her brother does. Or maybe she's too angry to play along, because she picks Lottie up and storms toward the car, leaving me standing awkwardly on the sidewalk, my back to Carlie. I whip around to look at her, wishing I could pull my wool scarf over my face and run away.

But I can't.

I won't.

Carlie gapes at Reese and Lottie's retreating figures. Tears leave trails in her makeup. When the car door closes, Carlie's eyes snap to mine. "That was ... that was my little girl," she says in a shaky voice, heedless of the people pressing past us.

I nod. "You must be Carlie. I'm—"

"Millie. I know," she says in a thick Southern accent, but it's different than any I've heard. She looks at the man with her. His arm is around her protectively. "We saw the tabloids. Benoit follows Duke on social media and shows me any pictures of Lottie." Her voice cracks when she says her daughter's name. "This might be the most awkward introduction ever, right?"

I let out a dark laugh, and when a gust of icy wind passes over us, I wrap my arms around my vintage coat. "It's up there with Mr. Darcy and Elizabeth Bennett."

Carlie giggles, wiping a hand across her nose. "Benoit, be a dear and get us a couple of coffees from that stand?" She speaks so fast and thick, it takes me a beat to catch on to what she's saying.

"None for me," I say to Benoit, "but thank you."

Carlie hazards a step closer. "You are even prettier than the tabloid pictures. Those photographers like you a lot more than they liked me."

"I don't know..."

"Girl, stop. Nobody liked me for Duke. I was too low rent, and he was the pro-typical All-American quarterback." She means prototypical, but I don't say this, as it would only illustrate her point. "Duke didn't even like me for Duke," she says with a heavy snort.

"Um..."

"You don't have to say anythin'. I knew how bad I screwed up the second I walked outta that hotel room while he was in the hospital. But you gotta understand, it was like somethin' else had taken over. Like I was outside myself, and this tiny little part of me kept yelling at me to stop and go back, but this destructive side of me just wanted to burn it all down because I never thought I was worthy of it, anyway." My eyes widen at the confession, and she shrugs. "Dr. Phil."

And now I laugh. Harder than the comment deserves, maybe, but I can't stop myself. "I'm... I'm sorry?"

"Me too. Will you tell Duke that when you see him? I tried to, but he blocked my butt a long time ago."

"I'll try," I say. She nods, and her gaze moves beyond me, probably to Benoit. "You two seem really happy."

"We are," she says. "I think he's plannin' to propose this weekend, matter of fact." I'm not sure what she reads in my face, considering I don't move a muscle at this news, but she answers my unspoken question. "I didn't cheat with him. It's okay, everyone assumes I did, but it was actually someone on his team. I'm French. Did Duke say? Don't matter. I grew up in Louisiana, and my grandparents are French. Their English sucks."

She's telling me far too much for this setting, but I get the sense she needs to justify what happened to someone, and I'm the only person who'll listen. I already know her parents were a few steps short of an episode of Law and Order, and it sounds like her grandparents were cold, but stable. Her mom dropped her with them every time she moved in with some new guy or chased some fix. Then she'd get dumped or get clean or get back together with Carlie's dad, and Carlie would be sucked right back into the dysfunction. Watching soccer games in French with her grandfather was the highlight of her childhood and created in her a love for soccer that eventually extended to other sports. Benoit's teammate slid into her DMs a few months before Duke got sick. She'd been flattered but had never responded.

Not until the night something inside of her broke and she hopped on a plane to go and blow up her life.

I'm not sure how someone with a look so carefully curated can have such a clear lack of filter, and I'm not sure if she even wants me to respond until she stops abruptly.

"I cannot believe I'm tellin' you all this. I'm not normally such a flamin' dumpster wreck, I swear."

"It can't be easy for you to see Reese and Lottie like this," I say with a backward glance at our car.

"You can say that again. For reals, though, it ain't easy seein' you, either. I got curious after Benoit showed me the one with Lottie where you guys were at the Fall Festival. The way Duke looked at you." Carlie glances away, her eyes blinking slowly but deliberately, as if she's remembering something painful. "It's the way I looked at him."

"What do you mean?" I ask. I shouldn't ask, though, because it's cruel to make her satisfy my self-consciousness and stoke my ego at her expense. "Never mind, I don't mean to probe."

"Please," she says with a laugh. "Because I need probin' to talk? He worships you like I worshiped him. I thought that man hung the stars. He never looked at me like he's lookin' at you in those tabloid pics, though. Not the day we got married. Not the day I had Lottie. Never. You know, he never even said 'I love you?' When I'd say it, all I'd get back was 'love ya,' or 'you too.' He never said it first. It hurt."

As much as I wanted to hear her admit all these very things, I don't relish the wounds this is opening in her. "I'm sorry," I say, surprised by how much I mean it. I kind of like this bold, open, unfiltered woman who so clearly knows she messed up.

She shrugs, smiling at someone beyond me. I look over my shoulder to see Benoit coming back from a food cart, two cups of coffee in hand. "I shouldn't have left the way I did. I shoulda just divorced him. I'll regret it till the day I die. But I'm tryin' to turn the bad good. Maybe Lottie will be able to see it someday."

Our driver honks at the same time that Benoit kisses Carlie's cheek. I make my goodbyes, but not before asking Carlie one last question.

CHAPTER TWENTY-FOUR

DUKE

After the game, Reese told me I needed to get an exception from my coach to stay the night in Manhattan.

It's against every team rule, but we dominated against our toughest opponent tonight, basically clinching our playoff spot, so I caught Coach in a charitable mood.

Also, my back is killing me, and the chance to get a full night's sleep tonight rather than hopping on a plane and getting home in the middle of the night sounds like heaven.

I get to the hotel late after our win. Apart from a quick post-game hug, the NFL's strict pre-game and game day protocols mean that I haven't had any time with my girls in over twenty-four hours. And yes, I know Millie's a woman, not a girl, but Millie said she loves when I call them that, so I'm calling them that.

My girls.

I've missed them.

BABY LLAMA DRAMA

I itch for them. Itch to feel Lottie's arms squeeze my neck and push the air out of my cheeks and do all the silly things she does. I crave the feel of Millie's arms around my neck, too, but for an entirely different reason. I just hope she didn't watch the press conference after the game. Some of the personal questions were about her, and I answered them exactly as she and I have discussed, even if I hated every second of it.

But one of those questions was about something else entirely—someone else—and I don't want that question to throw a shadow over the celebration tonight.

For the record, celebration is code for making out. I don't want anything getting in the way of making out with her.

Even still, I *do* want to talk to her. I want to ask her how she liked the NFL wives in the VIP box. I want to ask her how Lottie did for so long without me. I want to hear how she liked my parents, who flew out this morning for the game.

I scan the key card Millie left for me in the lobby and enter my family's suite. I drop my bag immediately when I see Millie standing in the kitchen talking on the phone. Her eyes light up when she spots me, and she lets the person on the other line know she has to go.

I make a bee-line for Millie and scoop her up, taking three steps to deposit her on the counter. I lean in, and she throws her arms around my neck, and without a word, we're communicating a language so much better than talking. She kisses me with a dizzying intensity, running her hands through my hair, which hasn't quite dried from my post-game shower.

"Please tell me Lottie is asleep," I say between kisses.

"Yup," she says, my lip in her mouth. "And Reese went out with a friend."

"We're alone?" The thought both excites and frustrates me, on account of my total commitment to being married before we, ahem, consummate this relationship.

For the millionth time since I told her I love her, I wish we were married.

"We're alone." She's almost breathless, and the sound is making my willpower crumble, so I step back while I still can. She puts her hand on my shoulders as if to steady herself. "And you looking this sexy in a suit is not making it easy to be alone with you, did you know that?" She runs her eyes over me and bites her lip before saying, "Mmm."

Grinning, I come back in for a quick kiss that becomes several long, deep ones.

"Are you always going to be this happy to see me after a win, or only when you rush for three touchdowns in a single game?" she asks, putting her forehead against mine.

I smile and kiss her softly. "Is there anything sexier than you pretending you know what football terms mean?"

"Yes. You in this suit," she says in a husky voice.

I'm about to go back in for more when I remember about Brianna and step back. "Wait, how is your sister? Is the baby okay?"

She blinks and inhales deeply, leaning back on the kitchen counter. "Yes, she's fine. It was just some normal lady business stuff."

"Lady business?"

"Do you really want to know?" she asks. I shrug, and she eyes me appreciatively. "Okay, big man. It was a yeast infection."

"Ah. Yuck." I can handle all the period talk in the world, but infections aren't my strong suit. "But what a relief."

She laughs, but the sound fades quickly. "I need to talk to you about something else, though. Something kind of serious."

"Does this mean we're done making out for the night?" I sigh at her nod and back up against the opposite counter.

"We saw Carlie while we were shopping. Lottie didn't see her, but Reese and I did. Reese took Lottie into the car and ... I

BABY LLAMA DRAMA

talked to her, Duke. For maybe ten minutes while Lottie and Reese waited in the car."

I exhale a big blast of air. "Her boyfriend's team is here for an exhibition game," I say. She looks at me in surprise. "One of the reporters asked me if I was planning to see them while they're in town."

She shakes her head in disbelief. "At least they didn't confuse her with Gisele."

I snort darkly. "You're sure Lottie didn't see her?"

"Positive. But Duke..."

I cut her off, because I don't want her to feel a need to ... to *therapize* me the way she does everyone else in her life. "I already know what you're going to say. You think Lottie needs to see her, don't you? You think Carlie needs to be in her life even in some small capacity. There's some study somewhere about how much better children fare when they have a connection to their birth parents, especially when the child knows that her mom wasn't, in fact, stolen by a monster, so I need to suck it up and meet with Carlie and consider letting Carlie have a relationship with our daughter, even though I fully intend on someone else taking the primary maternal role in Lottie's life soon. Right?"

A smile creeps up her face, and her cheeks are that color of red that makes me weak in the knees. "Um, yeah. Pretty much. And I think we should probably talk about those intentions of yours sooner rather than later, don't you?"

I want to smile back, but I also don't know if I'm ready to let Carlie back in, and something tells me that Millie won't consider the latter until the former is settled.

And she's right.

"I don't know if I'm ready to let Carlie be a part of Lottie's life ever, let alone now. What if she leaves again? What if she and Carlie spend time together and Lottie loves her as much as ever and Carlie just leaves?"

"You don't have to let Carlie have unlimited access to her. I don't know her at all, so I don't know if her leaving was a one-off decision caused by extreme emotional duress or if she's an emotional decision maker. But you don't have to decide that immediately. You could start with just talking to Carlie. You could even decide to tell Lottie a little bit about her."

I huff. "How would I do that?"

She hops off the counter and walks over to me, standing close enough that I can smell her fruity conditioner.

"You'd start small. Tell her a story about when she was in Carlie's tummy. About how she has Carlie's Bambi eyes. Whatever. It doesn't have to be the whole story now, just bits and pieces. She doesn't remember Carlie, so the trauma of your divorce isn't going to be a lifelong issue for her, but the trauma of abandonment very well could be." She puts her hand up to my face and rubs her hand across my cheek. "She thinks a monster stole her mom, Duke. Don't you think it's better for her to know what actually happened?"

I lean my head into her hand. "Is it really better for her to think that her mom broke down and couldn't handle being a wife and mother anymore?"

"I could be way off base here, but my impression is that Carlie had a hard life and was never taught the skills she needed to handle trials. Your cancer was a trial that she didn't know how to live through anymore. Deep down, she felt she couldn't be the mom Lottie deserved, so she left to give you both the chance at finding that," she says, emotion pooling in her eyes. "That's not a perfect love, but it is still love, and it's the best Carlie knew how to give."

"And we're sure that's better than the story about the monster?"

Millie chuckles. "Yes, because it's the truth, right?"

I sigh and put my arms around her lower back, bringing her close. "Almost."

She cocks her head and peers up into my eyes. "Almost?"

"Can we sit?" I ask. I take her hand and lead her to the couch, where she sits next to me, throwing her legs over mine. I put my arm around her and tell her the rest of the story.

The part I've never wanted to talk about.

The part I'm afraid paints me as the villain in all of this.

Carlie left during my chemo. She walked out on our daughter and she cheated on me, on both of us. That much is true.

"I was a bad husband. I wasn't mean or cold, but I white-knuckled marriage to Carlie. She didn't notice immediately, but after a couple of years, she could tell something was wrong. She thought having a kid would make everything better, but it only made everything worse, because I loved Lottie so much that she could spot the difference between real and fake love after that. She knew I was giving her a counterfeit. That only made me try harder to cover it."

"That sounds exhausting," Millie says softly.

"It was. When I went through that first round of chemo and radiation, I couldn't fake it anymore. All I wanted was my family—my parents, Reese, and Lottie. Tripp and Rusty. That was it. I was in too much pain, too sick, and Carlie was so visibly uncomfortable with how much weight I was losing and how the radiation made my eyebrows fall out. She didn't have anyone to talk to. Her grandparents had already passed, and she didn't have real friends, just the NFL wives. She wanted to bring it all to social media—to her *instafam*—so she could get their 'support.' I refused to let anyone outside of our closest inner circle know, though. She never breathed a word, but she took to social media more and more, got more sponsorships, became even bigger. And I was just relieved she was finally leaving me alone."

My throat gets hot at the admission. Millie caresses my hand.

"She cried whenever she saw me, and she would tell me it

was because she loved me so much and couldn't stand seeing me in so much pain, but I was so resentful, Millie. The last thing I wanted was to worry about her emotions while I was throwing up.

"By the second round of chemo, I didn't even want to see her. I told her to bring Lottie and that she could wait outside of the room when she came to the hospital. I pretended it was for her sake, but it was all for me. I couldn't be around her. I couldn't think about how if I died, Lottie would be left with someone whose idea of mothering was photoshopping the applesauce from our child's cheek before she posted rather than just wiping the stuff off. Or, heaven forbid, not posting at all." I shake my head. "I know how unfair that sounds."

"You don't have to filter for me, Duke," Millie says. Her eyes are full of confidence in me.

"Chemo changed me. The radiation burned up my ability to fake it. I did everything I could to stay married but only because I was too big a coward to ask for a divorce. In trying to honor my marital vows, I wasn't true to either of us. Carlie left, in part because I gave her no path to stay."

"That is *not* true," Millie says, the warmth in her eyes sparking into an angry blaze. "She could have told you she was struggling. She could have asked your mom for a weekend off to figure things out—"

"There's more."

"Okay. I'm listening."

"She called me from the hotel."

"Which—"

"In Atlanta, next to the hospital. She called me before she left, Millie. She told me she loved me but she knew I didn't love her. She said she couldn't handle me pushing her away when all she wanted was to be there for me. She told me she'd do anything for me if I just told her I wanted her." The acid in my stomach sours and bubbles up into my throat. "Do you know what I did? I lost it."

The memory is so vivid, so forceful, I feel like I'm back in that lonely, sterile bed. Carlie crying, begging me to love her. Me being done.

Done.

"Carlie, I'm in the middle of a treatment that could very well kill me, and you're calling to talk about your feelings?" I asked, bewildered. "I thought something was wrong with Lottie—"

"It's always about Lottie for you!"

"Of course it is. I'm her dad."

"Yeah, and you're *my* husband? Or did you forget?"

"What have I done, Carlie? How exactly have I failed you?"

"You don't care about me!"

"In what way? I provide for our family. I support you in your career. I'm faithful. I've never even looked at another woman. How exactly do I not care?" I demanded.

"You don't love me!"

The shock of waking up one morning to find a wedding ring on my finger had faded years ago. But the resentment hadn't. And it was all coming to the surface, even as I tried to keep it down. "I show love for you—"

"But you don't *love* me. Go on. Admit it! You don't care about me! I'm just the mother of your child. The woman you made a commitment to, *and you always honor your commitments,* don't you?" she mocked.

"Yes. Always."

"It's all about duty, isn't it?" I stayed silent, so she went on. "Do you know what it feels like to be a *responsibility* instead of a spouse?"

"Do you know what it feels like to wake up married to someone you didn't want to marry?" I shouted.

"So you admit it!"

"Yes! I admit it! Are you happy? I never wanted to marry you! I'm sorry if that's too big a truth bomb for you. I never asked for this life. I'm doing the best I can with it, but I cannot sit here and pretend to worship you like one of your stupid followers. I know you want more from me, but you've had everything I can give. If you want validation, post another selfie."

And then I hung up.

A minute later, I received a text with seven words:

CARLIE: You asked for it, you got it

The next picture on her feed popped up thirty-six minutes later. It was her in the airport making a kissing face with the caption, "Au revoir."

Goodbye.

Millie puts her hands to the side of my face, but I can't look at her. "I broke Carlie," I say, my lungs tighter than my throat. "I couldn't give her what she needed, even with my best efforts, and I broke her. The same goes for Lottie. Who's to say I won't break you, too?"

"Someone thinks highly of himself," Millie says in the least empathetic, saltiest tone I've ever heard her use. It's like she's added extra sodium to her voice just to pour all over my wounds.

"Excuse me?"

"Duke, you don't have that much power, not over me and certainly not over Carlie."

"I notice you didn't mention Lottie."

"You're her dad, she's three, and you have a huge impact on her, but don't you *dare* say that she's broken."

"I know, you're right. But it's my fault Lottie was hurt. Carlie abandoned Lottie because of me."

"Wrong."

My frustration mounts. Is Millie purposefully misunderstanding me? "Did you listen to a word I said? I told Carlie I didn't want her."

"Did you know she was going to leave the hotel and hop on an international flight?"

"No, but if she'd told me she was going to, I probably would have bought the ticket myself! I don't want to push you away, but I can't promise who I'll be in the heat of the moment. I can't promise not to ... to hurt you—"

"Duke, you had an argument with your spouse at the lowest point of your life. If that's the worst I can expect, sign me up."

"Stop minimizing this," I say too sharply.

"Then stop catastrophizing it. You didn't make her leave."

I lean back. "Millie, take this seriously! Marriage is hard! You need to know what you're getting into with me before we talk about taking this further."

"Okay."

"And it's not just marriage! Parenting is hard! What if Lottie finds out that I pushed her mom away and she hates me for it? What if she hates you for 'replacing' Carlie? What if being a step-mom is too hard for you and you resent me for dragging you into a life you never wanted, like Carlie dragged me? I cannot live with that possibility. I can't—"

Millie pulls my face to hers, and before I can process what's happening, her mouth is on mine with a breathtaking intensity. I don't resist. I let her kisses soothe the guilt and shame I've lived with for two years and the regret of a loveless marriage for the five years before that.

Millie's lips are soft and inviting, but her grip on my face is strong. The kiss isn't scorching hot or demanding or even overly enticing.

It's like a form of wordless communication. She's trying to

tell me something by kissing me instead of talking. I'm sure of it.

I just don't have a clue what she's trying to say.

"What was that?" I ask with a low chuckle when we part.

"You were spiraling and I didn't know how else to shut you up."

I laugh weakly. "Is that your professional opinion?"

"Not even remotely. But hearing you beat yourself up for someone else's choices was just—" she kisses me—"so"—another kiss—"boring."

And now I laugh in earnest. "Wow. For a therapist, you suck at listening."

"I'm not your therapist," she says. "And you can't expect me to be that for you. I physically *can't* be on for you like that all the time."

What does that even mean? I think. But as quickly as the question arises the answer comes to me.

I'm not the quarterback for the Carolina Waves at home. I'm Duke Ogden, dad, boyfriend, and smoked meat enthusiast. If I had to perform for people every minute of the day, I wouldn't just burn out, I'd break down.

Is that what it's like for Millie? Everyone constantly asks her advice, both around town and over the phone. She talks to someone from her family every day, and more often than not, I've overheard her reassuring, validating, or otherwise working that therapist magic Jane and Tripp have accused her of having.

I haven't seen it once from her friends, though. The people she chooses to live with and spend her time with don't treat her like a therapist.

Do I?

Absolutely.

I seal my eyes shut and groan. "Millie."

"What?"

I lean my forehead into hers, but I feel sick yet again. And my back is spasming. The exhaustion from the game has caught up to me. "I treat you like a therapist. I swear, I'm not trying to keep you in that box."

"You did at first, but you haven't for a couple of weeks. But thanks for understanding," she says simply. She nestles into me and we fall into a quiet pattern of breathing in unison. "Boy, we've covered a lot of ground tonight," she says.

"Are you afraid?"

"Nope. Sorry, pal."

My relief is palpable.

"Should I have let Carlie have shared custody?"

"Are you asking my professional opinion or—"

"I'm asking you as the woman I want to grow old with."

"I think you should consider it."

"She signed the papers. She didn't contest anything. She took less than she could have without so much as a protest."

"Why?"

"I think she felt too guilty and too … "

"Unworthy?"

"Unworthy, yeah." I swallow hard. I feel like I'm on a roll, like the confessions can't stop tumbling out of me, so I let every dark and shameful secret out. "And I took advantage of that. She sent gifts for Christmas that year and for Lottie's birthday—tons of them—and I threw them out. I refused to give her any more access to Lottie after what she did." I cover my face with my free hand. "All the pain Lottie's experienced over the last two years could have been avoided if I'd have just let Carlie be in her life." My insides feel dark and slimy admitting all of this. Admitting that if I'd been a better man, a better Christian, I may have forgiven her and let her back. Or at least divorced her more amicably. Of course, if I'd been better, I never would have gotten myself into this situation with her in the first place. I wouldn't have dated her just because she was hot and funny and spoke her mind.

But then I wouldn't have Lottie ...
Or Millie.
A hand on my face pulls me out of my spiral of self-loathing. "Hey," Millie says, almost in a whisper. "You went through something brutally difficult, and you handled it the best you could have at the time." The lights in the suite are low, and we can see the bright city lights and hear the steady stream of humanity outside of our windows.

"I'm not sure about that. I had a lot of hatred in my heart."

She has a sweet, small smile on her face, the kind that says she's listening but also unimpressed with how I'm using myself as a punching bag. "Duke. I'm not sure anyone would have been able to give her custody after what she did. She abandoned her baby in a hotel. Yes, family was there, but she still left while you were going through a procedure that could have killed you. Full custody made total sense. Would you have fought for sole custody if she would have simply asked for a divorce?"

"No way."

"Okay, then let's have some perspective. You weren't a perfect husband, but you're not the villain here. No one should be judged on their lowest moments."

"You're not disappointed in me?" I ask, my brow tense with anticipation.

"How could I be? If you're asking if I'm worried you'll be a bad husband—" her breath quickens and the pink tinge to her cheeks deepens, "then no. I'm not. The fact that you're even entertaining letting Carlie back in tells me the kind of man you are." She pulls my face towards hers and brushes her lips across mine softly and tantalizingly. "And I love that man. Deeply."

My hand tightens around her leg. "Just when I think I couldn't be more in love with you ... " I say.

And the making out recommences.

And it's hot.

Man, is it hot. We are a tangle of limbs, but I never let myself lose control or forget the limits we've set, even if I want to throw them out the window. Making out with feelings as deep as mine are for Millie is almost transcendent. It's so far beyond just the physical connection, I could almost get emotional. Every kiss, every touch is an expression of pure love, not just lust (although there's plenty of that, to be frank), and it makes the whole thing that much better.

So it is with my intense displeasure that we are interrupted by my sister and a friend, who are giggling their heads off as they tiptoe into the suite.

And then my displeasure hits a new low, a drop I didn't know was possible.

Because the "friend" my sister has brought into our suite in her obviously drunken stupor?

It's Carlie.

And her boyfriend is only a step behind her.

CHAPTER TWENTY-FIVE

MILLIE

MILLIE: What are y'all up to? I'm currently waiting for Duke and his ex to finish their heart to heart after a literal all-nighter. While the ex's boyfriend sits on the couch snoring next to me.

I text this to my friends, hoping at least Jane will be up. She loves those early morning runs.

Her response is almost immediate.

JANE: WHAT? Carlie is there? And Benoit?? I need more details.

MILLIE: Yeah, and I need a punch to the face.

. . .

ASH: [Sends a GIF of Nacho Libre saying "Punch to the face"] There you go. And here's another one for Duke and Carlie. [More GIFs of people getting punched.]

JANE: What bizarro world is this that you're up already, AJ?

ASH: Excusez-moi? How dare you imply that I would get up at 6 am like some common investment banker or CEO? I will have you know that I, too, pulled an all-nighter. Working on the Grenadine account.

JANE: Phew! I was worried. Now back to CARLIEEEE.

MILLIE: We ran into her shopping yesterday out of nowhere. Wait, no, two days ago? Is it Monday? I'm out of my mind.

JANE: Understandable.

ASH: You and the Baron would have made out all night, anyway, so it's not like you're actually missing any sleep.

MILLIE: You give my feminine wiles too much credit. Duke sticks to that curfew like it's his job. Which I guess it is.

ASH: *snort*

. . .

MILLIE: Guys, is it weird that I kind of like Carlie? You know, apart from the way she abandoned her family, broke her daughter's heart, and showed up uninvited last night?

ASH: Yes, it's weird. You're a weirdo. Welcome to the club. We meet on Tuesdays.

JANE: Kind of weird, kind of not. She can't have been *all* bad. Duke may not have planned to marry her, but he saw enough in her to date her in the first place, right?

MILLIE: Good point.

ASH: Okay, but how the crap did she show up at your hotel at all?

MILLIE: Reese. I got Carlie's number and Reese asked for it after I told her everything she and I talked about. They went out to dinner and Reese was evidently pretty nervous, so she, well, over-served herself. She was so drunk that Carlie and Benoit brought her to the suite to make sure she made it back safely.

ASH: Um, that's legit thoughtful of them. Am *I* allowed to kind of like them?

MILLIE: See?

. . .

The suite is big enough that there are two separate sitting areas. Benoit and I are sitting on the couch in one of them. Benoit is fast asleep. Carlie and Duke are on the other side of the suite and have been talking for hours. I don't see how it's possible that neither of them has had to pee yet. Not that I watched them every second, mind you. Benoit and I took shifts.

"This is a little different, no?" he'd asked me in a thick French accent. "It is not normal to be in a hotel with your lover and their former lover like this?"

"No, it is not normal," I'd agreed, even though the word "lover" gives me the heebie-jeebies.

"This is good for Carlie. She needs the ... *comment dit-on* ... closing?"

"Closure."

"Yes, closure. She has so much regret. I don't think I can ask her to marry me until she can forgive herself, you know?"

We were both watching when Carlie and Duke gave each other a hug in the middle of the night, and I think we both expected that to be the end of it. But instead, it was like they'd just turned the page and started a new chapter. One that lasted another three hours.

A text from Jane pulls me back into the present.

JANE: How are you holding up? This has to be awkward.

MILLIE: Awkward but necessary. We need to chat IRL when I get back.

Speaking of which ... I have a plane to catch in three hours. I have to work today at the farm—my first animal assisted clients, including a ten year-old with a trauma history. As much as I want to cancel and stay here with Duke, I have to go.

I get up and rush to my room to start packing. It only takes a few minutes, but when I come out, Carlie and Benoit are standing at the exit talking to Duke. At a glance from him, I head over. He slides his arm around my shoulders, and I feel anchored for the first time all night.

"Thanks for bringing Reese home safely and for talking, Carlie," Duke says. "I needed this."

"Me too," she says with a sniff. They both look like they've cried their fair share of tears through the night. Carlie has cried through most of her makeup, including her false lashes, but she still looks beautiful. I look like a wet tomato when I cry. I'm red and sweaty and puffy. I can't imagine looking as good as she does.

Yet, Duke has seen me cry. Before we were even a thing, he'd seen me cry and had held me close, totally unfazed by my tears.

That matters. It matters a lot.

I'm glad to see Duke and Carlie reconciling. I hope this is the start of a relationship that includes Lottie one day. But for now, it's enough to know that they seem to have some closure and that they're looking to move forward without the dark cloud of infidelity and indifference looming over them.

I give Benoit and then Carlie a hug, and Carlie whispers, "Thank you for givin' Reese my number. And thanks for softenin' Duke's heart so we could do this."

I smile, squeezing her like she's squeezing me. "Thank you for teaching him how to be a husband. He owes a lot to you," I say sincerely.

Reese told me how cold he was with fans before Carlie helped him change his approach. She was thinking like an influencer, not trying to find a way to help him sincerely connect, but she saved him years of grief and headaches with fans and the media. The natural man in Duke is focused inward, and

Carlie helped him look beyond himself in a lot of ways, personally and professionally. He wouldn't be the man I fell in love with without Carlie. I will be grateful to her forever for that.

"Oh, and the CPR lessons!" Duke says, telling Carlie about the way he managed to do the Heimlich on me when I was choking because of the parenting classes she made him take with her.

"I'm glad they came in handy after all. I only made you take the classes so you'd see I was taking motherhood seriously," she says wistfully.

The brightness on his face fades into something milder. Kinder. "Let me talk to her, okay? I need to prep her. And then let's get you back into her life."

Fat tears roll down Carlie's cheeks and past the corner of her wide smile as she nods. "Thanks, Duke."

We see them out, and as soon as we're alone, Duke folds his arms around me and we stumble to the couch, not saying anything. I'm smooshed against his side, and as much as I want to fall asleep, I remind him about my flight and about my client, and he groans and kisses me. "When do you have to leave?"

"In about ten minutes," I add. "What about you? Is your coach furious?"

"Oh, he'll be furious all right. So will my trainer. I promised I'd rest..."

But he's already in a slow breathing pattern, which means he's already half asleep. I can only imagine the toll a four-hour football game has on a body, let alone coupling that with an emotional all-nighter. I tuck my curiosity away and instead kiss his cheek softly, slowly. A hint of whiskers greets my lips, and the sensation makes me long for something I've never had.

I love Duke. We played house for almost two weeks, and we've dated for two weeks more, and it's not enough. I don't want to say goodbye at the end of every night, I want to say goodnight. I want to stand in the bathroom with him at our dual sinks every morning and watch him shave. I want the NFL wives to talk to me, to accept me, not to see me as temporary. I want to stop the press speculation by wearing a ring, by making vows, by being his and making him mine.

Unbidden, I think of Carlie.

She wanted all of those same things. Rather than waiting to see if he would give them to her, she manipulated him into getting them. She tricked him. She *trapped* him. Yes, he could have annulled the marriage, but she knew him well enough to know how seriously he would take marriage vows. He's a once-in-a-lifetime guy. A forever guy. I know he wouldn't change it for anything, but she took that from him when she took advantage of him.

I won't put an ounce of pressure on him, I promise myself. No matter how badly I want to see us progress, no matter how badly I want my forever with him to start right now, I cannot become Carlie.

I wiggle out from under his arm and get up, not letting myself wish I could stay, not letting myself indulge in any feelings that will make this weekend more emotional than it's been. I bend over and kiss his lips. "I love you," I whisper. "Tell Lottie I'll see her tonight."

"We'll see you at home," he mumbles with closed eyes. He rolls over and sleepily says, "Love you."

It isn't until I'm in the cab on my way to the airport that I realize he didn't say "I love you." He said "love you." Like he used to with Carlie.

And maybe it's just the sleep deprivation combined with the overly emotional weekend, but I fixate on those two words for the entire flight home.

CHAPTER TWENTY-SIX

MILLIE

I'm just finishing my notes from my last session when I hear Jane say, "Howdy, stranger!"

"Hey!" I hop up and give her a quick hug, and then we both sit at the picnic table in the animal pen.

Louis has been standing next to me like a guard llama, but he wanders over to Jane, who gives him a snuggle. "Who's the best llapaca in the whole world?" she says in a cooing voice while she pets him.

"You two are friends, huh?" I ask.

"Duh. To know Louis is to love Louis."

I grin. "I've missed you."

"Back at you," she says. "Now tell me everything."

Jane is one of the few people in the world who's never relied on me for emotional support. If anything, she spent so many years feeling responsible for me and all of our friends that she struggled to fully let us in. Awful childhoods will do that to a person. But since she fell in love, she's been as open as a Walmart on Black Friday.

I give her the rundown of my weekend, and she gasps and tsks and sighs and winces at all the right places. I tell her how Duke has openly said he loves me and wants a future with me, but I admit that hearing him say "love you" threw me more than I care to admit.

"Does anything else in your experience with him make you concerned? Or is it just those two words after a dramatic and emotional weekend?"

"You sound like you're doing voice over for *The Bachelor*."

She drops her naturally sultry voice and over-enunciates each syllable. "This will be the most *shocking* and *dramatic* season yet."

"Exactly." I laugh, then sigh. "And no, not really. He withdrew after a day of knowing each other, but he explained that."

"How?"

"He was fighting feelings for me because he felt like he was broken and swore to never marry again."

"Yeah, he did. He used to grumble about how no one should ever get married. But that changed fast after he met you." She grins. "Now that you two are happily in love, I can tell you that he basically begged me to ask you to babysit for him."

"What? Tell me *everything*!"

And she does. She tells me about the call, and she gives me his every expression and reaction, and it's exactly what I need to remember that he loves me, and an emotional roller coaster of a weekend doesn't change that.

"I cannot wait to hold this over him," I say, rapping my fingertips against each other like a mad scientist. Two baby goats seem to interpret this movement as my having food, so they jump on me. I cuddle them before putting them down.

"As you should. Don't be afraid of Carlie. And don't let fear stop you from communicating with him. We've seen a thousand

Hallmark movies together. Don't let a simple miscommunication become part of your plot. Promise?"

"Promise."

"Also, Tripp and I are coming to the next away game. We already got tickets for the VIP boxes for the rest of the games this season, including the Super Bowl, because there's zero chance the Waves don't make it."

Her just saying that out loud gives me shivers. "Don't jinx us!"

Her mouth falls open, and her stormy blue eyes sparkle. "Did you just say *us* about a football team? Does Nordstrom Rack know you're cheating with the Adidas factory?"

I laugh, close my laptop, and follow her to her house to catch up ... and borrow a sweater that doesn't smell like goats and llamas.

That night, Tripp and Jane invite the whole crew over to the farm for a cookout, including Rusty and Duke and Lottie, of course. I'm setting the massive farm table when Duke and Lottie arrive. Lottie bursts into tears and runs over to me the second she sees me. Duke widens his eyes, which look almost bruised from his game and all-nighter. But the look he gives me conveys all the message I need.

It's been a bad day.

I wave to Jane, who points me in the direction of Tripp's office. I pick up Lottie and head into the office, only vaguely noticing the updates Jane and Tripp have made to the house on my way. Inside, I drop to a cushy armchair in one corner and let Lottie cry.

And cry.

And cry.

My borrowed sweater is soaking and Lottie's hair is sweaty and matted from crying, but I don't stop her. I just smooth her hair and rub her back and whisper, "I'm here. I love you and I'm here."

And I let her cry.

"I woke up," she sobs and hiccups, "and you were gone!"

"Oh, sweetie," I say, my heart aching thinking about her fear. We'd spent so much time reviewing how the weekend would go, how I would have to leave before she woke up but how I'd be there when she got back. "I'm sorry you were so sad. What were you thinking when that happened?"

"That a monster took you!" she cries. "You said you'd be home!"

I close my eyes and shake my head, holding her as tightly as I can. We have to talk about Carlie eventually, yes, but *I* did this. I promised I'd be at the house and I wasn't. I feel sick with guilt.

After a few more minutes, her crying slows. "I should have called and told your dad that I'd be at the farm when you got home. I can see why you'd be scared when you expected me to be there."

Her chest shudders against mine as she takes a double breath. "You promised to be home when I got home."

"You're right. My plans changed and I forgot to tell you. I'm sorry, Lottie."

"You weren't there," she says again and again and again.

I have her tell me the story from start to finish over and over, including how we're together now.

Twenty minutes later, Lottie has successfully navigated some big emotions and we've played a game of I Spy, which she's awful at. We giggle a lot and then make our way back to the kitchen. Parker, Lou, and the guys are standing on either side of the spacious soapstone counter talking about Duke's game, while Ash and Jane are laughing at Rusty's new Tik Tok from the last Farmer's Market. The renovated kitchen is so alive that I worry about Lottie getting overwhelmed again, but she just holds my hand and walks over to the guys and demands that Rusty pick her up. He hefts her onto his back and takes her for a piggyback ride around the loop of the kitchen, dining room, and family room, and her giggles fill the house.

"There's my girl," Duke says, pulling me into a hug that is firmly nudging PG-13 territory, in spite of the audience.

Tripp chuckles. Duke is so tall and broad that I forgot that Tripp is basically Duke on steroids. The first time I saw him, I thought he was the ultimate eye candy, but now I know better. He can't compare to Duke. No one can.

"When Jane told me this was inevitable, I thought she was crazy," Tripp says, folding his arms and leaning his massive Jack-Reacher-esque frame against the island behind him. He has a stronger accent than Duke's, though Rusty's is stronger still. Tripp's eyes dance with laughter as he looks at us. "You gave me so much grief about getting married. And here you are, seconds away from dropping to one knee."

"Bro, please." Duke groans. His voice sounds scratchy, almost like he's getting a cold. Worry spikes my pulse. Is he getting sick? "Don't play my hand for me. Have some respect."

"Request denied." Tripp's grin widens. "I've never seen you in love before. I'm going to bust your chops all night long, brother."

"I hate you," Duke says. I love the rumbling sound of his chest against my ear. And I love that I can hear the smile in his voice. "Even if you're not wrong."

"Told you!" Jane says, slipping underneath her husband's arm. "And what's the moral of the story?"

Tripp growls and leans his face into her neck. "Jane knows everything," he says. He nibbles on her neck, causing her to squeal. Then he whispers something that makes her eyes flash, and I have a stab of envy at what they have.

Forever.

Duke and I are on that path. He said as much in the hotel last night. I can't push it, but I know it. And that has to be enough for now. I don't get to swoop in and demand a timeframe after a month of knowing him, even if that month revealed as much as a year with anyone else.

I know Duke. I trust him. I can tolerate wanting more, as long as I have him and Lottie.

While our friends talk and laugh like the freewheeling bunch they are, Duke and I take turns addressing Lottie's needs. She sits between us, refusing to eat anything except cornbread and green beans until I convince her to try a bite of brisket by talking about how it's the best thing I've ever eaten. She tries one bite, but at least it's a bite! She throws a roll at Rusty when he doesn't stop his conversation with Ash to talk to her, so Duke pulls her aside to remind her how to act while everyone assures us that they don't mind. When she spills lemonade all over the table and herself, Duke goes to change her with spare clothes from the diaper bag while Jane helps me clean up the table.

Part of me feels like I should apologize. Part of me feels even a bit embarrassed that she doesn't have table manners.

And the other part of me wants to kick my own butt.

Every person at this table was a little kid once, and no one's stage in life warrants an apology. So I bite my tongue, right my thinking, and thank Jane for helping me as we take dishes into the kitchen.

"You're a natural," she tells me, washing the lemonade from her hands. "Motherhood suits you."

I can't help but beam. "It's all I've ever wanted."

"I know." Jane squeezes my arm. "I'm happy for you guys."

"I'm happy for *you*. You and Tripp could trend as 'hashtag marriage goals' for the next decade."

She smiles so big, she scrunches her nose. "Aren't we adorable? I love that man."

"I know the feeling."

Jane goes back to the table, but I peek around the main floor, looking for Duke and Lottie. From the hallway, I hear Duke speaking softly. I'm about to announce myself when I hear what they're talking about.

Duke is talking about Carlie.

He's telling her that a monster never took her mom and that she wasn't able to be the momma she wanted to be. He's explaining that her momma left so that they could find Lottie the momma she deserved. He tells Lottie that her first mom's name is Charlotte and that they named Lottie after her.

"But my name is Lottie not Char-lottie," she says, stressing the l's now that she's mastered them.

"That's right," Duke says gently. "Her name is Charlotte, but she goes by Carlie because when she was little, she couldn't say the *sh* sound in her name."

"Just like I couldn't say my l's!"

"That's right!" he gushes. "So she goes by Carlie and you go by Lottie. Your first mommy loves you, so we gave you a name like hers. You always have a piece of Momma Carlie with you. Isn't that cool?" Lottie doesn't answer, and I wish I could see what was going on between them. "What are you thinking, Bug?"

"I like that Lottie and Millie sound the same."

My heart could burst.

"I like that, too," he says.

"Daddy, is it okay if Carlie can be my first mommy but Millie can be my forever mommy?"

I hold my breath, not wanting to make a sound. Not wanting to break the spell.

"That's more than okay, pumpkin. I feel the same way. We just have to make sure Millie agrees."

An explosion of joy and excitement swirls around in my chest, almost propelling me forward, because I should definitely run into the room right now and scream yes, right? I won't, for the record, because I'm eavesdropping. But I want to. More than anything, I want to.

He feels the same way. He said the words out loud: he wants me forever.

They both want me forever.

Duke tells Lottie they should go back to the kitchen, so I do that awkward thing where I dart down the hall and turn around as if I'm just coming from the kitchen rather than having stood around the corner, hanging on their every word. I try to blink away my tears of joy.

"Oh, hey guys! I was just looking for you!" I say casually, except I'm panting just a bit and can't seem to control the volume of my voice.

But it's no big deal. It's subtle. I'm totally selling it.

"Why are you being so funny?" Lottie says, screwing up her face and cocking her head so far to the side, she might tip over.

I narrow my eyes and tickle her all the way back to the table.

When the three of us are sitting back down again, Duke drapes his arm over Lottie's chair, and his fingers trace along my collarbone. The sensation sends tingles from my neck through my chest, into my stuttering heart. He is gorgeous every second of every day, but something about the earnestness in his face and voice makes him harder to resist than ever. "We need some alone time. Tonight."

He holds my gaze, and I am a willing captive. "Yes, please."

CHAPTER TWENTY-SEVEN

DUKE

*A*s glad as I am to spend time with my best friends, I'm still annoyed that I didn't have time with Millie tonight. I have things I need to talk to her about. Big things. Important things. Big, important things. All those wasted hours talking to everyone else but her ...

Well, except Lottie.

I can't get over how well the conversation went. I was praying like a sinner the whole time, hoping she'd be able to accept the truth that Carlie is real, that Carlie loves her, and that Lottie is safe. Lottie fell asleep on the drive home, but Millie took her car, so she couldn't drive with us, anyway. It's only fifteen minutes, but I wanted those fifteen minutes. I want every minute with her.

I sneak Lottie into her room with no problem and then take the stairs up two at a time. By the time I've reached the top of the stairs, my lungs constrict, and I have to breathe harder than normal.

Man, I'm tired.

The game yesterday was one for the record books, but the post-game exhilaration has worn off, especially coupled with the late night. Coach is gonna flip tables if I'm not in peak form for next week's game. I grab my heating pad, wrap it around my back, and lay face down on the couch in the sitting room to wait for Millie to arrive.

The next thing I know, Millie is pressing a kiss to my temple. I lift up from the couch, but she just shushes me and lays down beside me on the oversized sectional. It was Carlie's idea to buy such a huge couch. I can chalk this up to yet another reason to thank her. I roll over, and Millie puts her back to my chest so that I'm spooning her. My arm is slung over hers, curving around her waist. We both sigh.

"I talked to Lottie about Carlie," I say into her hair. I feel goose bumps erupt on the exposed skin of her arm, and I smile. I will never tire of having an effect on her.

"Oh yeah?" she asks with a yawn.

I should be nervous to say the words that come next. I should feel my breath quicken, my pulse pound in my throat. But instead, I'm calm as a summer's day. "We agreed that we're thankful Carlie was her first mom, but you're our forever. If you'll take us."

Millie shifts and rolls around so that we're chest-to-chest. I peek to see that her eyes are open and she's staring at me. "Are you ... are you asking ... "

I smile as broadly as I can in this state of utter contentment. "No, but I'm warning you that I'm going to ask. Soon."

She rests her head on my shoulder. Her breath tickles my neck. "Warning me, huh? That sounds ominous."

I snort and channel my inner Count Dracula. "Be afraid. Be very afraid."

Millie starts shaking against me. "Do you only know how to

do bad Irish accents? You weren't trying to sound like a vampire, were you?"

I squeeze her tight in my arms, shaking my head. "I take it all back—"

"No!" she squeals. "No take backs. You said it. I heard it. It's official."

I kiss her forehead and revel in the feeling of her in my arms. "It will be soon enough."

She breathes in slowly, the rise and fall of her chest matching mine. "Promise?"

"I do if you do."

"I do."

"I do, too."

And with that promise, we fall asleep.

And with Lottie's knees digging into our sides, we wake up far too soon. Lottie hops on us like we're a trampoline, and I shift to protect Millie, who isn't accustomed to the feeling of Lottie's bony knees digging into sensitive areas. "Ouch," I say, curling around a hissing Millie. "Lottie, what have I told you about a knee to the kidneys?"

"They're right here! They're both here!" Lottie yells.

"Well, good morning, lovebirds," Reese says, pulling Lottie off of us.

"When we get married, we're locking the door," I mutter to Millie.

"Seconded," she says, rolling off of the couch before I have a chance to wish her a proper good morning. Not that my thoughts resemble anything proper. I gotta put a ring on this woman already. Although maybe I should get a glass of water first. Reese presses a button to open the curtains as I sit up. The light that streams into the sitting room stabs my eyes, and I wince, covering my face. Now that the pain of Lottie's knee has subsided, I notice I have a splitting headache.

"What time is it?" I ask with a groan.

"It's almost eight," Reese answers. I've yet to fully open my eyes, but I feel Millie drop down to the couch beside me.

"What's going on? Are you okay?"

I shake my head and blink a few times before looking at her. Her hair is gloriously messy and her mascara has flaked beneath her eyes. The sight makes me eager for a million mornings to come. "It's nothing. Just a headache. Reese, could you grab me a couple of Excedrin?"

"I got it," Millie says. She's up and in the kitchen before I can even say thank you.

My back spasms when I try to stand, and I sit back down. I got sacked once during the game, but I didn't ice it nearly enough. With it being so late in the morning, I won't have time to hop into the ice barrel before getting to the practice field. I try to roll out my shoulders and neck while Lottie and Reese go into the kitchen, but my entire spine is stiff as a board.

When Millie returns, I'm still trying to limber up. Her eyebrows pull together as she hands me two pills and a protein shake.

"I don't have much of an appetite," I tell her, taking the pills and swallowing them dry.

"Drink." She pushes the shaker bottle toward me. "I put in a scoop of BCAAs to help with recovery."

I take the bottle and stand more quickly than I should. My back protests, but I keep my face neutral. "You are an angel."

"An angel? Wow. I'm used to people cracking jokes about how redheads don't have souls. This is a nice change." She hugs me while I sip the shake. I'm normally ravenous in the mornings and have a shake as soon as I get up, but I can't seem to choke this down. I drink just enough to satisfy Millie and then excuse myself to go get ready for practice. Technically players aren't required to be in the facility on Tuesdays, but only rookies take days off, and with having missed part of yesterday traveling home late, I can't afford to look like I'm slacking. I'll go in to get extra treatment for my back and to study tape to get a jump on Sunday's opponent.

If only this headache would go away.

It takes me an embarrassingly long time to get the few things I need in my duffel bag. There's no dress code for going to practice like there is for games, so I change into a pair of joggers, a hat, and a hoodie. Dressed all in black, I'm the Johnny Cash of athletic wear.

Upstairs, Millie, Reese, and Lottie are chatting around the kitchen island. Millie doesn't typically eat before eleven a.m., so she's sipping a Diet Coke that she got from the fridge.

Yes, I stock Diet Coke for her. I'd install a soda fountain if that would make her happy.

Whoa.

Maybe it's the brain-pain talking, but is that the best wedding present idea anyone has ever had?

I tuck that away for later, hoping I'll remember it. The Excedrin hasn't kicked in yet, but at least I have years of experience faking not being in pain for the people around me. I smile and walk around the table, kissing Millie and Lottie's heads and giving Reese knuckles. "Okay, I'm off. Love you, girls. Remember who you are."

Millie and Lottie both hop up to give me a real hug, and while Lottie goes back to the table, Millie stays and looks into my eyes a bit too deeply. "Are you sure you're okay?"

I give her my most winning smile. "I'm fine. The all-nighter caught up with me, and that sack Sunday hit my back harder than I thought. I'll have the training staff take a look at it today."

She grabs my hands "Are you sure you should be going in on your day off?"

"I'm sure. You haven't had physical therapy until you've had

NFL physical therapy. They're going to stretch and massage and loosen everything in my body. We're talking force plate technology, red light therapy, ice baths, the works. I'll come home tonight feeling like a new man."

"Good." She stands on tiptoes to kiss me, and I make a point of not wincing at the way I have to crane my neck down. The kiss is worth it.

Several hours of treatment later, I'm just packing up at the facility when Sonny comes over. "My man," Sonny says, slapping my shoulder. "How's your back?"

"Not as bad as I feared." Six hours of targeted therapy will do that. My headache has been more stubborn, though I don't mention that. At least it hasn't exploded into a full-blown migraine. Yet. "How's your knee?"

"This ol' thing? Unstoppable," Sonny says. I hope he's right. We need him to have a shot at the Super Bowl this year. And I hope it is for his sake, too. He tore his ACL a couple of years ago, and everyone thought it would be career ending, but he bounced back better than ever. What the fans at home don't realize, though, is that making sure his knee stays strong is a full time job for him. "I'm superhuman, remember?"

"I seem to remember reading that on a site or ten. Was that one Sports Illustrated?"

"No, Bleacher Report. Sports Illustrated called my recovery 'jaw-dropping.'" His smile shows more teeth than a human should be able to have and still look so good.

"I'm glad it didn't go to your head."

Sonny laughs so unselfconsciously, I know why reporters love him. Everyone respects me well enough. I'm a consummate professional, thanks to Carlie's help, but Millie has helped me see that I can make the entire fame experience work for me better if I think about it as a chance to connect with people.

But what I have to work to do, Sonny does effortlessly. He

has a way of making reporters feel like their questions are valid even when they're not and perceptive even when they're clickbait. He treats them all like friends rather than people who would gladly dance at his funeral if they thought they'd sell more articles. And it works. The press loves him, and fans love him even more.

"Have you seen any of the Janes lately?" he asks.

"Yeah, actually. We just had dinner with them last night."

He pauses, pulling a shirt over his head. "All of them?"

What is he getting at? "Yup. They're all doing well."

"Cool. Cool cool cool."

His tone is odd, but then I remember that they're all old friends. "You should come to Lottie's birthday party in a couple of weeks at the farm. We're renting a bunch of those bouncy houses. Bring your nieces and nephews. Heck, bring the whole Luciano fam."

He nods, zipping his his duffel bag. "Yeah, that would be fun. Text me the info?"

"Will do. See you tomorrow."

I call Millie on my way out, eager to talk to her as I always am, but I get that tone that tells me she's on another call. After it goes to voicemail, I hang up. I listen to a podcast for a few minutes and then try again. She's still on the call. No problem. It's probably a client, come to think of it. I can wait for forty-five minutes. I'm in love, not addicted.

I may be a little addicted.

I don't hear from her on the whole drive home, and no amount of telling myself that she's talking to a client is helping. After basically proposing last night and feeling too off this morning to really connect with her, I'm weirdly nervous. That really did happen last night, right? I just want to hear her voice. Want to feel her in my arms and taste her lips and have her tell me she's all in like I am.

Once I get home, I expect to hear the usual: Millie gasping and saying, "Daddy's home!" and Lottie squealing for me, and then the sound of two pairs of feet running for me.

What I hear instead is crying.

Crying and chaos.

CHAPTER TWENTY-EIGHT

DUKE

I rush into the kitchen to find Lottie in full meltdown mode, while Parker and Ash, of all people, are crouched down around Lottie, trying to calm her.

"We can watch Bluey!"

"I'll give you candy!"

"You can use my lipstick!"

"What's going on? Where's Millie? Where's Reese?" I ask.

Parker and Ash both stand, visibly relieved. Ash is sweaty and red-faced, while Parker's hair is sticking out of her high ponytail at odd angles.

Parker smoothes her hair and then her pencil skirt, inhaling sharply. "Millie's in your office. She texted that there was a family emergency and needed help with Lottie. I guess she gave Reese the night off? Millie ran for the office the second we got here."

"Is it something with the baby?" I ask in alarm.

Ash's shoulders rise and fall. "It sounds like it. Millie texted us a 911 an hour ago. We got here to see her pacing around the kitchen while Lottie was crying at her feet. Not that Millie was doing anything wrong! She wasn't ignoring her!" Ash's words jumble over themselves as she tries to reassure me.

"I'm not worried about that," I say. "Is everything okay?"

Parker's gaze narrows. "Millie's in full crisis management mode. Whatever's happening, her family is not managing it well."

"Tell me something I don't know," I grumble. Parker nods knowingly. "I'm sorry y'all had to come over last minute, but thanks for the help."

"Anytime," Ash says. "Will you keep us posted? I don't know when she's flying out, but if you need help with Lottie, let us know."

I thank them both on their way out, but my thoughts are spiraling.

Flying out?

I bend down to pick up Lottie, but my back is tender, and I tweak it on the way down. I wince and bite back a string of curses that have much more to do with concern over Millie's family than with my stupid, finicky back. "Lottie, you gotta calm down, pumpkin. You gotta breathe," I say over her cries. I heft her up, but she's throwing her body all over, and the movement is undoing half of the treatment I had done earlier. I engage my core to take the brunt of her thrashing.

Screams meet my words. Screams and kicking. "Please, Lottie, just breathe! Calm down!"

More screams.

What am I supposed to do? Anxiety churns and swells in my gut, making me want to scream right back. I hate it when she's like this. I feel so powerless. What is wrong with me that I can't even calm down my own child? How am I supposed to handle this if Millie has to fly home, even for a few days? I can't do this by myself. I can't go back to trying to do all of this without her.

I don't know how long I'm holding a shrieking, kicking Lottie, but eventually, Millie comes out. Her face is a deep red, and she looks as upset as I've ever seen her. She hasn't been crying, though. She looks like she's trying hard to contain too much pressure, like a shaken up bottle of soda.

I know the feeling.

"Thank goodness you're out," I blurt. Her eyes go wide, and I shake my head. "No, that's not how I mean it. Are you okay?"

A sob escapes her throat. "Of course. I'm always okay for everyone." She comes over to grab Lottie, but I pull back. "She's fine. I got this."

Lottie wails and lunges for Millie. "Right. Because that wasn't a grimace of pain I just saw?" Millie says. And she takes Lottie from me.

"You can't go!" Lottie screams. "I hate you! You can't go!"

Lottie's words strike Millie like a blow. Tears fill up her eyes and start streaming down her face. "Well, I love you anyway," she says. Her mouth is pulled down around the corners, and the sight of her in so much pain makes me want to lash out at her stupid family.

"What's going on with your family?" I ask too harshly.

"Bri's in the hospital. She's been bleeding pretty badly, and …" she pauses over Lottie's cries. "My mom doesn't think the baby will make it."

I'm aghast. Sick to my stomach. All the while, Lottie is raging against Millie. Hitting her now, and Millie's just taking it. "Lottie, stop!" I say. "Do not hit her!"

"Don't yell at her!" Millie yells.

Lottie slams her fists against Millie's shoulders and screams how much she hates her. "Lottie, enough!" I take Lottie from Millie's arms, but Lottie's legs are wrapped too tightly around Millie, so I have to pull to free her. When Lottie is in my arms, I grunt.

"Duke, stop!" Millie shouts. "I can handle her!"

"You shouldn't have to! She shouldn't be treating you like this!"

"I hate you! You're stupid! You're a stupid person and I hate you!" Lottie screams. "Leave me alone! Go away!"

"Millie's not going away!" I say.

She shakes her head. "You can't say that. I *am* going. Bri is out of her mind with fear, Greg is practically catatonic, my dad and brother are totally checked out, and my mom can't stop crying. None of them are equipped to handle any of this."

"What's her diagnosis?"

"Like I stopped to ask? They *need* me."

"They *use* you, Millie. I get why you want to go support Bri, but they treat you like an emotional punching bag."

"They're my family, Duke, and they're scared."

"They're lucky to have you. They have no idea how lucky they are," I spit.

"Maybe not, but that doesn't change things. I need to pack."

I startle at the news. "What do you mean? We'll fly out tomorrow—"

"I already bought my ticket. I leave at midnight."

"What? You already bought your ticket?"

"My sister is in the hospital! Yes, I bought the ticket. We're not actually married."

"Obviously we're not married, or you would've talked to me."

Her jaw drops. "If we *were* married, I *still* would have bought the ticket, just as I'd expect you to do if Reese needed you!"

"The difference is that I would tell you first. I'd, I don't know, see if you wanted to come along." I hate the sarcasm in my voice, but I can't stop it. I can't stop anything. I'm in too much pain. The pressure in my head is set to explode, and my back is spasming so badly, I want to throw up. A part of my brain warns me to keep quiet, tells me that we are a time bomb, and the countdown will start if I don't shut up already.

I don't shut up.

"Are we even a consideration for you at this point?"

Tick.

Her nostrils flare. "Oh right, because you're going to miss practice? Your coach would lose it."

"Maybe, maybe not, but would it have hurt to wait five minutes and call me to let me know? Let me try to help book a private flight or get Bri transferred to a better hospital? Or was that the last ticket? The only plane going to Columbus tomorrow?"

Her cheeks are a dark red from our fighting, but the skin on her neck turns pink. Ha! There were probably thirty open seats and another flight first thing in the morning. "I'm not used to running decisions by someone."

"I see that." Tick. *Shut up! Stop now!* But I can't. I'm getting an aura from my headache. The kitchen lights stab deep into my brain. Whatever filter my better angel is trying to convince me to use is currently beyond my bandwidth. "And what about Lottie? If we were married, would you be taking her with you? Would you leave her? Hope I found a sitter?"

Tick.

She bites the inside of her lip. "That's not fair. Your sister—"

"Won't be here forever." Tick. "When you're a parent, you don't have the luxury of relying on someone else. You have to put other people first."

Boom.

I want the words back immediately. Her eyes widen as big as her mouth. She looks like she's been slapped. Stabbed. Shot. She looks like the man she loves just said the cruelest thing imaginable. She closes her mouth as tears spill down her cheeks and drip to the floor. I feel my own chin start to tremble, because as hurt and scared as I am, the only thing worse is knowing that I've hurt and scared her.

"I'm sorry. I didn't mean that," I say. "I shouldn't have—"

"I'm going home to pack."

"Millie, wait—"

Her head shakes quickly. Her lips are pursed as she comes over and gives Lottie a hug and a kiss. "I love you, sweetie. My sister's sick, so I need to go help her. I would never go if it weren't important. Auntie Reese will be back tonight and I'll call you tomorrow, okay? You're safe and I love you," she whispers.

I don't know when Lottie's screaming stopped, but she's shedding quiet tears now. She reaches for Millie, and they cling to each other and sob together, and all I can think is how I should be hugging and crying with them, but I can't. I don't get to. Shame coats my insides.

"Millie, please—"

But she slams her eyes closed and turns away from me, holding my weeping daughter. "I have to go, sweetie. Be good for your daddy, okay? I love you and I'll talk to you tomorrow," she whispers. She kisses Lottie's hand and tells her to hold it to her heart whenever she misses her. Then she passes Lottie back to me without a word and leaves the house too quickly and too quietly.

And Lottie and I are alone.

CHAPTER TWENTY-NINE

MILLIE

*M*y flight is canceled.
The next one is at 9 a.m.

I tell no one. I find a quiet-ish place in the terminal at the Columbia airport and lay down, using my coat and suitcase as a pillow.

A coat and suitcase are not a pillow. Shocker!

So instead of sleeping, I think and stew and worry. I worry about Duke and me. I worry about Lottie. I worry about Bri.

Oh, how I worry about Bri.

When Bri showed up at home with a baby the summer after my freshman year of college, no one was surprised. She's four years older than I am and two years older than Jason, but she always acted like the younger, rebellious sister, and more often than not, I was the one to bail her out.

Sophie was diagnosed with a critical congenital heart defect shortly after birth, and it changed something in Bri. Rather than running, for the first time in her life, she rose to the occasion.

She got a job and health benefits. She enrolled in night classes and doubled up during the summer to get her degree done.

Watching my niece grow meant the world to me, as did seeing my sister grow with her. Sophie was so funny and precocious, so full of love and life. Her hugs were magical. She had the most amazing, joyous little soul, and soon, I couldn't wait to be a mom so I could have a little Sophie of my own.

A week before her fourth birthday, Sophie grew tired and drawn. I was home for the summer. We took her immediately to the hospital, and we all got the chance to tell her we loved her before she went into emergency surgery. On the operating table, her amazing little heart bravely beat its final beat.

Losing her was the worst pain I've ever felt.

Worse than any ovarian cysts or surgeries. Worse than any breakup or rejection.

Lou's first song was about how loving someone is doubling your pain.

She was right. Times infinity.

I miss Sophie every day. And as bad as it is for me, it's a million times worse for Bri. After Sophie's death, we all worried Bri would backslide. My parents were beside themselves. I deferred my enrollment in my Master's of Social Work program and moved home. I spent a year picking up the pieces and encouraging her to eat, shower, and exercise for her mental health. I listened to my mom cry whenever she wasn't at work and cooked and cleaned while everyone grieved. I let my dad theorize and philosophize, as if mourning was an equation he could figure out if he thought hard enough. I tried to involve my brother and he punted it all back to me anytime I took so much as a weekend away to see my friends. All year, I begged them to go to therapy. And all year, they said, "Why would we go to therapy when we have you?"

When I announced I was going back to Chicago, my family protested. Bri had to convince them that she was okay. She went

BABY LLAMA DRAMA

back to work and school and insisted they could all move forward together.

They, not we. Because in all that time, *I* never got to grieve.

Loving someone has opened me up to so much pain and risk. *Anything* could happen. An accident, a diagnosis, abandonment, anything. How could Bri let herself fall in love and get married and get pregnant knowing full well how it could all end?

How have I?

Duke's accusation plays on repeat in my head. I didn't think about them. I only thought about myself.

Ha! As if I'm ever able to think about myself! Does he really think I wanted to jump on the first plane out of Columbia to watch my sister in a hospital bed while I act as the family life preserver? We should be planning our life together and instead, I'm hopping in a time machine to relive the worst experience of my life.

The flight and car ride to the hospital are a blur. My friends text me, and I try to update them, but my head gets foggier the longer I go without sleep. I call Reese on the drive, though, and talk to Lottie. She cries but puts on a braver face than I could have dreamed. She tells me how she understands that I need to help my sister but that she knows I love her and will see her soon.

I will, won't I? How do Duke and I get past a fight like that?

In the hospital, Mom runs to me. Her once red hair has faded to a light strawberry blonde, well on its way to going white. She's bundled in a sweater and scarf like the rest of us, but I feel how bony she is through her coat. She always says she has too much to do to remember to eat. Yet another thing I'll be responsible for while I'm here. She cries in my ear. "How could you take so long? I needed you!"

My dad hugs me next. "We've been waiting for you to come."

"Glad you could finally make it," Jason says.

Greg just cries.

Acid gurgles in my chest. Do they think I personally sabotaged the electrical equipment, or something? "I took the first flight out. What else could I have done?" I ask. I'm never this bold with them, and they're all taken aback.

"Whoa, no need to get upset," Mom says. "You have no idea how hard this has been for us. We're just relieved you're here."

Relieved. Not grateful. Not happy. Relieved.

And *I* have no idea how hard this has been? Do they forget that I'm part of the family? That it's my sister in the hospital bed? As out of line as Duke was last night, he's not totally wrong. My family over-uses me for emotional support. When Greg called me, he was on the verge of a panic attack. I talked him through it, but then he handed the phone to my mom, who was in hysterics herself. My dad kept saying in the background, "Millie will know what to do. Listen to Millie."

Did he even try to help her himself? He was settled enough when I talked to him after Mom. When I asked him how he was, he said he was fine but that they needed me there. They *all* said that.

Sometimes it feels like my family needs me more than they want me around. I don't get invited home for Christmas, I get coaxed home for a crisis.

That is so unfair of me. So calloused and unfair. My sister is going through something huge and scary. I'm devastated about it. I want to be here to support her.

But who supports me?

Mom pulls me to the seating area and tells me all about how she only slept five hours last night and how she hasn't eaten all day. Dad says, "I couldn't get her to eat a thing," and points to her, as if to say, *she's your problem now.*

I convince Dad to take Mom home to rest and instruct them to grab a sandwich on the way. They dutifully agree. "But no chips," I say. "Get a salad with it. If you haven't eaten all day, you don't want all that gunk messing with your system."

Mom clasps her hands and nods. "Thank you, sweetie. I don't know how we could do this without you."

Next it's Greg's turn. I adore Greg. I really do. But he has the emotional resilience of a Chihuahua. He comes from money and works for his parents—and from what I can tell, he didn't have to work too hard to get to where he is. Some wealthy families expect a lot of their kids while others pamper them to the point of uselessness. Greg is the world's biggest sweetheart, but his parents coddled him whenever things got hard. His mom joked about it at the wedding, how her goal in life was to never let her baby boy cry.

Pro tip: NEVER DO THAT.

What a shocker that he doesn't know how to deal with heavy emotions.

Greg verbally vomits all his fears and worries on me. He's scared for Bri, scared for the baby. Obviously. But it turns back to him more than to Bri. How will he handle losing the baby? How will he handle Bri being hurt? How is he supposed to act with her? It's not that he doesn't have compassion for her, but he doesn't have the perspective to look outside himself. He doesn't know how to compartmentalize or put someone else's needs ahead of his own. I don't know Bri's diagnosis, but the prospects must be brutal for how everyone is acting. But as bad as all of this is for him, it's worse for her.

"You're a good husband going through something hard," I tell him. "Why don't you take a step back and think about what this all means for Bri right now?"

"Great idea. Yes. Great." He says, nodding. "How do I do that?"

Give me strength.

I talk slowly. "Don't hover so much, and don't try to fill the silence. Just sit with her. Sit with the pain. Tell her you love her and that you'll get through this together, no matter what. And then let *her* talk. Don't interrupt, don't try to solve her problems. Just listen and love her."

"Love her?"

"Yes. Listen and show her how much you love her."

"Okay." He pauses, doing what looks like mental math. "But love like ... *love* love?" he asks with raised brows.

I stare at him. Is this real? Is this my life? "Do you think I mean sex, Greg?"

"No?"

"No. I do not. I don't know exactly what's going on, but if she's bleeding, I'm pretty sure sex wouldn't help. At all."

"Right. Good. Because I can't tell you how hard that would be. Well, not *hard* hard, because let me tell you, that's never a problem. But emotionally—"

I want to smack him upside the head, but I settle instead on a look that screams *you're an idiot*. But with affection. "Greg?"

"Yeah?"

"Stop it."

"Got it. Okay. This is good stuff. Keep going."

"GREG."

"Yes?"

"Do you understand what we're talking about?"

"Loving Bri?"

"If by 'loving Bri,' you mean, 'supporting Bri in a loving manner,' then yes. Do you know how to do that?"

He looks away, his eyes darting around as if he's trying to think. "Sit with her and tell her I love her and that we'll get through this, and then ... "

"And then you shut your mouth and listen. Listen for as long as it takes. Can you do that?"

He exhales noisily. "Yeah. I can. Thanks, Millie. I don't know how I'd get through this without you."

I've heard that one before.

CHAPTER THIRTY

DUKE

After a brutal day of practice, I come home to screaming. I follow the sound to the movie room, where Reese looks like she's at her wit's end and Lottie is five stops past tantrum town. I know she talked to Millie earlier, because Reese texted me to say how well Lottie handled it. But she's not handling it anymore.

Unless this is about ice cream. Man, my girl can cry about ice cream.

"Rough day?" I ask Reese.

"No, actually. She was totally fine until the internet cut out about ten minutes ago. I reset it and told her we needed to wait for it to come back on, and ... " she points down to my explosive angel.

I tell Reese to take the rest of the night off, and she leaves without argument. I feel lost watching Lottie. It's like she's the embodiment of my inner turmoil. She's experienced so much in the few short years of her life, and I don't know how anyone could expect her to handle it differently. The thought of her suffering without knowing how to express it makes my eyes well.

My back is feeling a bit better, but my normal urge to bring her to my level evaporates. Instead of picking her up, I drop to the floor beside her and run my hands through her hair.

I've been afraid for a while now how badly I'm botching things up for my little girl. What if I mess up so badly that no amount of therapy can help Lottie recover from my mistakes? How will I live with myself when all I want is for her to be happy? When I love her so much, it's physically painful to see her in pain?

I wish Millie were here.

Not because she would magically fix everything, but because the force of her love is so powerful. It's changed me. It's changed both of us.

"You are amazing, Lottie," I whisper, smoothing her hair over and over again. "You've been through so much pain, and you've handled it so much better than I have."

She rolls over and puts her head in my lap and continues crying. I keep running my hands over her hair. "I'm here, pumpkin. I'm here and you're safe." After another minute, her cries start to slow and calm until she starts to sit up. I pull her into my lap, facing me, and her little arms curl around my neck. She sighs against my chest.

"I miss Millie," she says softly.

"I do, too."

"Did the monster take her?"

"Pumpkin, a monster never took Momma Carlie, remember? She couldn't be the mom you deserved, so she left to let us find that momma."

"But I thought Momma Millie was 'posed to be my Momma, and now she's gone."

Seated, I sway back and forth like I used to when she was a baby. "Tell me where Momma Millie is. Do you know?"

"Her sister is sick. Momma Millie's helping."

"That's right. Good job listening," I say. "Is she coming back?"

"She said so, but she didn't come home today."

"I know, pumpkin. She said she'll be home in five sleeps. Remember?"

Lottie nods against me.

"She got mad. You got mad."

The tension in my shoulders releases, and I almost slump realizing I never talked to Lottie about last night. "Did we scare you when we were mad?" She nods again. "We should never have gotten mad, especially not in front of you, Lottie. I'm sorry we scared you."

"Don't get mad at her, Daddy. I love her!"

"I love her, too."

"But you made her cry!"

Ouch.

"I messed up. Will you forgive me?"

"Okay," she says easily.

"Do you think Millie will?"

"Yes. She loves you. But I love her most."

I lean back so we can look in each other's eyes. "Hey. What about me?" I say in a fake grumpy voice. A smile quirks her lips. "What about Daddy?" I poke her side, and she flinches and giggles. "You love Daddy, right?" I pinch her knee, and she giggles harder. "Right?" I tickle her sides and soon I'm chasing her around the theater, pretending to fall and being unable to catch her. She creeps up to me when I'm on the ground.

"Can't catch me!" she taunts. I shoot an arm out to grab her, earning another peal of laughter that makes my proverbial cup run over. I blow raspberries on her belly, and she squeals, "I love you, Daddy! I love you!" and I pull her into a bear hug.

"I love you, too."

The rest of the night is as good a night as I can remember with her. She helps me make dinner. We have a dance party, do bath tub karaoke, and read books. She holds her two new dolls close and falls asleep in her bed while I'm reading to her. Instead of creeping away instantly, I sit on the bed beside her and gaze at the perfect little girl who has my whole heart.

It isn't until I'm upstairs cleaning up from dinner that I realize how quickly her tantrum subsided. I realize, too, that I handled things totally differently than normal. I didn't lose it. I didn't bargain or plead or beg. I didn't threaten or cajole. I simply sat with her and let her feel until she was ready to talk. I wasn't filled with despair seeing her tantrum, I was filled with compassion.

The fog from my migraine seems to clear, and it's like a shaft of sunlight hits me.

Maybe Lottie doesn't need me to solve her problems. Maybe she needs me to see that she actually *has* problems. Maybe she needs to know I accept and love her, no matter how she behaves.

Maybe she needs to know that her outbursts could never, ever drive me away.

Tears spring to my eyes at the thought.

I want to run downstairs and hug her and reassure her that nothing she could do will ever drive me away, but waking her up would be selfish. Instead, I vow to myself that I'll tell her during every tantrum from now on.

You're safe. Your feelings don't scare me. I'm right here, I think, practicing the words in my head.

Just like I did all those weeks ago, I have an uncontrollable urge to call Millie. Why did we have to get into that stupid fight last night? Why couldn't I have been supportive and understanding? I already sent a handful of apologies, but there's been nothing but radio silence on her end.

I screwed up. I fought with her. I *hurt* her. *In front of Lottie.*

As I beat myself up, another thought nags at me.

Why didn't she think about us?

I don't know if that's fair or not of me to think. She didn't actually do anything wrong, but it hurt all the same. We were abandoned by a wife and mother. Should I be concerned that she didn't even think about all we've been through or am I the one being selfish? Her sister could be miscarrying, after all, but her family is also manipulative. I *know* they are. Does she not see it?

I get why she wanted to go. Of course I do. But why didn't she think to tell me? Why couldn't she have taken two minutes to include me? To think about how we could tell Lottie together? Is it a product of the newness of our relationship? The fact that, even though it feels like we're on a path to forever, it's barely been a month since we met?

Or is it possible she's not as committed as we are?

I'm nauseated considering the idea, but I can't dismiss it. If that's the case, I hope she'll tell me before we get in any deeper.

Assuming we can get any deeper at all.

CHAPTER THIRTY-ONE

MILLIE

"Do you need to get that?" Bri asks from her hospital bed later that night. Her auburn hair is a bit more brown than red, and she has fewer freckles than I have, but we otherwise look alike. Except that she's always been stick thin and flat as a board, where I'm more athletic. She's even paler than normal, though, and in the hospital bed, she looks so delicate and frail. Almost like Sophie did...

I put my phone in my back pocket. "It's nothing," I say with a cheery façade I won't let her see behind. "I'll call him in a bit."

"You two and your fairytale life," she says. I don't laugh in her face, though I want to.

"It's definitely been like a dream." One that veered into nightmare territory with our fight.

Nurses come in every twenty minutes, checking on tubes and screens, and no one tells us anything. I'm worn down from not sleeping a wink last night on the tails of my recent all-nighter. The room spins around me every time I move. Come to think of it, I missed dinner last night and haven't eaten at all today. It's been almost twenty-eight hours. I do intermittent fasting often enough that I don't feel sick, but I also typically drink electrolytes in my water throughout the day. I don't even know if I've had anything but Diet Coke today. As much as I love the stuff, it doesn't replace water.

Bri is asking me something, but I have no idea what. "Sorry, I spaced out. What?"

She rolls her eyes affectionately. "Are you missing your insta-family?" Bri has the rare ability to not covet what other people have. As she's suffering in a hospital, she can be happy for someone else. I love that about her.

"Oh, something like that," I say dismissively.

"What does that mean?" She adjusts herself in her bed. "Is everything okay?"

"Of course."

"Millie."

"It's nothing."

"Mills. Spill it."

"Breezy, it's nothing."

"You know you can tell me, right?"

"You're in a hospital bed."

"So? Are my ears broken?"

Does she really want to hear this? I've never confided in Bri like she has in me. Bearing people's burdens is *my* role. But the expectant way she looks at me makes me wonder if I *could* tell her. At least a little.

"We had a fight last night. That's it."

"Whoa. *You* had a fight?" Bri looks like this is the best news she's had all day.

"A small one." Times a hundred.

She must read the lie on my face, because her excitement only increases. "Oh my gosh, it was huge, wasn't it? You guys *fought* fought. Don't you see how great this is?"

"Great? You obviously weren't there. There was nothing *great* about it."

"I'm not talking about whatever stupid thing you both said and wish you could take back. I'm talking about the fact that you fought. Millie Jane Campbell, the girl who always monitors her emotions and never fights with anyone."

Little lights are forming in my vision, so I sit down in a chair across from her bed. "Whatever. We all fought constantly in high school."

"Over chores and hair brushes. Not about real stuff. You don't fight with anyone. Ever. You play the magic therapist card and stay cool, and it drives the rest of us crazy."

"What do you mean?" I'm racking my brain for an example that will let me prove her wrong, but nothing's coming. Not with an ex, not with my parents, not even with my crappy freshman roommate who used all of my eczema lotion without telling me and left me to figure it out during a flare up.

"You must love him a lot to confront him about something, that's all."

I frown. "I do love him a lot, but this was a nasty fight, Bri. We didn't end it in a good place."

"Why is he angry?"

I can't tell her the whole story. She would feel too guilty. "I bought my plane ticket without telling him. Can you believe that? How dare he get upset about me flying out without his approval like I'm his property, or something."

Bri tilts her head, wincing. "I'm sorry."

"Thanks. I'm still mad about it," I say. Bri bites the side of her lip, as if she's debating saying more. "What?"

"I appreciate that you bought your plane ticket without hesitating, and I get what you're saying, but you can see his point, too, right?"

His point?

"No. I'm not some doting housewife who has to have dinner

on the table promptly at 5:30 p.m. to ensure his happiness. I work. I have my own career and my own life."

"Yeah, and so does he. Does he not run things by you?"

"Sure, but it's not like this kind of thing has come up before."

The more she talks, the more color comes back to her cheeks. "Not for you, it hasn't. But for him?"

I roll my lips together. She has a point. Duke was married. He was probably used to running decisions by Carlie and Carlie running decisions by him. "That doesn't mean I was wrong," I say weakly.

"It isn't about right or wrong. You weren't *wrong* for making a decision to fly out and he wasn't *wrong* for wanting you to coordinate with him. It's about the kind of relationship you want to have. Obviously Duke wants a relationship where his partner seeks his input. Do you?" Her question is so astute that I'm annoyed I didn't consider it. "And can I say one more thing without you hating me?"

I glare at her. "I'm not sure."

"Carlie left without telling them. Isn't it understandable that he'd be sensitive to you doing the same."

My mouth goes dry. How did I miss something so obvious? "When did you become the paragon of emotional intelligence?"

"When my little sister became a therapist. I realized it was time for me to focus on healing."

Time slows. "Have you been going to therapy?"

"Not exactly. I joined a grief support group a while ago." The set of her jaw shows me that she's proud of her decision. So am I. I marvel at my sister. I'm getting progressively more light-headed, but I grip the handles of my chair to hold myself in place.

"Wow, Bri. That's a huge step. Good for you."

"That's where I met Greg, actually." My eyes pop. "We never told you guys, because he doesn't like talking about it. His older brother died when he was in high school. His parents never let them experience difficulty, and between you and me, I don't think he knows how to handle emotions very well."

"You don't say," I quip, and then the room spins.

"Millie! Are you okay?"

I grab the arm of my chair. "Yeah, just hungry. I forgot to eat."

"Go, now. Go downstairs and eat something. Don't stop for Mom or Dad or Greg. Don't let Jason bully you. Don't come back until you feel better. Promise?"

I nod. She air-kisses me, and I walk out of the room and toward the elevator where I spot Greg, who's on his phone in the lounge. He tries to get my attention, but because he doesn't stop talking to the person on the other end of the call, I walk past him with just a wave.

Jason is reading Nietzsche a few seats away. Because of course he's reading Nietzsche while his sister is in the hospital. He catches my eye and looks meaningfully at Greg. The subtext couldn't be clearer: are you gonna do something about this?

I ignore him. I feel dizzy on the elevator and the whole way to the cafeteria. In line, I order two pork chops, a large chicken Caesar salad and two waters. I dump salt into the first bottle of water to replenish my electrolytes, and then I drain the bottle before devouring most of the food at my corner table. I'm glad it's empty in here, because I'm sure I look like I'm training for a food eating competition.

When I'm finished eating, my head no longer feels like it's on a swivel. I open the second bottle of water and sip it while I look through Duke's texts. I haven't read a single one yet, stewing instead in my hurt and anger.

I have seventeen missed texts and three missed calls, complete with actual voicemails.

He sent so many apologies. So many expressions of concern for Bri. So many requests for updates. He thanks me for talking to Lottie and tells me that they both understand why I had to go help my sister. They love me. They can't wait for me to come home, but they'll wait as long as I need.

Nowhere does he excuse himself or accuse me of anything. His apology is as good as they come.

So why am I still hesitating? Why are the embers of my anger still smoking? Why am I reading the transcripts of his voicemails rather than listening to his lightly accented voice?

The slick feeling in my throat that I can't swallow down tells me exactly why:

Guilt.

Bri nailed it when she talked about Carlie. I'm embarrassed at how oblivious I was that leaving out of nowhere would be painful for Duke and Lottie. She was spot on when she asked me what kind of relationship I want with Duke. He makes me part of every decision, whereas I didn't consider him or Lottie when I told my family that I'd fly out immediately. And I told them right in front of Lottie, without even talking to her or preparing her first.

I've spent so much time being my family's therapist—even before I got my license—that I didn't even stop and ask what was actually going on with Bri. I launched right into that familiar role without question, without a quick conversation to determine how to balance the needs of the people I love. *All* the people I love.

They were abandoned! Lottie just found out about her mom and then I vanished the next day! Duke was in obvious pain last night to the point that he made Bri look like the picture of health. He was ashen, and his eyes were so pinched that the lights must have been agonizing him. And what did he do that was so cruel? Point out the obvious? He was tactless, and I'm still fired up that he would ever talk like that in front of Lottie … but I did, too. I could have stopped us at any point, and I didn't.

I open up my phone and look at pictures of us. One of him

and Lottie and Louis the llama at the farm. One of us sharing a turkey leg. Workout selfies that we're both too private to post but that we take, all the same. Kissing selfies that we're also too private to post but that we take, all the same. Pictures with me and Lottie snuggling and watching a movie, laughing, cooking.

I ache with longing. Missing them feels like a gaping wound in my chest. Am I going to let our relationship end because I'm too afraid to face tough emotions? Am I going to just walk away because I'm ashamed of how thoughtless I was?

No. I promised Jane and myself that I wouldn't let a miscommunication become a plot device in my relationship. I have to make good on that promise, no matter how it ends.

I FaceTime Duke.

CHAPTER THIRTY-TWO

MILLIE

He picks up on the first ring.

"I was hoping you'd have time to call," he says. Happiness and concern war endearingly on his face. His exhausted face. I noticed it last night, but it's even worse now. The shadows under his eyes look like dark bruises.

"You look awful!" I blurt. "I mean ... are you feeling okay?"

He laughs darkly. "Not quite the first thing I was hoping to hear you say, but I am so glad to see you, I'll take it." Am I hearing things, or does his accent come out more when he's tired?

"You didn't answer my question. Are you okay?"

"It's a migraine. It's nothing."

"A migraine is not nothing. You need rest."

"Rest isn't in the cards. I'll power through." He shrugs, and this only incenses me.

"There are some things you can't power through, Duke! How

are you supposed to recover? How are you supposed to even perform when you're in so much pain?"

"The same way I always have. This isn't the first time I've felt sick during the season. The team doctor will assess me, as he always does. If he doesn't think I can perform, then I'll sit out."

"Like your team doctor will make a decision that isn't in the best interest of the team."

Duke looks like he's rearing up for a fight, but instead, he pauses. His eyes rove over my face, and that makes me look at my image instead of his.

"How's Bri?"

A sob escapes me. "Terrible. Apparently she has an … incompetent cervix?"

He hisses. "That's hard. I'm sorry."

"It is," I agree, my chin quivering. "The hospital gave Greg a pamphlet about it, but I haven't had the heart to even look up the symptoms, because I know if I do, I'll start panicking, and I can't be the rock they all need me to be. But I don't know how I can just sit here and watch my sister have a miscarriage after everything—" I cover my face with a hand and fight back tears. "I don't know how to do this, Duke. I'm so scared."

"Tell me about it."

"You don't want to hear about it," I protest weakly.

"I do, Millie. Tell me."

I start slowly, in control of the narrative. But soon, his understanding opens me up, and my emotions rush out in a stream of consciousness, along with feelings and thoughts I've never said aloud. I tell him about coming home every summer to help with my niece and about delaying my master's to help everyone mourn. I tell him how my dad and brother have always deferred responsibility to me. I tell him how Greg and my mom and even sometimes Bri call me with every little bump and bruise, emotionally or physically, and how I'm drained from bearing all of their fears and burdens and how sometimes, I wish I could just stop taking their calls altogether.

Duke just listens. I know it's theoretically possible for a guy to listen without trying to fix everything, but I've never experienced it.

It's epic.

Half of the things I say seem to come out of nowhere, but as I express my fears over what's going to happen to Bri and her baby, my grief over losing Sophie comes into full effect. And talking about Sophie, about the last time we cuddled on a couch watching a movie together, about her symptoms coming on hard and fast and us rushing her to the hospital, makes me realize the real reason I'm so upset with Duke.

I'm terrified I'm going to lose him, too.

There's another reason I haven't researched Bri's condition. Because I know if I do, nothing will be able to keep me from also looking up Hodgkin's Lymphoma. Nothing will be able to keep me from reading into every single symptom Duke has. Nothing will help me sleep at night knowing that he could be taken from me at any minute. Not just him, but Lottie, too.

I'm the happiest I've ever been, and I know that it can all be taken from me in an instant.

When I admit this to Duke, I'm crying angry tears. "And now I have another person I have to worry about who doesn't care about his own health, and I don't know how I—"

"What?" he snaps. "Are you talking about *me?*" There's no mistaking the offense etched into the faint lines of his squinting eyes. "I don't need *anyone* worrying about that. You've lived with me. You've seen how seriously I take my health. I eat clean. I work out. Apart from this last week, I observe the strictest possible curfew. I do multiple therapies for longevity and healing, including a friggin' *ice barrel*. I see my oncologist like clockwork, take blood tests throughout the year, and have a doctor observing me weekly. And you don't think I care? I'm a single dad. *I have a daughter to take care of.* Listen, I love you, and I can't tell you not to worry, but don't you dare accuse me of being cavalier about my health."

The muscles in his jaw clench, accentuating his dimpled chin and his flawless bone structure. His chest heaves with barely restrained anger. His eyes glint like metal in the low light of his bedroom at home.

He is stunning.

"You're right."

"I know I'm right," he says, still fuming. "Millie Jane, I want you as badly as I've ever wanted anyone or anything in my life. But I don't need you. Not for a babysitter, not for a therapist, and certainly not for a doctor. I want a partner or nothing at all."

He's so angry that I imagine he wanted his words to sting like a jellyfish.

They don't.

They are a balm on my wounded soul. They are a salve, healing a thousand cuts I've protected others from seeing over the years. They are the feeling of an immense, unseen load finally being lifted from my shoulders.

They are relief.

Pure and simple.

"I love you," I sob.

His eyes widen. "Uh, yeah, good. I love you, too. You fight weird."

My laugh is snotty and disgusting. I have to wipe my face with a napkin, and this only makes me laugh harder. "We fight weird," I correct him.

He chuckles wryly, his lips curved into a puzzled half smile. "I guess so."

"I shouldn't have ordered my ticket without running it by you. I didn't think about how that would feel to you and Lottie after everything you've been through. I'm sorry. I want you to be part of my decisions, big and small. Duke, I want to take care of you and Lottie, and I want you to take care of Lottie and me, too. But I want it to be mutual, give and take. I can't have one more relationship in my life where someone drains me dry."

"Is that what it feels like I've done?" He doesn't sound accusatory but genuinely concerned, and I love him even more for that.

"No," I say immediately. Honestly. "Not since that first week. You're the only person I've ever felt safe to break down in front of, because I know you can handle it. And I know you love me enough to help me pick up the pieces."

He drops his voice and raises his eyebrows suggestively. "Girl, I'll pick up your pieces anytime." I laugh. "It hurt when I thought you didn't care enough about us to talk to me about it first," he says. "But I'm sorry for not understanding your fear and for not approaching it better, especially with an audience."

"I get it now. I'm sorry for not getting it then. I promise to put you two first everyday for the rest of my life. If you still want—"

"I do. I still want you, Millie. I want you more than ever, and I want you *forever*. And next time one of us has something worth fighting over, we wait until Lottie's in bed."

"Agreed. But are you already planning our next fight?" I tease.

"No, just fast forwarding to when we can make up." His words ignite a fire low in my belly. I miss him to my soul. "Can I revisit Bri's situation for a minute?" he asks. "Have you heard from the doctor directly about what's going on?"

"No, only what Greg and my mom have said. She has an 'incompetent cervix' and they're just waiting for her to miscarry."

His brow furrows. "You remember how I told you that Carlie spotted? She had an incompetent cervix. She took a progesterone shot every week and was on bed rest for a few weeks after the bleeding. She took it easy throughout her pregnancy, but she gave birth to Lottie at thirty-nine weeks. Maybe Bri's condition is a lot more serious than Carlie's was, but her doctor said miscarriage is the exception, not the rule. I think you'll feel better if you hear from the doctor directly."

Hope flickers to life inside me. "That's a really good idea. Thanks."

His smile is small. "You are the most beautiful thing I've ever seen. I miss you."

It's a mystery how he can say it like he means it, even when I have yesterday's mascara, bags under my eyes, and dry shampoo frosting my hair like a cake. But I believe him. "I miss you both so badly."

"I wish we were married already so I could call this a family emergency and be there for you."

"Name the time and place," I say. And I mean it.

"Soon," he promises. "I love you."

He's said it dozens of times, but hearing him say it first after such an emotional few days is like getting a cast off and seeing my injury fully healed. "I love you, too"

CHAPTER THIRTY-THREE

MILLIE

*B*ri insisted that I go home and sleep last night around eleven p.m. I argued that I came to help, but she was adamant that she and Greg could manage. Surprisingly, I believed her, so I took a car home. Mom almost had a heart attack when I showed up.

"What are you doing? Who's going to watch after Bri if you're here?" she fussed before swatting my dad's leg and asking him to talk some sense into me. Dad gave me a tired look before going back to his phone. "What did you even come home for if not to help?"

Her words were a slap to my face.

"Jason is still there."

"Oh, Jason doesn't know how to help. You should have stayed. I only came home because I thought you were taking care of her."

"She's married, Mom. What help would I be while she

sleeps? Greg's in the extra bed. Or did you want me to sit and watch and micromanage the nurses?"

"Don't talk to your mother like that," Dad said, not looking up from his phone. Knowing him, he was probably getting into an argument with someone on Facebook about the most effective method to de-ice winter roads.

"I have a headache. I'm going to bed." I told them and walked upstairs to my room without waiting for more argument.

The ride to the hospital this morning has been exactly what I expected: Dad listening to NPR while Mom tells us to brace ourselves because the worst has probably already happened. Her doom and gloom mentality is so pervasive that it seems to draw storm clouds to us. Like attracts like.

I chide myself mentally, reminding myself that Mom has suffered, too. That she mourned Sophie's loss and that she was already a supremely anxious woman before that. Fear has ruled her my whole life, but she refuses to get help. When I've asked my dad to intercede, he's reminded me that that's what I'm for, as if it's a compliment instead of another boulder in my emotional backpack.

At the hospital, I tell my parents I'm going to the cafeteria and will meet them upstairs in Bri's room. Mom pauses. "Are you okay?" She asks this like she's remembering my health scare from a few years ago. It's nice thinking of her caring, but I don't want her to worry, especially because I'm fine.

"Fit as a fiddle, Mom. My symptoms are totally in check when I eat well."

"Good for you, sweetie. If only that diet could fix every problem so easily."

If only.

I eat my bacon on the way up, holding Bri's platter in my other hand. When I finish, I feel my phone vibrate against my butt and pull it out to see a text from Duke. It's a picture of him and Lottie around the kitchen island eating breakfast, telling me they love me.

I send a picture of myself blowing them kisses and tell them how much I love them. It's not enough, though. Being here without them is like being here without a vital organ. The pain of missing them is visceral. A gnawing, twisting, stabbing pain, like an ovarian torsion … but a torsion of my heart.

I paste on a smile and walk into the hospital room with Bri's food and a deck of Uno cards. Both are greeted with cheers from Bri, who looks better after even the crappy night's sleep that a hospital provides.

Bri's doctor, Doctor Yee, shows up only twenty minutes later. Greg, Bri, Jason, and I are playing Uno while Mom paces and Dad is on his phone playing Wordle.

"Hail, hail, the gang's all here," Dr. Yee says brightly when she sees us all. "Bri, do you want everyone to leave, or … "

"Whatever they want," she says. Dad and Jason excuse themselves, while Greg reaches for the cards. In his haste, he knocks them, and they go flying off the bed, scattering all over the floor. He apologizes and drops to his knees to pick up the cards.

I drop down beside him and whisper. "I got this, Greg. Sit with your wife and listen to Dr. Yee."

"You'll stay, right?"

I'm nervous enough to want to run, but Duke is right. I have to talk to the doctor. I have to hear her say what's really going on.

"I'll stay," I whisper.

He nods and thanks me, his eyes wide and his breathing ramping up like he's racing Usain Bolt. I pick up the cards quickly and then wash my hands for a full thirty seconds, because touching a hospital floor has a way of making my whole body feel like it's crawling with germs. Also, I have to prep myself to be the rock my family needs.

You can do it, I tell myself. *They need you. You can do it.*

Dr. Yee is in the middle of her ultrasound of Bri's cervix, but she's not explaining what she's seeing. She's talking about, of all things, the weather. There's a big storm coming down from Canada that's expected to hit in the next day or two.

Greg holds Bri's hand, but it's more like he's wringing it. I expect his anxiety to send Bri's nerves through the roof, but if it bugs her at all, she has an unreadable poker face. Mom chews her fingernails like a mouse eating cheese.

"How's everything looking?" Bri asks.

"Good. Your little peanut is holding on strong, and your cervix is, too."

The seed of hope Duke planted in me last night starts growing roots. They're both holding strong? How strong? What does that mean?

"For now," Mom says, rubbing Bri's shoulder.

Dr. Yee's brow wrinkles. "Well, yes, for now. And if we do things right, for the next thirty weeks."

Does this mean what I think it means?

"But you're saying there's a chance it won't. We need to prepare ourselves for the worst," Mom says almost firmly.

Dr. Yee puts her ultrasound wand away. "Well, miscarriage is rare, especially with us catching it so early. But—"

"Exactly," Mom says almost triumphantly.

Dr. Yee seems so unfazed, so casual I'm almost shocked. Isn't this an enormous deal? I look at Bri, who is wilting. She was able to stay strong while Greg squeezed the life from her hand, but Mom's pessimism seems beyond what she can bear.

"You said her cervix will hold strong if we do things right. What does 'right' entail?" I ask.

Dr. Yee throws her gloves into the trash and crosses to the sink. "Progesterone shots, weekly monitoring through the second trimester. We can do a cerclage where we sew the cervix shut until thirty-seven weeks, if we need to. She'll want to take it easy for the next few weeks, but the vast majority of women with this diagnosis deliver a healthy baby."

"But not all." Mom says.

"*Mom!*" Those aren't my words, but Greg's. "We need you to step out of the room. We'll invite you back in when Dr. Yee leaves."

Bri stares up at her husband with the same awe I feel. Go Greg!

Mom's jaw drops. "Greg, sweetie, I'm just trying to be practical."

"But you're not being practical. You're being alarmist." He looks at Dr. Yee. "Do you see any reason now to think Bri will be the exception?"

"No. We caught it early and will monitor her, but I'm confident in the treatment and in your ability to help Bri not overdo it." She smiles warmly.

"But—"

I grab Mom's arm. "Thank you, Dr. Yee. This is wonderful news!" I say as I pull Mom out.

In the hallway, Mom spins on her heels. Her face is puce, and she looks like she could spit fire. "How dare that woman give them false hope! And you, just congratulating them like it's all going to be fine! We need to prepare ourselves for what's to come, not fill Bri's poor head with this wishful thinking! That's what got us into trouble with Sophie!"

She yells this last part, and I glance at Dad, who's sitting in a chair only a few feet away. He looks up cautiously and then puts his head back in his phone. But his ears are red. He's upset or embarrassed, maybe. But he's not doing anything. Not a single thing.

I pull Mom's arm over to where Dad and Jason are sitting. "Come with us." Dad stands, and I pull Jason's ear phone off. "You too. Come, now."

I find a quiet corner in an equally quiet hallway and I spin on them. "This isn't working," I tell them. "I know you're mourning Sophie still. We *all* are. But living in constant anticipation of someone else dying isn't going to bring her back, and it's hurting us."

"I'm not hurting anyone," Mom bites back. "It's foolish to hope like that doctor's been saying."

Been saying?

BEEN SAYING?

"What do you mean? Are you saying this isn't the first time Dr. Yee told you that Bri and the baby would be okay?" Mom hems, Dad seems to shrink, and Jason grinds his foot into an imaginary spot on the floor. "When did the doctor say this?"

Mom doesn't answer.

Dad doesn't answer.

Jason doesn't answer.

Anger flares in my chest until my lungs are burning. "Did you know when you called me? Did you know that Bri's own doctor isn't actually concerned?" No one meets my eye. "You did! You convinced me that I was coming here to help Bri go through something unimaginable, and nothing is happening! You lied to get me to come!"

"We didn't lie! I told you that we're just waiting for her to miscarry, and we are. *I* am." Mom's voice breaks, but my normal well of empathy is bone dry.

"Dad? Jason? Anything you want to add?"

Jason shakes his head. "Oh, come on, Millie. She's been like this since we were kids. What do you want me to do about it?"

My mouth parts in shock.

Dad doubles down on Jason's unbelievably awful comment. "You know how dramatic she can be. She doesn't listen to me. You're the only one who can ever get through to her."

"It's not that she gets through to me," Mom snaps, "It's that *she listens*. Not that you'd know anything about that."

Dad closes his eyes long-sufferingly, but it's faker than a knockoff Gucci bag.

"Talk about being dramatic," I say. "You don't think it's dramatic to hide away from your problems, ignore your wife, leave your daughter and son-in-law spiraling, and expect your other daughter to carry the entire load while you catch up on your news and correct people on the internet?"

"That's not all I do!"

"That's how it feels," Mom says, tearing up.

"I tried caring!" Dad's voice quivers. "And look what it got me."

"Oh, come on, Dad," Jason says. "You may have cared, but you've never gotten involved."

"Like father, like son," Mom says.

"Take a valium, Mom."

"Don't talk to your mother like that."

"Oh, so *now* you listen?" Mom snaps.

"See why I want you around?" Jason asks me. "I don't need this crap."

"But I do. Right?" I ask.

"You know what I mean. You're better at handling this stuff than we are."

"I'm better at it because I *do* it, and not just for a living. You guys put me in this role when I was a *teenager*. I've never had another option."

Jason looks at my dad and rolls his eyes.

I want to say so many things, want to walk them through *all* of this baggage, but snow catches my eye through the window, and something Dr. Yee said makes my spine stiffen.

Suddenly, my desire to rip them all a new one burns away, falling to the ground like ashes.

"I love you guys too much to be your therapist, so I'm officially firing myself. Mom, you have profound anxiety. You need to see someone. Dad, your refusal to deal with your grief is unhealthy. Jason, I love you, but you suck. The three of you need to pull yourselves together and get some counseling, or something tells me Greg is going to prove a very faithful guard dog for Bri over the next thirty weeks. And for every week of that baby's life thereafter. I'll talk to you after your third appointment with your therapist, and not a minute earlier."

I give them all a hug and tell them I love them before striding off.

"Where are you going?" Mom cries.

"Home."

"Millie!" Dad calls.

"Don't be like that," Jason says.

But I don't stop. I rush into Bri's room. She and Greg are in the middle of an intense conversation, but Bri waves me in. I give her a hug. "What did Dr. Yee say after we left?"

"Nothing new. She fully expects Baby and me to be good."

"And do you believe her?"

Bri looks at Greg. "Yeah. We do. Right, Greg?"

Greg nods. "We do," he says firmly. "And if we forget, we will talk about it in group. Right Breezy?" he says to Bri.

"Right, Greggo."

"I'm glad to hear you say that. I love you guys, and you know you can call me anytime, but I think your grief group is the place for a lot of these conversations."

"And not you," Greg supplies.

"Maybe not," I agree.

Bri purses her lips. "I'm sorry, Mills. I should have believed Dr. Yee the first time. I shouldn't have let Mom talk me into believing the worst and should have stopped her from calling you."

"No, you shouldn't have. I wish I'd known more about your situation, but I would have come quickly, anyway."

"Thanks. I love you."

"You too, sis." I hug her again, feeling the muscles in her lean back for the first time. She's stronger than I give her credit for, physically and emotionally. "Now, I need to ask Greg a favor."

CHAPTER THIRTY-FOUR

MILLIE

I wheel my suitcase through the terminal at a breakneck pace, catching the eye of more than one security guard. There must be a ton of flights today, because I've never seen the airport so crowded. I'm lucky to have made it back to Columbia at all. There was one last seat on the noon flight, and I only made it in time because Greg agreed to drive me. If I'd had to wait even a few minutes for a driver to pick me up, I'd have missed it.

And now I'm here, finally, where I should have been all along. I run as quickly as the crowds will let me, and when I jostle into someone, a guard clears his throat.

"Watch it, miss," he says. Is it my imagination, or have I seen this guard before? Is he following me?

Never mind if he is. Guards have to walk around the airport, and it's not like I'm doing anything wrong. People run through airports all the time.

Including me. Because I cannot wait to get home and see Duke and Lottie.

Speaking of Lottie, I hear a little voice that sounds so much like hers, a fist seems to squeeze my heart. I can't believe how much I miss her after only a couple of days. Longing sweeps over me.

Then I hear the voice again, louder. And louder and clearer still.

"MOMMA MILLIE!"

"Lottie?" The voice that calls my name is the most beautiful voice I've ever heard. I whip around in the terminal to see two chestnut pigtails two feet above the rest of the crowd. And below those pigtails is the elated face of the most gorgeous man I've ever seen. Tears come unbidden as I fly through the crowds, sprinting at top speed. "Duke!" I cry. I drop my luggage at some point because it's slowing me down, but I can't seem to care about that as I run toward the loves of my life. Toward my family.

Duke sets Lottie down and they open their arms.

I anticipate the feeling of being enveloped in their embrace.

And that's when I get tackled from the side.

And yelled at.

And handcuffed.

By security.

TSA INTERVIEW TRANSCRIPT
SECURITY AGENT BEAU BROWN
MILLIE J. CAMPBELL DETAINED ON SUSPICION

Security Agent Beau Brown: Tell me about your plan here.

Detainee: What plan? What do you mean?

Agent Brown: We saw you running through the airport after you dropped your bag.

Detainee: Is that what this is about? Oh, good.

Agent Brown: 'Good?' How is leaving a bag and yelling 'Duck!' good?

Detainee: I wasn't yelling 'duck,' I was yelling Duke. Duke Ogden?

Agent Brown: So Duke Ogden was your target? The football player?

Detainee: He wasn't my target, I was running for him.

Agent Brown: So you dropped your bomb—

Detainee: BOMB? Who said anything about a bomb?

Agent Brown: Isn't that why you dropped your bag?

Detainee: No, I dropped my bag by accident. I was just running to see my family.

Agent Brown: But you wanted to attack Duke Ogden first. Is that why you flew from, where is it?

Detainee: Columbus. And no, I didn't come to attack him! This is all a big misunderstanding. I flew home early to be with my family and they weren't supposed to be here.

Agent Brown: But you flew "home" to be with them.

Detainee: Yes, but not *here* home, home home.

Agent Brown: I don't understand.

Detainee: I know this sounds crazy. I went for a family emergency but then I found out it wasn't as much an emergency as an inability to handle hard things, so I left my family to deal with their crap and flew home to be with my family—

Agent Brown: You left your family to be with your family?

Detainee: My parents and brother and my sister and her goofy but well-meaning husband, yes.

Agent Brown: Which family are they? The family you left or the family you flew home to?

Detainee: The ones I left.

Agent Brown: And who did you fly home to?

Detainee: To Duke. My fian—boyfriend and his daughter.

Agent Brown: You don't know if Duke Ogden is your fiancé or your boyfriend? And whose daughter are you talking about?

Detainee: Duke's. He's my boyfriend but we're talking marriage. And she's legally his daughter, but I love her like she's mine, because she will be.

Agent Brown: Are you saying you're planning to kidnap Duke Ogden's daughter?

Detainee: NO! *hits head against desk* Can I call my Attorney?

Detainee given a glass of water and allowed a bathroom break.

Attorney Lucy Jane Williams arrived at 19:04

Interview Commenced at 19:15

Agent Brown: You're Ms. Campbell's Attorney?

Attorney: Yes, I'm Lucy Williams, Ms. Campbell's attorney. What is she being held for?

Agent Brown: Suspicious behavior. Your voice sounds familiar—"

Attorney: We don't know each other. What exactly did she do that was suspicious?

Agent Brown: She dropped her bag and yelled 'duck' in an airport.

Detainee: I was saying *Duke*.

Attorney: Have you examined the bag?

Agent Brown: Yes.

Attorney: Was there anything suspicious in it?

Agent Brown: No.

Attorney: Then why hasn't she been released?

Agent Brown: We have reason to believe that she was planning to harm someone.

Attorney: Who?

Agent Brown: Duke Ogden.

Attorney: Do you? Can I see the video?

Note that Agent Brown and Attorney reviewed video.

Attorney: What potential harm do you see here?

Agent Brown: She's running toward her target and yelling "duck."

Attorney: She's looking at him and clearly saying "Duke." Why would she say duck?

Agent Brown: Because we believe she was trying to hurt him.

Attorney: And you believe, what, that she was warning him? Giving him a heads up that she wanted to hurt him?

Agent Brown: *no response*

Attorney: And let's be clear on "him." You mean Duke Ogden? The man with his daughter who is smiling and calling my client's name?

Agent Brown: Yes.

Attorney: The man who is clearly holding his arms open to embrace her? Is he pressing charges?

TSA INTERVIEW TRANSCRIPT

Agent Brown: Not yet.

Attorney: Not *yet*? But he's planning to?

Agent Brown: *no response*

Attorney: Have you interviewed him?

Agent Brown: Airport security has, yes.

Attorney: Airport security? Because you're not airport security, right?

Agent Brown: No, ma'am.

Attorney: Is he considering pressing charges?

Agent Brown: No, not at this time.

Attorney: Again, you keep phrasing that with a qualifier. Is Mr. Ogden planning to press charges: yes or no?

Agent Brown: *pauses* No, but we take his safety very seriously.

Attorney: I can't help but notice your Carolina Waves lanyard. Are you a fan?

Agent Brown: This isn't about me.

Attorney: It's clearly not about a threat to Mr. Ogden's safety, either. So why are you holding my client?

Agent Brown: *no response*

Attorney: I repeat: why are you holding my client?

Agent Brown: We'd like to interview Mr. Ogden one more time.

Attorney: 'We?' Airport security already interviewed him.

Agent Brown: I would like to be thorough.

Attorney: Okay. I see what's happening. You're hoping to speak to Duke Ogden, aren't you?

Detainee: What? Is he ... are you doing all of this to meet my boyfriend? Seriously?

Agent Brown: *no response*

Detainee: If I can get you an autograph, will you let me go already?

Agent Brown: I would never accept a bribe.

Attorney: How about a lawsuit for wrongful detention?

Would you accept that? No crime has been committed here and no one has pressed charges. You have no legal authority for detention. Or did you want to talk to my friend in Homeland Security? You know what? Let me give him a call. He's in Augusta, but I'm sure he could—

Agent Brown: That won't be necessary.

Attorney: So are we through here?

Detainee: Lou, you are the Queen of the Courtroom. Or TSA office.

Attorney: I'm waiting.

Agent Brown: *no response*

Attorney: *no response*

Detainee: *chuckles*

Agent Brown: Do you think I could take a selfie with him?

Detainee: I'm sure that can be arranged.

CHAPTER THIRTY-FIVE

DUKE

*W*hen Bri called and told me Millie was on her way back home, Lottie and I came straight to the airport. We couldn't wait another minute.

We didn't realize we'd wait three hours, instead.

Fortunately, I remembered to download the Paw Patrol movie. Which she has watched twice now.

"Momma Millie!" Lottie drops her device and launches herself at Millie the second the TSA officer's door opens. Millie grins and sweeps her up into a huge hug.

"I have missed you so much!" Millie says.

I hop up and put my arms around them both, feeling whole for the first time in days. I bend my neck down to kiss Millie, but Lottie's pigtail gets in the way.

"Ew," I say, spitting out hair.

"Nasty," Millie agrees with a laugh. She moves her face farther out from Lottie's hair, and I pull her into as long a kiss as Lottie will let me. Millie snakes her arm beneath mine, feeling my back with a lot more interest than I would typically expect in the middle of a TSA office. Her lips taste like peanuts and peach lip gloss, and I let myself taste them again and again.

"A-hem," Lou says, ending the reunion party far too soon. "Duke, we promised this nice agent that he could have an autograph and selfie with you. And then we can get going."

I want to groan. Was that what this was all about? Of all the times and places to have an obsessed fan, it just had to be now.

"Sorry," Millie whispers, bumping her head into my shoulder.

I look at the agent, a guy in his mid-30s who looks like he wanted to play football in high school but never made varsity. He's a bit too pale and a bit too sweaty for me to believe he plays in a rec league on the weekends, but I bet his fantasy football team gets more than enough attention. I know this kind of guy. He wears a jersey to watch games and turns his phone to Do Not Disturb when I play.

And he's looking at me with naked devotion, reminding me of why I've always hated talking to fans. Millie squeezes my arm, as if she knows exactly how I'm feeling.

But for the first time maybe ever, she's wrong.

"Hey, I'm Duke," I say, holding my hand out to this super fan.

His eyes light up and he holds out his hand. Yes, it's sweaty. "I'm Beau Brown," he says in a thick Upstate accent. He has a goatee—no mustache, just the chin hair—and an earnest smile. "I'm a big fan."

"Thanks for being a fan, Beau. That means a lot. Did you ever play?"

Beau looks like he just won the lottery. "Sure did. It was just JV, but I was pretty good."

"If you played JV in the South, that's like playing college anywhere else."

He grins. "You know that's right."

"Beau, I wish I could talk longer, but I need to get my

daughter home for bed. Could ... could I ask you a huge favor, though?"

"Anything, Mr. Ogden!"

I pull up the camera on my phone and hand it to him. "Could you record this?"

"Of course!"

He moves toward me, ready to take a selfie, but Lou grabs his shoulders and points him at me. "Record *them*," Lou says. She gives me a wink, obviously knowing what's coming, because she has her phone out, too.

Millie looks at us in confusion. I whisper in Lottie's ear, and she pushes out of Millie's arms and then stands right next to me. I nod to her and drop to one knee.

Millie's hands fly to her mouth.

Lottie looks at me excitedly, but she waits, as we discussed. If for some reason Millie turns me down, I don't want Lottie to get turned down, too.

The very possibility hits me like a 300-pound linebacker. I'm sick at the memory of Millie leaving just the other night. I could so easily go back to that dark, bitter path I was on before she came into my life. It was clear, uncomplicated, easy to navigate. It held no surprises except for the ones coming from the car seat behind me.

But there was no one in the passenger seat. No one to enjoy the journey with, no one who could even understand it. No one to drive for me when I got tired or keep me awake when the road became more than I could bear. No one to help me fix a flat or fill up the tank. No one to laugh with or listen to a book with. No one to tease me as I sing along to the radio. No one to hold my hand and enjoy the drive.

It was a one-way highway with no exits and no turns.

Just me and my backseat driver forever.

It was enough, once. It would still be enough if I hadn't met Millie.

That solitary road holds nothing for me now, though. It's time to get off and enjoy the journey with Lottie and Millie. Forever.

With all these thoughts and words swirling around my mind, I open my mouth.

And I can't remember a single thing I planned to say.

So I gaze up at Millie, mouth agape, thinking of how she deserves a sonnet and I can't even give her a one-liner.

But I can give her forever.

"I had planned to say something really meaningful, but now that I'm looking at you, I can't remember anything except how much I love you and want you with me forever." Millie laughs and bites her lip. I take her long, thin left hand in mine. Beau snickers, and I remember that I have him recording this. What was I thinking? I should have proposed after we were home. But Beau's presence sparks something. "When I'm playing, sometimes I'll have this moment in the crush of players where I can see the end zone so clearly that everything else disappears. It's not that there are no obstacles, but it's like I can see exactly how to navigate the field in order to score. That's how I've felt ever since I met you, Millie."

Her eyes twinkle as she squeezes my hand. "It's always about scoring with you, isn't it?" she says.

I laugh, but it's nothing compared to Beau's, which is a guffaw plus a snort that makes us all laugh harder. "Maybe more about victory," I say, which makes her raise her brows saucily. "No, teamwork? Listen, I'm losing the metaphor, okay? But I don't need a clever metaphor, I need you. I *want* you. Millie Jane Campbell, will you marry me?"

Her grin spreads across her face like a sunrise. "Yes!" I don't rise, and confusion flits across her face. The confusion clears in an instant, blossoming into pure, unadulterated love when she sees Lottie drop to one knee beside me.

"Momma Millie," Lottie says, looking up at Millie. She sways on her little knee, so I put an arm on her back, holding her steady. Millie starts to cry the fattest happy tears I've ever seen. They roll down into her smile, leaving a trail that glimmers in the fluorescent lights overhead. "You are the best mommy in the world. I like how you make me feel safe and I like when we pet llamas together and I like when we wear matching dresses. I like how you hold me when I'm sad and how you hug me. I wanted you to be my mommy the first time I met you under the table when I gave you cheese," she says, rambling far less than I did and remembering every word she told me she wanted to say. Millie laughs through her tears. "I think you're the best person in the whole world. Sorry, Daddy. Will you be my Forever Mommy?"

Millie falls to her knees and throws her arms around Lottie, kissing her little cheeks a hundred times. "Yes yes yes yes yes!" she says between kisses. "I love you so much, sweet girl. I want to be your mommy more than anything in the world."

Lottie starts crying now, too, and because I'm nothing if not a supportive father and future husband, so do I. I grab both my girls into a bear hug and squeeze them tightly, kissing them both until Lottie squeals. It's the best moment of my life. I've never felt so whole, so full, so excited about what comes next. It's the Super Bowl of life, and I've already won just by getting to play the game with these two.

Applause erupts around us, and we move apart just enough to see that the entire TSA office is full of employees, and the glass door leading out to the airport is swarming with people, their phones trained on us.

This is the most private, special, intimate moment of my life, and of course there's a crowd. Of course it's streaming live on the internet. I groan, but Millie just bumps her forehead against mine.

"They came for the show," she says. "Let's make it worth their while." And then she tilts her head and presses her lips to mine softly, tantalizingly. Long enough to make for a satisfactory conclusion to the reels they're going to post, but nowhere nearly long enough or deep enough for my liking.

But it's perfect for the moment. Her reaction, her ability to hang with the chaos that is my life ... it's salt on my steak.

And it's absolutely delicious.

I jump to my feet and pull Lottie and Millie up with me. "We're getting married, y'all!" I yell, and everyone yells with us.

Beau is wiping tears from his cheeks when he hands me back my phone. "That was beautiful, man. Thanks for letting me be a part of that."

"Couldn't have done it without you, buddy," I say. "Now ... is there a back exit out of here, by any chance?"

Beau leads us out the employee exit where a car picks us all up and drives us back home ... after a quick selfie with my new friend.

CHAPTER THIRTY-SIX

DUKE

My baby girl is four today, and after weeks of planning, I have the best birthday present ever lined up for her.

It's Tuesday, our day off in the NFL, and Lottie's party is in full swing at the farm. The Janes are running point around the venue like it's their job, even though they're invited guests. When Millie and I told them our idea, they launched into planning mode.

They've outdone themselves.

Somehow, Parker has managed to make it both kid-approved and tasteful. The bounce houses are even white. Who knew they made white bounce houses?

And because I remembered my mental note to self, there's also a Diet Coke bar.

Parker went with a Southern Tea Party theme, and the guests have shown up accordingly. Most of them look like they're ready for the Kentucky Derby, and Lottie is here for it.

She has an adorable, poofy party dress on, and she keeps curtsying to her guests. After getting engaged, we got a little excited about Lottie's big day. We blew up the guest list and invited my whole team, half the town, our favorite TSA agent, Beau, and, of course, Millie's family.

Her sister hasn't had any problems since the hospital, and she was cleared to fly, on condition that she moved very little. So I chartered a private plane, hired drivers, and got a motorized scooter for her to make sure she's as comfortable as possible.

Millie's family has been sweet and respectful. Her parents love Lottie already, even if they seem wary. They act like everything could be taken away any second.

I get it.

But instead of making them afraid to enjoy life, I hope it makes them afraid *not* to.

Nothing is guaranteed. But life is too precious to avoid the things that make us happy. I've found my forever in Millie, and I don't want to waste another second being hurt, scared, or prideful.

It's only 9:20 a.m., but Parker's already giving guests a warning that Lottie will open presents in ten minutes. If anyone thinks opening presents so early into a party is odd, they don't say anything.

Sonny gathers his nephews and nieces from the bounce house at the same time that I get Lottie.

He's wearing a casual light gray suit with a white turtleneck and suede low top sneakers, which he kicks off as he comes on to the bounce house.

"What's up, GQ?" I ask.

Sonny gives me his trademark smile, but I can't help noticing him looking over his shoulder at Parker. Millie told me her suspicion that neither of them ever got over the other, and

I'm sure she's right. Sonny's a flirt, but I haven't known him to have real eyes for anyone.

He bounces over to grab his youngest nephew, who's biting Lottie's dress, as little kids do.

"How's the birthday girl doing?" Sonny asks Lottie.

"Good," Lottie says as she pulls her dress from the toddler's clenched teeth. The fabric yanks free, and she smoothes her dress and then her hair. I've seen Millie smooth her hair exactly like that.

Like mother, like daughter.

Parker rings a triangle, again alerting people that presents are starting.

"I didn't know it was possible for the ding of a triangle to sound so commanding," I say.

"Then you don't know Parker like I do," Sonny says.

We scoop up kids, deposit them at the exit of the bounce house, then take turns trying to fit our absurdly oversized bodies through the stupidly child-sized door.

"What the—"

"Who designed this thing? Not dads, that's for sure."

We squeeze and roll and jam our bodies out until we're standing on the grass, both a little worse for the wear.

I am, at any rate. Sonny looks untouched by the demon bounce house.

He straightens my collar as the kids run off.

"What are you getting Lottie?" Sonny asks. "I overheard Jane and Ash talking about how you found the perfect gift."

I scan the crowd for Millie, who's talking to Parker. Parker taps her wrist and looks over to confirm I'm ready.

Boy, am I ever.

"You're about to find out, brother," I tell him with a slap to his shoulder.

"Go get 'em, tiger," Sonny says.

I meet Millie at the Diet Coke bar. She can't keep the smile off her face, which means neither can I.

"Fancy meeting you here," she says, getting a large soda with coconut cream, lime, and sugar free coconut syrup.

"I'll have what she's having," I tell the barkeeper. The guy's brother owns the bar in the town over and is kind of a recluse, but I've always liked him. I like him even better for arranging a soda bar on such short notice.

Reese brings Lottie over a moment later, and Lottie says, "Excuse me? I'll have a Caffeine Free Diet Coke with coconut cream, lime, and coconut syrup, please."

I look at Millie, who's beaming in pride. "That's my girl," she says, pulling Lottie close. Lottie stands on her tiptoes and Millie bends down to kiss her cheek.

I look at the two loves of my life as we hold our sodas. "Cheers to the best day ever." I hold out my drink and both girls bump theirs into mine.

Then I tip it back. My soda spills all down the front of my shirt and pants. Oh. Oh man. Oh wow. Ice-crotch is not the vibe I was going for today, of all days. I shiver.

"Whoops," I say. All around me, friends point and laugh. "That was silly."

"Real classy stuff, bro," one of my teammates calls.

I raise my glass. "Thanks, pal. I try."

Lottie giggles, sipping her drink carefully through her straw. She normally spills everything, because she's a kid, but she's being extra steady in her dress.

Meanwhile, Millie is sniggering as she sucks her drink down. None of the cups have lids, and this isn't quite what we agreed on.

"Enjoying yourself?" I ask her.

"Yes," she says, eyeing me warily. She knows what's coming. This was her idea, after all.

"Don't you have something you need to do?" Her 32-ounce is rapidly shrinking. It's more like a 12-ounce at this point.

"In a sec." She puts her red lips back on the straw, and I shake my head.

"No way. Do the thing."

Her eyebrows pull together. "Do I have to?"

"This was your idea!"

"I was wrong?"

"Nice try, Duchess," I say. Then I reach for the bottom of her cup and tip it all over her dress.

She gasps and sputters. "Duke Ogden!"

"What, uh, what color you got under there?" I ask.

"Wouldn't you like to know?"

"Yes, I would."

The look she gives is hot enough to dry us both.

And then Lottie says, "What are you guys doing?" Her eyes are jumping between us. I pick her up into a big hug, and she squeals. "Daddy! You got my pretty party dress all wet!"

Reese shakes her head. "You two need to keep it in your pants," she mutters as she reaches for Lottie. "Here, Lottie-bug. I have *another* party dress for you! Would you believe it?"

And she whisks Lottie away to go get changed.

The second they're gone, I pull Millie in tight and close. Our wet bodies press against each other. My breathing quickens, not out of fear or nerves but out of excitement. Anticipation.

I lean down and whisper in her ear. "Are you ready?"

"I've never wanted anything more," she says. My cheek brushes against hers as I bring my head back up, but she throws her arms around my neck and pulls me down for a scorchingly hot kiss that makes my knees buckle. For a moment, my world is nothing but Millie's arms and the taste of Diet Coke and peach lip gloss. And I like it. I love it.

But it's not enough.

"As much as I'd love to stay here all day, I have somewhere I gotta be."

"Oh, a big date, huh? Is she hot?"

"Hotter than the sun," I tell her. I give her one last kiss and then push her away. "Now go! You have five minutes."

"Five?" she gasps. "I need ten!"

"Then you should have rethought that kiss. Move that cute butt, Campbell!"

She smacks my own butt and yells "Good luck!" as she runs for a tent a few dozen yards past the white barn.

I take a moment to admire how insanely attractive she is while she runs. And then I dart for another tent, where my friends are waiting.

It's showtime.

EPILOGUE

MILLIE

When Duke sees me, his eyes and jaw both open wide, and I can't help but be gratified by the naked appreciation in his stare. "How did I get so lucky?" he asks me.

I bite my lip. I've gotten more than a few looks from our guests. This dress is a little much for a birthday tea party, but I don't care. In fact, that's the whole point.

This dress is *amazing* on me. It's a vintage Dior dress made from silk chiffon with a gorgeous corset, panels of vintage lace, and a skirt made from layers of pleated chiffon. One guess who found it for me.

Nico!

When he heard what happened at the airport, he left me a message that he was on the hunt. That's right, Nico and I are friends now (and even better friends since he found me this dress). Also, I'm not ashamed to admit this: I feel like a better version of myself wearing Dior. I think half of people's crankiness must come from not knowing how good the right clothes could possibly look and feel on them. Duke is still gaping appreciatively.

"The feeling is mutual," I say, admiring him in his sexy slim cut burgundy suit. The color makes the blue of his eyes even more intense.

My legs almost give out.

Lottie tears into her gifts, and she's as spoiled and loved as I could ever want for the little girl who captured my heart.

Emphasis on the spoiled.

She gets an Apple Watch, four iPads, two Nintendo Switches, two electric ride-on cars, a vespa, a Dolce and Gabana dress for her American Girl doll, and more.

"Wow. Really? Y'all," Duke says loudly after yet another extravagant gift. "*She's four.* Ever hear of a scooter? A pogo stick? What's she going to do with a Prada backpack?"

"Same thing she'd do with a backpack from the Piggly Wiggly, I reckon," Beau calls out.

Duke puts his face on my shoulder and laughs. "We're donating all of this, right?"

"Maybe we let her keep just a couple of things."

"Softie."

Duke's parents and Reese give Lottie their present next. They're staying in town for the next week, but tonight, they're taking her on an overnight trip to an indoor water park. They leave right after the party.

Okay, that one's more for Duke and me. And fortunately, she's elated.

After she hugs her grandparents, Duke says, "Millie and I have one last present for you, pumpkin. But it's in the barn. Do you think you could come with us?"

Lottie squeals and takes both of our hands, pulling us into the beautiful white barn where my best friend got married not even two months ago.

As we walk hand-in-hand, Pachelbel's Canon in D starts playing, and a gasp sounds behind us. Followed by another and another.

I risk a glance behind me and see that almost every adult here has guessed Lottie's birthday surprise.

Duke stops us when we get to the open barn doors. Lottie looks at us and seems to notice my dress for the first time.

"I love your dress! You look like a princess!" she gushes.

"Thank you! You look like a queen," I say. Her chestnut brown hair is down in pretty curls, and her white dress is fluffy and twirly and perfect.

"That's because I'm going to be a queen one day," she says matter-of-factly, swishing her dress from side to side. "Now where is my present?" she asks in a commanding way.

Duke whispers in Lottie's ear, and suddenly, Lottie is screaming.

"Yes!" She jumps like she's on a trampoline. The guests laugh and sniffle. "Yes! I'm getting a mommy for my birthday!"

She throws her arms around my legs, and I bend down to hug her. My eyes well with tears, but I don't let them fall. Not yet.

Parker speaks into a microphone, and the next thing we know, Louis the llama is walking down the aisle in front of us. Everyone inside oohs and awes at the adorable sight.

Then I shift my flowers into my other hand, and Duke and I both grab one of Lottie's hands so that the three of us can walk down the aisle together.

Everyone in the barn is in tears.

Everyone except Lottie.

She's grinning like the magnificent little queen she is. This is such a big moment for her. She's walking through a crowd of people, some she just met, and she isn't retreating or clinging to us! She squeezes my hand tighter when we get to the end, and I sense a tick of nerves in her. I model taking a deep breath and blowing it out slowly, and she mimics me. Then she looks at Duke, and he does the same, nodding and smiling at her. She hugs his legs tightly and then takes a step back on the dais, holding her flowers tightly in front of her with one hand and petting Louis with the other. She breathes slowly, and she doesn't scream or cry or throw a tantrum. She's emotionally regulating!

With Louis and Lottie both situated, Duke and I stand across from each other in front of the pastor and our loved ones, beaming.

I miss half of what the pastor says. I don't even know how I make it through my vows. I'm in a blissful, joyful, marveling fog.

When we're made husband and wife, Duke sweeps me into a low dip and kisses me like we're in a movie. And it's every bit as romantic as it is on the screen. Our lips part, and he gazes into my eyes, still holding me low.

"I love you, Duchess."

"I love you, too. Pinky."

He gives me a quizzical look before realization dawns on his face. And excitement. "Seriously?"

I grin. "Seriously."

He pulls me up and spins me around, yelling, "Hot pink, baby!" And I laugh as everyone we love laughs and cheers along with us.

When he sets me down, my heart is bursting. I look in awe at my friends, at the family I'm working hard to set boundaries with, and at the new family who has become my everything.

Duke wanted to give Lottie the best present possible today, and in doing so, he gave me everything *I* ever wanted, too.

And it's better than I ever imagined.

BONUS EPILOGUE
SUPER BOWL SUNDAY

PARKER

I pace nervously in the VIP box as the time runs down in the fourth quarter.

Millie and I pass each other. Seeing her deeply furrowed brow reminds me to get a handle on my own emotions. I stop, fold my arms, and fix my attention on the field. I'm dimly aware that the rest of our friends are here with Duke's family. I'm a bit more attuned to the presence of my ex's family in the VIP box, but not even that can distract me from this play.

We're down by three with seven seconds left in the game. It's fourth and goal. If we kick, at best, we go into overtime. Duke and Sonny have shone throughout the game, but our offensive line hasn't. Duke's been sacked twice, and Sonny's had a couple of rough tackles and near misses that have had his parents, brothers, and sister yelling.

But not me.

My guts twist every time someone crashes into him, but I

can't let anyone see that, especially not his family. They remember me. When Sonny's dad saw me at Duke and Millie's wedding a few months ago, he said, "If it isn't Parker Emerson, the one that got away." Sonny's mom swatted his dad's arm and gave me a hug, reminding me of the warmth I felt each time his parents came into town when we were dating in college.

It also reminds me of the fact that I can't remember the last time either of my parents hugged me like that. And the fact that I definitely remember my last hug with Sonny ...

I yank my thoughts firmly back to the present, where they belong. That ship sailed years ago, a voyage I encouraged when Sonny first talked about transferring from University of Chicago to Clemson. He red-shirted his freshman year, but he trained hard that whole year and was so dominant when he finally started, he had division one teams beating down his door. Clemson has one of the best programs in college football, and playing for them was almost a guaranteed shot at the NFL. It was a no-brainer.

Even if he wanted to stay for me or for me to transfer with him or for us to try long distance.

As if.

We fell in love at nineteen. The stats on college sweethearts getting married are abysmal. I did us a favor by breaking things off at the end of our sophomore year. It would have been so much more painful if I'd transferred with him just to break up later or, heaven forbid, if I'd let us try dating long distance. It would have impacted his play, and that would have led to him resenting me.

I could handle not having Sonny Luciano in my life, but I could never handle him resenting me. Not for anything.

Head in the game, I chide myself just as the center snaps the ball to Duke. Our offensive line holds for only a couple of seconds, so Duke has to scramble to get away from the defensive end chasing him. One of our linemen stops the defender short, but another is hot on Duke's heels.

With a defender bearing down on Duke and nowhere to run, he spots Sonny in the end zone at the last second. The ball shoots from Duke's hand like a cannon. He has to beat the middle linebacker jumping to intercept the ball. But Sonny is the better athlete. His jump is so high, he could easily be dunking a basketball. For a moment, I marvel at how graceful he is. It's art watching him play the game he loves so much. He reaches high overhead and the ball hits his fingertips, bobbling for only a second before ...

He gets it!

Of course he gets it.

He brings the ball straight to his chest, cradling it for the landing.

But the landing doesn't come.

At least not as expected.

Another defender hurls into Sonny, taking him out at the knees. Sonny crashes to his side, the defender slamming on top of him as another follows and another. With so many players piled on him, the announcers can't call the play. A ref runs over to clear the pileup, and we all wait with baited breath. Sonny's brothers are hitting each other's shoulders as they watch and wonder. Did he lose the ball? Is he okay? I tense, watching man after man get off until finally, we see.

The ball is still in his hands!

TOUCHDOWN!

The Waves win the Super Bowl!

The sound in the stadium is ear-splitting. The entire box shakes with the vibration of a hundred thousand fans losing their ever-loving minds. In the luxury box, we all scream and jump and hug each other, and more than a few people are crying.

But as Jane runs over to hug me, the hair on the back of my neck stands up.

What happened with Sonny?

I spin around mid-hug, trying to spot him on the field, but I don't see him anywhere. I shoot a look toward his family. His brothers and mom are cheering and hugging. His dad, though, has the same look of concern on his face that I'm not allowing on mine. He catches my eye, or maybe I catch his, and a flicker of understanding passes between us.

Sonny's absence can only mean one thing: he was rushed off the field.

Dread fills me, dropping my stomach until I feel physically ill. That hit to his knees. That pileup.

His bad knee.

The one that already had what should have been a career ending surgery.

Mrs. Luciano turns to bring her husband into the family's festivities, but she stops, following his eyes as they scan the field. She puts the pieces together instantly.

"No. Oh no. Where is he?" She whips around, looking for the owner of the Waves, but he's nowhere to be seen. "Where's Sonny?"

"He probably needed a bathroom break," Sonny's oldest brother, Anthony, says. "Watch. He'll be back out in a sec."

His other brother, Gabe, eyes him. "Huh? Who would take a bathroom break when they just won the Super Bowl?"

Sonny's big sister, Sienna, rubs her mom's shoulders. "Sonny's a fighter, Momma. He'll be okay."

Sienna spots me watching them, so I quickly turn away and focus on the interviews happening on the field. Millie, Lottie, and the rest of Duke's family were escorted downstairs to celebrate with Duke already.

Mrs. Luciano pretends their weak efforts to comfort her are helping, but it's a lie that they go along with rather than something any of them believes. Because to a person, each of the Luciano's eyebrows are drawn as they watch the interviews and celebrations.

And unlike the rest of the NFL families, they're the only ones in the suite who don't get escorted down to the field to celebrate.

Duke is named MVP, an honor he more than earned. My excitement for him can't let me forget the pit in my stomach, though. I try to ignore the dread until a security guard whispers something in Mr. Luciano's ear. The rest of the family rallies together, saying a quick prayer, and then they follow security out.

Envy pierces my heart, but I don't let myself dwell on the feeling. Not for an instant. Sonny and I are ancient history. I made the right choice.

I made the *only* choice.

We were fire and ice. Sunshine and darkness. I was always dousing his flame and he was always setting my world ablaze. When I wanted to study, he wanted to explore. When I was making lists, he was planning adventures. He could turn a trip to the grocery store into a game, and he did. Frequently.

It was exhausting.

And maybe a *tiny bit* exhilarating.

Not that I ever let him know that. I couldn't encourage him. If I asked a simple question about a Saturday hike, his plan would balloon into an elaborate scheme to switch our classes to online, rent an RV, and travel to every national park in the country.

He was incorrigible. A dreamer. He scattered sunshine so relentlessly, I needed SPF 50 just to be around him.

It didn't matter that I loved the burn.

It mattered that I loved him enough to make him take his dreams seriously.

If we had stayed together, he wouldn't be playing football.

He's always loved the sport, but he lacked discipline and focus. A huge part of the success he saw at University of Chicago and beyond was *my* training schedule for him. He probably would have quit football altogether to spend time with me and host a morning radio show, if I'd let him. But he was on a football scholarship! I pushed him and challenged him to help him. I stayed on him to make sure he trained and practiced relentlessly. And it worked.

He claimed it worked too well when I broke up with him, but his shiny new Super Bowl ring would say otherwise.

And what about me? If we had stayed together, my grades would have suffered worse than they already had. My relationship with my parents would have gone from strained to nonexistent. They would have cut me out of their lives completely.

And what would have happened then? I'd have felt pressured to make safe decisions. I never would have left a toxic job to start a marketing agency with my best friends. I'd still be a low-level account executive doing work way above my pay grade, having men *literally pat me on my head and tell me how adorable I was* during an interview for a promotion that I knew they'd never give me in spite of the fact that I was the most qualified candidate and was already doing the boss's job and ... and ...

Let it go, I tell myself. *It happened. It's over. You and Sonny both moved on, exactly as you should have. Let. It. Go.*

I don't like Disney movies as a general rule, but that *Frozen* chick knows a thing or two about coping with stress. You have to bottle that junk up or move on. There's no in between.

Only a few minutes have passed from the time that Sonny's family was escorted downstairs. Tripp, Jane, and our other friends are still reveling in the celebrations. Ash is talking to someone I know for a fact has a star on the Hollywood Walk of Fame, and he looks like he's trying to get her number, even while our friend Rusty keeps an eye on him.

I feel a tap on my shoulder at the same time a beefy security guard says, "Ms. Emerson? Mr. Luciano is asking for you."

I glance around. "Mr. Luciano?" As in Sonny's dad?

"Sonny Luciano, yes. He'd like to see you."

I swallow and hold my head up, acting like my heart isn't a runaway train. "Lead the way."

I follow him through secure hallways and elevators until I'm in the belly of one of the most famous stadiums in the country. He leads me through a locker room of elated NFL players. The men are in the peak of their revelry, shouting, singing, and spraying champagne on each other. Not all of the Waves are here—fewer than half of them—but based on the way most of them are eyeing me, these are the ones who don't have families or girlfriends to celebrate with.

I suppress a groan.

I am a lot of impressive things, if I do say so myself. I was a level nine gymnast and competed in the Junior Olympics. I attended an elite institution on a full-ride scholarship and was captain of the debate team. I'm the CFO of a marketing firm I started with my best friends, and we're killing it.

But does that matter to any of these guys? No. The only thing this locker room full of big, buff jocks cares about is that I am tiny and attractive. (I know, I know. It's not a universal law. But it's close.)

I'm not saying I mind the attention, but I'm not interested in any man in this room. I'm not interested in the man I'm being led to right now, either, I remind myself. I'm only following this security guard to see Sonny because it's the polite thing to do. What kind of a jerk would I be to deny his request?

I'm doing this to be polite, I tell the swarm of bees in my stomach.

It doesn't mean anything, I tell my rapidly beating heart.

All of my reminders fly out the window when I see Sonny

propped up on a stretcher in one of the medical offices. He lights up like a Christmas tree when he sees me, his bright aqua eyes expanding so that I could drown in them. But just as fast as the enthusiasm appeared, I watch him rein it in. The way he fights to keep his generous smile smaller and the way he makes himself sit back after reaching for me ... the movements are daggers to my heart. After all these years of watching him on TV, I thought I knew him as well as I ever did.

But the worry lines forming between his eyebrows are new. And the quick blinking shows an expression on his gorgeous face that I've never seen before: hesitation.

"How are you?" I ask as neutrally as I can. I can't let him see how much the sight of him on a stretcher worries me. I can't let him know that the ice on his wrapped knee is thawing my frozen heart. "After that catch, I imagine you must feel like you're walking on sunshine."

WALKING ON SUNSHINE? WHAT IS THE MATTER WITH ME?

He cocks his head to the side. "Still trying to figure out what to do with big emotions, huh PJ?"

I put a hand on one hip. "Still saying the first thing that comes to your mind, huh Sonny?"

A smile slowly stretches across his face, and I look at his lips. He has always had the absolute sexiest smile. Ask anyone. Ask the internet. The boy's lips were made to be kissed.

Stop looking at his mouth!

I snap my eyes up, but based on how Sonny releases his shoulders, he knows he still has an affect on me. I need to control myself, and I need to get back in control of this conversation before Sonny pulls a fast one on me and I'm being sucked into his dreams. And life.

"I'm sure you're wondering why I asked you to come down."

"I am."

BABY LLAMA DRAMA

"My family told me that you were upstairs and they said you looked worried when I was taken off the field."

I glance away, hoping I look casual instead of busted. "Yeah, along with half the stadium."

"That's all it was? A fan worrying about the star running back?"

The shortness in his voice pulls my eyes back to his. "It wasn't just that, and you know it." I flush at the admission, then purposefully slow my breathing to steady my pulse and draw the heat from my face.

"Worried about an old friend, then?"

"Of course. I'll always care about you and want the best for you." My light tone is solid. Convincing. I almost believe it myself.

"Okay. Thanks for the concern. I hope you enjoyed the game. Good seeing you," he says. Then he nods to the security guard, who puts his hand on my elbow.

What? That's it?

I smile sweetly. "Good seeing you, too. Good luck with … rehab?" I hazard. It's just rehab, right? He won't need surgery?

Sonny smiles as big as a shark, and I could kick myself for dangling my question like bait. "See you around, PJ."

I fume the entire way back to the luxury suite. And the entire drive home with Ash and Lou. And while I get ready for bed.

When I can take it no longer, I pull out my phone and shoot off a text.

PARKER: You never did say what's going on with your knee.

Three dots appear.

And then disappear.

And they don't reappear for at least a minute.

Why is he torturing me like this?

Wait, does he even have the same number? Does he still have *my* number?

When his reply comes in, it's wholly insufficient.

SONNY: No, I didn't, did I?

G'night, PJ.

And then my phone notifies me that he's put *his* phone on silent mode.

How dare he?

How dare he show up in my life out of nowhere again? How dare he draw me in and then leave me hanging like this? How dare he get hurt and not tell me if he's okay or not?

How dare he not be wrecked like I am to see him again?

I force myself to put down my phone and to not check it all night long.

Even if I don't sleep a wink.

Because if I know anything about myself, it's that for all of my carefully erected walls, for all of the armor I meticulously put on every day, I only have one weakness.

Sonny.

It's always Sonny.

Want more of Parker and Sonny's grumpy-sunshine, second chance romance vibes? Pre-order It's Always Sonny *now!*

Stay in the know with all things Sweet as Sugar Maple *by signing up for my newsletter: www.katewatsonbooks.net/newsletter*

Subscribe and get a free novella

Let's Connect!
Instagram @KateWatsonBooks
Facebook Clean Romcom Reader Group

YOU'LL ALSO LOVE...

Did you like Millie, Duke, and Lottie's story? Then you'll love Strawberry Fields for Never, featuring Jane and Tripp (and where Lottie and Millie first meet)!

She's the desperate CEO hired to rebrand a sleepy Southern orchard. He's the stubborn heir determined to see her fail.

All's fair in love and farming.

As CEO of my marketing firm, my friends' careers rest on my shoulders. And my shoulders—and company—are failing. Rebranding a famous farm is my final chance to fix what I've broken, and nothing can get in my way.

But flirting with a gorgeous farm worker can't hurt. Right?

We have an instant—and hot—connection...until he tries to sabotage my every move. Turns out, this hunky local is actually Tag Carville III, the wealthy new heir to Sugar Maple Farms. When he finds out why I'm really visiting his sleepy Southern town, he goes from ally to enemy so fast, it takes my breath away.

My new nemesis clearly has his own agenda, and it's in direct opposition to mine. I will save this farm and my company, even if he seems determined to stop me. Even if our fighting feels more and more like flirting.

Even if I'm starting to fall.

But in the battle over heart and home, only one of us will win.

Strawberry Fields for Never is a laugh-out-loud closed-door romantic comedy with sizzling chemistry, enemies to more, and a swoon-worthy guy who falls first. And, of course, a happily-ever-after.

Find my books on Amazon!

And if you enjoyed this book, I hope you'll consider reviewing it on Amazon. Reviews mean the world to indie authors.

ACKNOWLEDGMENTS

People always say that raising kids takes a village, but in my experience, writing a book takes an even bigger one. Becky and Sam, thank you for being amazing critique partners and friends! Kaylee, Raneé, and Krysti, thanks for all the help, advice, commiseration, and support. To the bookstagram community—including Meredith, Jenn, Lindsey, Sarah, and Susan—thank you for all the support and boosting. You are amazing! Caitlin, thank you for your wonderful proofing eye!

To my ARC team: I truly couldn't do this without you. To all my readers, thank you for making Little Kate's dreams come true. I always said I wanted to be an author when I grew up, and you've made it possible.

To my genius therapist sisters for helping me make Millie and Lottie more authentic, thank you. Mollsies, thanks for walking me through EMDR in a kid-friendly manner and for all the character help.

To my kids for inspiring all the best parts of Lottie, I sure love you. To my Jeffy, Stevenflo is definitely the Pearl Jam tribute name for you. I'll get my "I'm With the Band" t-shirt ready.

To my loving, merciful, enabling God, thank You.

ABOUT THE AUTHOR

Kate Watson is a fan of cheeky romantic comedies and delightfully witty banter. Originally from Canada, she attended college in the States and holds a BA in Philosophy from Brigham Young University. A lover of travel, speaking in accents, and experiencing new cultures, she has also lived in Israel, Brazil, the American South, and she now calls Arizona home.

She started writing at six years old and sold her first book, "The Heart People," for $0.25 to her parents. It received rave reviews. Since then, she's written many books, including the acclaimed Off Script, a 2020 Junior Library Guild selection. She writes stories full of heart, humor, and happily-ever-afters.

She is currently living her own happily-ever-after with her super cute husband and their four wild and wonderful kids. She runs on caffeine, swoons, and Jesus.